How the Stock Market Really Works

How the Stock Market Really Works

The guerrilla investor's secret Handbook

An imprint of **Pearson Education**
London / New York / San Francisco / Toronto / Sydney / Tokyo / Singapore
Hong Kong / Cape Town / Madrid / Paris / Milan / Munich / Amsterdam

3rd Edition

Leo Gough

PEARSON EDUCATION LIMITED

Head Office:
Edinburgh Gate
Harlow CM20 2JE
Tel: +44 (0)1279 623623
Fax: +44 (0)1279 431059
Website: www.pearsoned.co.uk

First published in Great Britain in 2001

ISBN 0 273 65435 7

Figs. 8.5 & 8.6 reproduced from *The Millennium Book: A Century of Investment Returns*, by Elroy Dimson, Paul Marsh and Mike Staunton, ABN AMRO/LBS 2000.

British Library Cataloguing in Publication Data
A CIP catalogue record for this book can be obtained from the British Library

10 9 8 7 6 5 4

Typeset by Northern Phototypesetting Co. Ltd, Bolton
Printed and bound in Great Britain by Ashford Colour Press, Hampshire

The Publishers' policy is to use paper manufactured from sustainable forests.

To Rob Ormsby

Contents

Introduction

If you were living in Europe during World War 2, you probably have little difficulty in entertaining the notion that the authorities are not always fair or honest. If, however, you were brought up in post-war Britain – or in many other European countries, for that matter – you might well have trouble with this idea, but if you are to do well in the stock market, you need to get used to it.

Now you want to be an investor. The first thing to do is to take stock of yourself and your circumstances, and to develop a capacity for clear-mindedness and good judgement. As a small investor, you will find that governments, the institutions, financial advisers and the professional classes are not your friends – if you do as they urge, and leave the decisions about your money to them, you are likely to end up with less of it than you had before. It is not simply a question of fraud, although as we will see in this book, the financial world is an adventure playground for fraudsters, with ludicrously mild punishments in the unlikely event of their conviction. It is also that the rules of the game are weighted against you.

Many of the savings and investment 'opportunities' available to the public are designed to prevent you from getting rich. Inflation, fluctuating interest rates and exchange rates, government regulation and taxes have a tendency to catch out the individual. In this book I have tried to explain how the financial markets work, and to suggest strategies for increasing and preserving capital. It is possible to do this, but only, unless you are unusually lucky, by taking investment seriously and learning as much as you can about it – like life, investment really is a 'do-it-yourself' project.

You may find some of the views expressed in this book controversial. This is intended. To develop the capacity to discriminate, which all successful investors must have, you must allow yourself to be exposed to new and different ideas that may conflict with what you already know, or what you are constantly being told on radio and television. Investing combines theory and practice in a complex and imperfect world; you may not always get it right, but that should not be your objective. Prosperity and coming out 'on top' in the long run is far more important. May you achieve this worthy goal!

Please note that since new legislation and financial products are being introduced all the time, some of the details in this book may be out of date by the time you read them; these will be rectified in future editions. In the meantime, remember that while you should always check the precise details of an investment before committing yourself, you can be confident that the basic principles of investment will not change.

I would like to thank Elaine Lee Yu Lian, Phyllis Reed, Simon Reed, Tony Jay, Trevor Pepperell, Barry Riley and Nick Henderson for their valuable help and advice. The opinions and any mistakes herein are mine, not theirs.

Preface to the third edition

Much to my surprise, this book has been consistently popular throughout the six years since I first wrote it. Free markets, globalization, technological change and all kinds of political and economic reforms have made stock markets not only open, but vitally important, to the average person. Not least of these changes has been a general recognition throughout Europe that, given our aging populations, people are going to have to take financial responsibility for their old age.

When I first wrote this book, many points were considered wildly controversial, and people were eager to tell me so. Today, with a much larger financial press, it is becoming increasingly common to read about, for instance, how not to be ripped off by investment products of poor value, and more and more people realize the value of consumer protection in financial matters.

This is not to claim that I got everything right. Most notably, I completely failed to realise that the Japanese economy would descend into the stagnation where it currently languishes. It's a reminder to me to stick to the iron rule for guerrilla investors: don't make predictions!

We are living in something of a golden age of stock market investment. Nothing lasts for ever, and it may be that within a few years other asset classes will perform better for a decade or two. This is nothing to worry about. The stock market is the most flexible and efficient way of funding industry that has ever been devised, and I have little doubt that there will be many bull markets for shares in the future. The banker J. P. Morgan famously growled, when asked what he thought shares would do during the 1929 Wall Street Crash, that they would 'fluctuate'. That's what shares do, and that's what stock markets are designed to allow them to do. If you can get to grips with this, the chances are that you will prosper as an investor.

Leo Gough
May 2001

The 'guerrilla investor'

This book is for people who want to make money. If you think that having money is wrong, or unfair, this book is not for you. Don't despair, though, if you don't have any money yet; it is possible to accumulate capital if you are determined to do so, whatever your disadvantages when you are starting out. In this chapter we will look at the basic things you need to understand before investing.

The topics are:

- *The 'guerrilla investor' concept*
- *Net worth*
- *Income and expenditure*
- *Employment*
- *Educating yourself about money*
- *Should you own your own home?*
- *Preparing for the stock market*
- *Choosing a financial adviser*
- *Gough's five golden rules for guerrillas*
- *Payback*
- *Simple and compound interest*
- *Liquidity*
- *Inflation*
- *How long will it take to double your money?*

- *Introducing risk*
- *What is a risky investment?*

The 'guerrilla investor' concept

The private investor has vastly superior forces arrayed against him in the struggle for wealth – they have better information, better equipment, more experience, incomparably more money, and political influence. In this respect, the private investor is in a similar position to a real guerrilla; the way to fight back is to exploit the opportunities that being small gives. In the Vietnam War, the North Vietnamese forces had, on paper, no chance against the overwhelming US military, yet they fought on until the enemy left. After a battle, guerrillas were trained to pick up every usable cartridge case for refilling. A black market trade in US arms grew up. By the end of the war, almost all of the equipment used by the guerrilla forces was American, stolen, captured or bought from the opposition. Guerrillas were expected to live off the land, on a tiny amount of food; they were prepared to sit in a tree for a week waiting for the enemy to pass by. They were determined not to give up, and they used their greater flexibility to move faster than the cumbersome organization they opposed.

So it is with the private investor: what would be a small gain to, say, a merchant bank is a large gain for an individual. You cannot compete on the same terms as the huge financial institutions and companies that dominate the world's economy. You must adopt a survival strategy entirely different from the way in which the big boys operate.

MAKING THE MOST OF THE PRIVATE INVESTOR'S ADVANTAGES

You might be surprised to know that private investors have a number of real advantages over the financial institutions. The key to making the most of these is to refuse to play the game on their terms.

Like most large corporations, financial institutions don't enjoy a great deal of loyalty from their employees, who move from company to company in search of better-paid jobs. Managing in this environment means constantly checking on your employees' performance, and being judged on your own. This is one of the factors behind the tendency towards 'short-termism' among the institutions – they tend to focus on quick profits. People don't get fired for making profits! To some extent, they can afford to think short-term, since they only pay a tiny fraction of the share-dealing costs that you and I must pay.

Let's look at the private investor's competitive advantages:

- As a private investor, you don't have to justify your decisions to a board. You don't have angry customers telephoning you to ask why you haven't invested in the latest craze.
- You're not in competition with anybody, and no one need ever know how well, or badly, you are doing.
- You aren't under pressure to produce huge gains every quarter, which inevitably exposes you to high risk – you can afford to buy something and sit on it for years, if you believe in it.
- No one can fire you.
- You don't have to worry about your reputation. You can take a position in an unknown but promising company that many institutions simply aren't allowed to touch because of the rules that govern them. You can purchase stocks abroad in any market that will allow you to do so. You can go against the grain and ignore conventional wisdom.

All this points to the need for private investors to concentrate on medium-to long-term investing, not short-term trading. To do this well, you need to do research – which is a scary word to many people. Research simply means developing an understanding of the businesses and industries that you are following, and you can now use the internet to help you do this.

It is often pointed out that investors only really need one or two big successes in their lifetimes to become really well off. Getting to know a winning company over a decade or two, watching it grow and grow and grow beyond all expectations, and continuing to purchase more of its shares out of your income, will give you the results you want. Notice the time frame – decades, not months, or a year or two. Keeping your big winners, and buying more, for a very long time, is likely to serve you better than endlessly churning your portfolio in search of a quick profit.

There are professional investors who take the long view and refuse to be swayed by all the pressures of corporate life, but they are in the minority. Most of these own their own firms, have autonomy within a larger organization, or work for a small firm that has loyal clients who respect their investment philosophy.

GUERRILLA STRATEGY AND TACTICS

Traditionally, investors are supposed to fall into two categories: those who want capital growth (i.e. to get more money) and those who want to live on the income they get from investing the money they already have. The notion of 'widows and orphans', middle-class people with no job but a little capital, used to be used as a symbol for the investors who wanted income – advisers felt that it was their duty to keep such individuals in the safest possible investments because they were unlikely to be able to recover if they suffered a serious loss. With the advent of social welfare, the situation has changed – widows and orphans will not starve in the gutter if they lose their capital – so I believe that these traditional categories are no longer helpful. After all, we all want capital growth if we can get it.

Here is a list of questions you should ask yourself regularly:

- What is my net worth?
- What are my total income and expenditure?
- Am I getting richer or poorer? Why?
- What are my future employment prospects?
- What do I know about money?
- Am I in a position to buy my own home?

Net worth

Net worth is simply the difference between the value of all the things that you have and all the money that you owe. Most people on this planet have no net worth. Even in the richest countries of the world, most people only have some clothes, a car and a few sticks of furniture – not much to show for a lifetime's toil. The reason why this is so is that the system is constantly ripping them off. They buy life assurance products and then give them up after a couple of years, making a loss. They buy consumer goods at retail prices and borrow money at high interest rates to do so. They run up expensive overdrafts and live off credit cards. They buy things to make themselves feel they are richer than they really are. They borrow too much money in boom times to buy houses and fail to anticipate the inevitable bust. When they are old, they are put into a retirement home and their last remaining assets are spent on nursing costs. On and on it goes. Financially speaking, most people are abused and pushed around all their lives. The guerrilla fights back!

To fight back, you have to be in command of your own resources; first and foremost this means knowing what you've got and how much it is worth. Naturally, it is hard to estimate the value of some things, particularly houses, so take the trouble to get realistic valuations and be conservative. The market value of assets goes up and down all the time, which is why you must frequently take a 'snapshot' of how you are doing. Make your net worth the benchmark by which you measure your performance.

Companies have to work out their net worth regularly too; it's called a 'balance sheet'. The principle is exactly the same:

1. List all the things you own and put a realistic but conservative resale value against each of them.
2. List all your debts
3. Subtract (2) from (1) to find your net worth.

EXAMPLE

Julia is 32 and owns her own home.
Her assets are:

A flat		£80,000
A car		£2,000
A pension fund		£10,000
Cash in a building society		£5,000
	Total	£97,000

Her debts are:

A mortgage		£60,000
A five-year bank loan		£2,000
A bank overdraft		£500
Credit card loan		£1,000
Sundry bills		£2,000
	Total	£65,500
Net worth	Total	£31,500

Knowing your net worth is vital, because it gives you your 'score' in the game of increasing your wealth. Of course, not all of Julia's £31,500 can be spent right away – much of it is tied up in her house and her pension – but it is still 'real' money.

Income and expenditure

Working out how much you earn and how much you spend is a mundane housekeeping activity that most people practise. However, they don't usually go far enough. Simply aiming to cover your bills leaves you exposed, although it is a cardinal principle for accumulating capital. Engrave this on your mind:

Don't consume more than you earn.

Most people waste their money on things they don't need. By all means buy the best you can afford – the best quality is usually the best value in the long run – but look for bargains and ways of reducing your expenditure. Examine each category in your regular budget, and try to think of ways of cutting it down. A guerrilla has few resources, and must put them to the best use. Don't worry if you don't buy things that your peers do. Your job must be to generate regular savings out of your income.

The foundation of successful investing is to save money out of your income

The foundation of successful investing is to save money out of your income. It is your savings that you use to add to your investment holdings. This may appear obvious, but in practice it is easy to start to think of your investment gains as extra cash you can spend. The real secret of long-term investment gains is to stay invested for as long as possible.

Conventionally, people are told that in retirement they can expect to start drawing out money from their investments. This is true enough, if you are no longer earning an income. Successful investors often manage to make their assets grow substantially during retirement. The more money you have, the easier this is, since you are not under pressure to keep dipping into your funds to pay for your living expenses.

Employment

Investors need income from non-investment sources to pay for their living expenses. Trying to live on investment gains severely reduces your chances of making your investments grow satisfactorily. For most people, this non-investment income has to come from working.

The world of employment is uncertain. If you have a good salary, there is no excuse not to save, but many high earners manage to get into debt nevertheless. In old age you may not be able to get a job – don't rely on your pension, start saving!

Many of us don't earn as much as we'd like. If you can, re-train, and get a better job. Self-employment is an option, and has tax advantages, but it is not something to be taken on lightly. The whole mentality of the self-employed is different: it's lonely, you must bear more responsibility, it is uncertain, and it often takes years of struggle to get established. If you get it right, though, it is very rewarding.

Educate yourself about money

Sportspeople often say that people's general unfitness and lack of body awareness is as great a form of ignorance as not being able to read and write. I believe that the same holds true for financial matters. If you were not fortunate enough to have been born into a business-minded family, you will have to learn it all for yourself. Talk to people who are richer than you are and know something about the subject. Read widely. When you have run though your local library, try using university libraries (you don't normally have to join) and talk to academics, who will be scrupulously careful to give you a balanced view. There are many uncertainties and unanswered questions in the world of investment. Developing a deep appreciation of this will help your judgement.

Should you own your own home?

Buying a property is usually a good investment in the long term. We all have to live somewhere, and if the alternative is renting at market rates, you should find that the cost of servicing a mortgage is equivalent to the rent you would otherwise pay. In the long term, property has been a good hedge against inflation, and if prices go up you are using the 'leverage' of your mortgage to increase the value of your equity.

EXAMPLE

If you buy a £60,000 flat with a £40,000 mortgage and £20,000 of savings, and after a few years the flat's value increases to £90,000, your equity will increase from £20,000 to £50,000, or 150 per cent. If you had bought the flat entirely with your own money, your equity would have increased by a lower percentage – from £60,000 to £90,000, or 50 per cent.

Another good thing about property is that it is a way of forcing yourself to save. As you pay off your mortgage, your equity in your home increases. This is tough in the early years, but gets easier as time goes by. Sometimes people argue that they cannot consider selling their homes, so their equity is useless. That is their choice. There is nothing necessarily wrong with moving down the housing ladder in order to release some capital for other investment purposes.

People are often nervous about property because of the potential problems when values crash and interest rates go up.

There are two things to do to stay safe:

- Don't borrow more than you can afford, taking into account possible interest rate hikes.
- Be careful what you buy. Location is the most important factor – is the area growing or dying? Soundness of the property is also important; do all the searches and surveys properly before you buy.

Preparing for the stock market

Let's assume that you have a regular income, a home of your own, and that by saving regularly you have accumulated a capital sum. You have practised all the bourgeois virtues and now you feel ready to spread your wings. Investing in the stock market will probably give you a better return on your money than any other kind of passive investment; but try not to be greedy. Trying to 'beat the market' almost always means taking more risk, so you are much more likely to lose money. The safest way to invest in shares is to buy good ones and hold them for a long time. Constantly buying and selling shares is expensive because of the commissions you pay.

Choosing a financial adviser

Your best financial adviser is yourself – you care more than anyone else what will happen to your money. Before seeking professional advice on a matter, read everything you can about it and try to understand it. This will help you to get the best out of your advisers. A very experienced businessman once told me that there are two kinds of customers who get the best treatment: the ones who spend a lot of money, and the 'difficult' ones who never stop badgering, looking for a bargain, insisting on their rights and making demands. Be a difficult customer – it's your money, and you are the person who cares most about it. Don't be afraid to be rude or pushy if necessary, and don't let yourself be pushed around – there is always someone else if your adviser doesn't want your business.

Your best financial adviser is yourself

As with most things, a personal recommendation from someone whose business judgement you really respect is the best way to find a good adviser. Nevertheless, there are general points about financial advisers that are worth considering. They are basically of two kinds, the 'tied agents' and the 'independent financial advisers' (IFAs). Advisory stockbrokers are also sometimes sources of good advice, not only on shares and bonds, but also on general investment matters.

TIED AGENTS

Tied agents represent a company, most often an insurance company, and only sell the products offered by that company. They don't have to tell you how much commission they are making, but they do have to tell you that they are tied. The high street banks and most building societies are tied agents, since they will only sell financial products offered by a particular company. Before dismissing tied agents out of hand, you should recognize that, since they are backed by large companies, they are unlikely to go bust, and they may, sometimes, be able to give you the best deal on a particular product. Never sign an agreement that contains a penalty clause specifying that if you allow, say, an insurance policy or mortgage to lapse you will pay a percentage of the sum to the agent.

INDEPENDENT FINANCIAL ADVISERS (IFAS)

IFAs can be stockbrokers, accountants, insurance brokers, solicitors and some building society managers. They may also be individuals without professional qualifications other than having passed the Financial Planning Certificate exams. IFAs have to tell you about their charges and any commissions they make, if you ask them, and are obliged by law to give you the best advice for your circumstances. IFAs who live on commissions are arguably less independent than ones who only charge fees. The latter type may rebate any commissions they earn to you. Never rely on the regulation of IFAs to give you complete protection; check them out very thoroughly before you part with any money. Such checks would include getting references, confirming that they are members of the relevant regulatory bodies, making sure that you have obtained, and understood, all the relevant paperwork, and verifying that they are insured against professional negligence.

Remember to be careful when writing cheques. A cheque should be made out to a company, not an individual, to minimize the chances of fraud.

STOCKBROKERS

The days of the old-fashioned stockbroking firm are disappearing, but you can still find brokers who have not been swallowed up by the mega-corporations. Stockbrokers make their money from commissions on the investments you buy and sell, so it is in their interest to get you to buy and sell as often as possible. This isn't quite as sinister as it sounds, as good stockbrokers take pride in their work and often go out of their way to protect you from doing anything silly. Often they have sensible advice to give about all kinds of investment matters, not just shares.

There are three types of service generally on offer, discretionary, advisory and execution-only:

● The discretionary service is the poshest. You leave all the decisions to your broker while you go off skiing with the royals or hunting elephants in Kenya. Not surprisingly, it tends to cost the most. Unless your portfolio is worth at least £150,000, you will probably not find a broker to offer you this service, although some may take you on if you have as little as £50,000.

- The advisory service is where you are allowed to nag your broker for advice during office hours – and sometimes at night, too! It costs less than the discretionary service, but make sure you understand all the charges.
- The execution-only service is the cheapest and gives no advice at all. You issue your instructions and the broker obeys them without comment. With the advent of the internet, some specialist execution-only brokers have websites chock-full of research for you to digest on your own. Commission costs are low, but the quality of service varies greatly. You need to make sure that you are buying the right shares (some companies have more than one kind) and that you have done all the calculations correctly; for instance, if a company has altered the number of shares in issue and you haven't checked, you could make a nasty mistake.

Some investors like to use both an advisory broker and an execution-only service. This may be a bit rough on the advisory broker, but it enables you to have the best of both worlds. Brokers never know everything, so sometimes you have to go elsewhere. For example, you might use an execution-only service to buy the latest hot high-tech stock in the USA, and a London advisory broker to trade in a British blue chip company. If you do embark on this approach, remember to keep the advisory brokers happy by putting some deals through them – they'll get upset if you just milk them for advice and go elsewhere for your execution-only deals.

Gough's five golden rules for guerrillas

It is said that one can't be taken seriously these days unless one propounds laws, so here are 'Gough's five golden rules' for achieving prosperity:

- Don't put your faith in governments, especially over money.
- Don't spend more than you earn.
- If a deal looks too good to be true, it *is* too good to be true.

- Get rich slowly.
- Trust yourself.

If these rules seem a bit simple-minded, think about the people you know who have grown rich through their own efforts. They are often not particularly clever or well educated, and their methods are often surprisingly unsophisticated. In my view, succeeding as an investor is not so much about trying to outsmart everyone else as it is about steadiness, common sense and self-reliance. As one multimillionaire I know likes to say, 'Keep it simple!'

A little financial maths

People don't like doing sums, but if you are going to be a successful investor you will have to learn how. This section introduces a few important notions which you need to be familiar with.

PAYBACK

Payback is a remarkably simple rule-of-thumb method of assessing investment propositions. It is used in the boardrooms of large companies to help decide whether or not to go ahead with, say, the introduction of a new product or the building of a new factory.

Suppose the cost of purchasing a widget-making machine is £5 million. How long will it take for the profits on the widgets it makes to reach £5 million? That's the 'payback' time – the time it takes to recoup the initial investment. Companies like to see a short payback period, preferably under five years.

SIMPLE AND COMPOUND INTEREST

Interest is the amount that you pay when you borrow money from someone else for a given length of time. It is also the amount that someone will pay you for borrowing your money. If you put money into a bank or a building society, you are lending it money, so make sure that you receive some interest!

Since the amount of interest paid is related to the length of time that the money is borrowed, interest is calculated as a percentage of the sum borrowed per a fixed time period, usually a year. Thus, if you lent a building society £1,000 and it is paying 10 per cent interest per annum, you could get your money back at the end of the year with interest as well: 10 per cent of £1,000 is £100, so you would have £1,100.

If only life were so simple! Unfortunately, governments have found out about interest, and like to take some of it in tax, so your building society might have to offer, say, a gross rate of interest of 10 per cent, which only non-tax-payers can get, and a net rate of 7.5 per cent for most tax-payers. The remainder is taken by the government directly from the building society.

Another complication is that your £1,000 might not buy as much at the end of the year as it would have done at the beginning – this is because of inflation. The 10 per cent interest that you earned should compensate you for the reduced buying power of your £1,000, but the inflation has taken another bite out of your profit. Out of the gross interest of 10 per cent, you might have made only 2 per cent profit after tax and inflation on your original £1,000. The £1,000, by the way, is the 'capital' that you have lent.

The interest rate offered to you will vary, taking tax and inflation into account. A point to notice is:

Interest rates are usually quoted as the interest you will get or give for a year's lending or borrowing, but not always, so you should check.

The kind of interest we are talking about at the moment is called 'simple interest'.

EXAMPLE

If you lent £1,000 for five years at 10 per cent simple interest p.a. (per annum), you would earn £100 per year:

	10 per cent interest
Year 1	£100
Year 2	£100
Year 3	£100
Year 4	£100
Year 5	£100
Total	£500

At the end of the fifth year you would have your original £1,000 back, plus the £500 interest, totalling £1,500. The value of what you lent at the beginning (£1,000) is the 'present value', and what you will get at the end of five years (£1,500) is the 'future value'.

Compound interest

If you were getting £100 in simple interest every year, you could also lend that, and get interest on it.

EXAMPLE

If you lent a bank £1,000 for five years and received 10 per cent interest a year, you could re-invest the 10 per cent (£100) each year and earn interest on that too. If you did this by leaving the interest in a deposit account, the £100 that you received in the first year would earn £10 in the second year, so by the end of the second year you would have:

The capital	£1,000
10% interest on capital in Year 1	£100
10% interest on capital in Year 2	£100
Interest in Year 2 on Year 1's interest	£10
Total	£1,210

Interest plus the interest on the interest is called 'compound interest'. How much compound interest you get depends on how often the bank gives you the interest. If you deposit £2 million in a bank at 10 per cent p.a. and it only gives you the interest at the end of the year, you would have £200,000 in interest at the end of the year, but what if it calculated the interest every six months? The annual interest rate would be the same, but the interest you earned in the first six months, (half of £200,000 = £100,000), would earn interest in the second half. You would earn an extra £5,000, which is half of 10 per cent of £100,000. The intervals between the times when the bank calculates the interest is called the 'conversion period'. The shorter the conversion period, the more the interest will be compounded, and the more money you will make for a given annual rate.

Why compounding is so important

Compounding is one of the great joys of investment, and is the largest part of the investment gains you make over the long term. The longer you invest at a positive rate of return, the more significant the effect of compounding becomes.

The secret of successful investing is patience. The longer you hold an investment, the more it is likely to grow, simply through the effect of compound interest.

In the stock market, which is a risky type of investment in the short term, shares have consistently outperformed cash and bonds over the long term. If you hold shares for the long term, either directly or through managed funds like unit trusts or investment trusts, the risks of volatility (violent changes in price) are ironed out.

EXAMPLE

Here's what would happen if you invested a lump sum of £25,000 in the stock market and achieved an annual rate of return of 8 per cent, and then if you achieved a rate of 10 per cent on the same sum:

Years invested	8%	10%
1	£27,000	£27,500
5	£36,700	£40,300
10	£54,000	£64,800
15	£79,300	£104,000
20	£116,500	£168,200
25	£171,200	£270,900

The longer you hold your investment, the more it grows – and in the later years, the growth becomes remarkably large. Notice that the apparently small difference in the rate of return – only 2 per cent – makes a huge difference in the long run because of the effect of compounding. In the table, an 8 per cent return produces £171,200 after 25 years while a 10, per cent return produces £270,900, a difference of nearly £100,000, or four times the original investment.

LIQUIDITY

You can distinguish assets from one another by their liquidity, which simply means how fast the asset can be turned into cash.

While shares and bonds are highly liquid – although you may not be able to sell for the price you paid – property and businesses are not. In the case of a property, you might expect to sell it within a few months, while a business could take years to sell.

You need some liquidity to give you the freedom to adapt to sudden changes in your circumstances. For example, if you have a house worth a million pounds and no money in the bank, you'll be in a panic if you suddenly have to pay for a new roof.

You often, but not always, get better returns on illiquid assets than highly liquid ones. Keeping all your money in an instant access account will give you great liquidity, for instance, but not much hope of a good return. In the long run, in fact, you might even get a negative return!

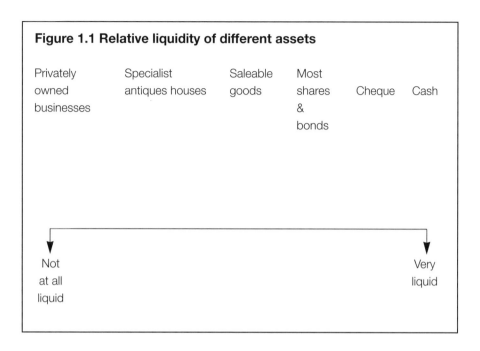

Figure 1.1 Relative liquidity of different assets

| Privately owned businesses | Specialist antiques houses | Saleable goods | Most shares & bonds | Cheque | Cash |

Not at all liquid   Very liquid

Shares in heavily traded companies are highly liquid, since you can sell them with one phone call or internet message, but they may also produce good returns if you hold them for many years.

A useful rule of thumb that is well accepted in the USA, but less talked-about in the UK, is that it is a good idea to keep a percentage of your assets in cash on short-term deposit at all times: 5–10 per cent of your net worth is usually considered appropriate. For eager share traders, this is particularly useful since it prevents you from selling your shares too soon in order to pay for some emergency living expense.

INFLATION

Inflation was remarkably low across the developed world during the 1990s, but there is no reason to expect that it will remain low indefinitely. We may well experience periods of high inflation in the future as we have in the past.

Inflation can be defined as a general increase in prices. It's a chain reaction where price rises are passed on from one supplier to the next until they reach the consumer, who has to pay up. In times of high inflation, people on fixed incomes tend to suffer because their cash can buy less than it could previously.

Inflation figures are published regularly in the national press, and it is worth keeping an eye on them. Increasing inflation can eat into your investment returns – you may be delighted at a return of 15 per cent one year, but what if inflation was at 16 per cent? You would actually be making a loss.

To monitor the effects of inflation, adjust your investment returns downward by the annual rate of inflation that year, from the published figures. This will give you the 'real', or 'inflation-adjusted', return, which is more accurate.

EXAMPLE

On 1 January Joe invests £100,000 in a one-year fixed-term deposit that pays 10 per cent. At the end of the year he receives £110,000 back. If inflation during that time was 2 per cent, his £110,000 would only have the 1 January buying power of £107,800, so his inflation-adjusted return is 7.8 per cent, not 10 per cent.

Coping with inflation

Inflation is genuinely unpredictable over the medium to long term, but there are a variety of investment products designed to protect against inflation shocks. These are discussed in Chapter 2.

The people who are hurt most by rising inflation are those who have little room for manoeuvre, either because their money is tied up or because they have retired and are no longer earning an income. In the famous Weimar inflation in Germany in the 1920s, respectable old ladies literally starved because their bonds were inflated into worthlessness.

You can protect against inflation to some extent by diversifying your assets – some assets tend to increase in value during inflationary periods. We'll look at diversification in more detail in Chapter 8.

HOW LONG WILL IT TAKE TO DOUBLE YOUR MONEY?

To work out approximately how long it will take your money to double from an investment producing a given rate of return, simply divide the annual rate

EXAMPLE:

You are contemplating an investment that will yield 10 per cent a year.

$72 \div 10 = 7.2$

Your money will double approximately every 7.2 years.

of return into 72.

... And to treble your money?

Divide the annual return into 115 to find out roughly how long it will take for

EXAMPLE:

You are contemplating an investment that will yield 10 per cent a year.

$115 \div 10 = 11.5$

Your money will treble approximately every 11.5 years.

your money to treble.

Compounding again!

The doubling and trebling rule is another way of looking at the compounding effect.

EXAMPLE:

If you invest £100,000 to produce an inflation-adjusted average return of 10 per cent a year:

After approximately 7.2 years it will be worth £200,000.
After approximately 14.4 years it will be worth £400,000.
After approximately 21.6 years it will be worth £800,000.
After approximately 28.8 years it will be worth £1,600,000.

Most people don't start investing with a lump sum, so they add to their investments out of saved income over many years, but the same effect applies.

Introducing risk

Investment is not a one-size-fits-all process. We are all different, with different needs and aspirations. Part of the art of successful investing is in tailoring your plans to suit yourself. To do this, you should consider your own attitudes towards risk.

Nothing is 100 per cent certain and there is no such thing as zero risk. This is another way of saying that nobody, not even the Treasury, can predict the future with much certainty. In the investment business, you will come across many pompous individuals who pretend to be able to forecast the future. If you pressed them, they would admit that they don't know for certain, but it is easy to get the impression from watching TV or reading the papers that these prophets are certainly correct. They are not! It is not possible to predict the future with absolute confidence.

It is not possible to predict the future with absolute confidence.
In practice, we have to rely on probability

In practice, we have to rely on probability. It is very *unlikely* that extraterrestrials will conquer Birmingham this year, but it is very *likely* that the sun will come up tomorrow morning.

In investment, we assess risk constantly. Some risks are much easier to judge than others, and it is often possible to calculate likely outcomes given certain assumptions. For instance, gilts, which are bonds guaranteed by the British government, are considered to be completely safe. Over the centuries, the British government has always honoured its gilt obligations, so we make the assumption that gilts carry zero risk. Given that assumption, it is possible to predict accurately the return on gilts held for the life of the loan by simply doing sums.

An ordinary building society account is also considered to have virtually no risk: 90 per cent of the first £20,000 in the account is guaranteed by the government, so it is just a little riskier than a gilt.

Various kinds of investment schemes are structured to give you more risk in return for the chance of getting a better return. Shares are more risky, but they may give you an even better return.

As a general rule, the more risk you are willing to accept, the higher your returns may be. That's why cash deposits in banks and building societies don't pay you a high rate of interest – there is little or no risk of losing your money.

WHAT IS A RISKY INVESTMENT?

Risk is a truly fascinating subject, and it is surprising how few people are willing to contemplate risks in a sober and rational fashion. As an investor, if you train yourself to become a better judge of risk, you may be able to achieve good returns by finding investments that are less risky than they appear.

Some types of asset are inherently more risky than others:

Least risky:
- Cash at the bank
- Bonds
- Second-hand endowment policies

Medium risk:
- Property
- Shares

Very risky:
- Your own business
- Derivatives and commodities

It is important to understand that borrowing, say, £150,000 to buy a house is inherently less risky than borrowing £150,000 to start your own business. This is because businesses are unpredictable and much harder to control than houses, and also because a house loan is secured on the property, so it can be recovered.

Don't assume that an investment is not risky just because most assets of its kind are not thought risky. A bad bank, a problematic house or a troubled corporation may all turn out to be bad investments. Remember to consider worst-case scenarios and how you would act if they occurred.

If you want to be good at investing, don't be silly about risk, either by taking wild plunges that are almost certain to fail or else by dismissing everything as too risky. There is risk in not saving and investing too – the risk of ending up with no money at all! Successful risk-takers take carefully considered gambles with which they can live comfortably. To master risk, you need to master your own emotions. If a certain investment will keep you up worrying every night, it is not worth having – stick to investments that won't make your life a misery, and you'll make better decisions.

2

Shares

In this chapter we will look at the basics of share ownership and stock markets. If you are a UK taxpayer you should read the section on Individual Savings Accounts (ISAs) carefully. These are currently a very attractive way to invest in shares. The topics covered in this chapter are:

- *What are shares?*
- *The London Stock Exchange*
- *Managed funds – unit trusts, OEICs and investment trusts*
- *Individual Savings Accounts (ISAs)*
- *Buying and selling shares*
- *Yields and price/earnings ratios*
- *Net asset value (NAV)*
- *Investment strategies*
- *Stock indices*
- *Index investing*
- *The world's stock markets*
- *American Depositary Receipts (ADRs)*

What are shares?

A company that is quoted on a stock exchange offers shares in its ownership to anyone who wants to buy them. A large company may have issued millions of shares. There are several types of shares, but the most common are called 'ordinary' shares. If you buy one, you are a part owner, or shareholder, in the company, with the right to share in its profits, to attend board meetings and to vote on key issues and appointments. You can sell your shares if someone is willing to buy them.

The price of a share changes all the time: it may bear little relation to the cash value of the company if you were to sell all its assets. There have been many cases, for instance, where the buildings owned by a company were grossly undervalued and its share price was much lower than it 'should' have been. These days, when the stock markets of the world are booming, many companies are valued at much higher prices in the stock market than their 'real' value. And there are new challenges to valuation – how, for example, do you value a high-tech company whose products change every few months and whose real earning power resides in the brains of its talented employees? The constantly changing difference between the market capitalization – which is essentially the total value of all a company's shares at the current market price – and 'real' value is one of the great themes of stock market analysis.

Shares are volatile – they go up and down all the time as people buy and sell them. All sorts of factors influence the prices of shares, including company analyses, political change, natural disasters, wars and economic fluctuations, but one of the main influences is the behaviour of people who buy shares, or, as some would have it, 'the madness of crowds'. If many investors think that the price of a share is going to go up and buy it, the price of the share will go up until they stop buying. This may have nothing to do with the essential soundness of the company. As we will see, this kind of volatility is temporary. In the long term, shares in good companies are thought to be better investments than those in bad ones, which might seem obvious, but in the intense world of the stock market, it is often forgotten!

This capitalist system of financing big business is fundamental to the world's present economic system. Following the collapse of the USSR, there is no other system that is a serious contender with it. Thus, like it or not, people who want to increase or preserve their assets must learn how it works, and will probably decide to participate in it at some time in their lives.

Shares are also called 'equities'. Outside the UK, shares are often called 'stocks'. This can cause confusion since, in the UK, bonds are traditionally referred to as 'stocks'.

HOW SHAREHOLDERS MAKE PROFITS

There are two main ways:

- by selling their shares at a higher price than they paid for them; and secondly,
- by receiving 'dividends', which are a distribution of profits that the company has made.

Another way is to sell 'short', which means, in effect, to bet that a share's price will drop. This is neither easy nor advisable unless you are a very experienced investor.

THE QUALITY OF SHARES

The soundest, best-established companies are known as 'blue chips'. The term 'blue chip' comes from the world of the casino, where blue chips are those with the highest value. Next come the 'secondary issues', which are shares in solid companies. These receive slightly less confidence than the blue chips. 'Growth stocks' are shares in newer companies which are expected to do well in the future, but which may not do so. Finally, there are 'penny shares', which are those of companies with a low value, but which may increase for some reason.

Don't become fixated on the apparent safety of 'blue chips'

Growth stocks become blue chips, blue chips become dinosaurs, and the stock market jungle is always throwing up new possibilities. Don't become fixated on the apparent safety of 'blue chips'; an American friend of mine likes to refer to them as 'blue gyps' (a slang term in the USA for a swindle).

KINDS OF SHARES

Companies usually start out by being privately owned. When they get big enough the owners may decide to 'go public' and sell some of the shares of their company on a stock market. The rules for going public are quite strict, to make sure that the company is worth buying. The advantage to the original owners of selling their shares is that, if the offering is successful, they can realize very large sums of cash. Some owners, however, prefer to keep control by staying private, while others have been known to buy back all the shares and return the company to private ownership.

Companies can issue several kinds of shares, usually labelled 'A', 'B', 'C', and so on. Each class of share will have different rules, different market prices and different dividends.

Most shares are 'ordinary' shares, putting the shareholders at the back of the queue of creditors if the company goes bust, and giving them equal voting rights and dividends to all other holders of ordinary shares in a company. Less common are 'preference' shares, which give the holder a slightly better chance of recovering some money in the event of a liquidation, often pay a fixed dividend, and usually don't give voting rights. The rights of preference shares vary from company to company, so you should always examine the rules in detail before buying. 'Convertible' preference shares give the holder the option to change them to ordinary shares at a fixed future price and date.

Companies sometimes issue warrants. These give the holder the right to 'subscribe' for shares at a fixed price at some point in the future. If the share price then rises higher than the subscription price, the warrant can be sold in the market. People who buy company bonds (see Chapter 4) are sometimes given warrants as an inducement to hold on to their bonds, thus helping the company to prosper.

When considering the purchase of obscure shares, always investigate the number of market makers (see immediately below) in the share and its marketability before investing. A share with only one market maker may be very expensive, in terms of the 'spread' (see immediately below), to buy and sell, and it may not be possible to sell the share at all for long periods of time.

The London Stock Exchange

Since the 'Big Bang' reform in 1986, groups of financial services have been formed, combining several kinds of business that used to be kept separate:

- **Market making** – this means dealing in certain shares 'wholesale', guaranteeing to buy or sell these shares at all times, which ensures that investors can trade with them whenever they want to. Market makers sell shares at more than they buy them for in order to make a profit. The difference between the price at which they will buy ('bid') and the price at which they will sell ('offer') is called the bid/offer spread. On popular shares in large companies the spread is quite small, while on less popular companies the spread gets wider.
- **Broker/dealing** – this is the business of buying shares on behalf of investors.

- **Investment analysis** – this is the detailed study of the performance and prospects of companies and industries.
- **Merchant banking** – principally, this involves bringing new companies to the market, arranging rights issues and advising companies on takeover bids and defences.

These groups are called securities houses. The different parts of the organization often have access to privileged information which, in order to keep the market fair, they are not supposed to share with other parts of the group. For example, if the merchant banking part of a securities house is privately advising a company on a planned takeover bid, it is not supposed to tell the broker/dealers or the others in its own group because they would use this 'inside' information by buying shares in the company targeted for takeover in the hope of a quick profit.

In order to prevent this kind of conflict of interest, 'Chinese Walls' exist between the various arms of the securities houses. They are intended to keep sensitive information secret. Often, the different arms are housed in separate buildings, but many people feel that Chinese Walls don't really work.

Since the Big Bang, shares have been dealt via computer. There are very few places left in the world where dealers actually crowd together waving bits of paper. These days, almost everyone sits in front of a computer screen.

Managed funds

The latest acronym for managed funds is 'CIV' (collective investment vehicles). The principle is simple: a large number of people put savings into a fund that is managed by professionals. The idea is that the professionals will be able to get better deals and discounts on their stock market and other investments because of the huge size of the fund (which is true) and that they will make better investment decisions than private investors (which may not be, see page 50).

Managed funds come in different varieties, which are discussed below. Guerrilla investors should appreciate that the companies and individuals who manage such funds often make most of their money from deducting charges from the funds. Depending on the contract, a manager can draw down huge sums from the fund, irrespective of whether or not the fund is profitable.

A report in late 2000 by Professor Merlin Stone of Bristol Business School (*Stealth Financial Charges and the Mass Affluent*) suggested that financial advisers recommend products that are overpriced and that the 'mass affluent' in the UK have paid £3.8 billion in unnecessary investment charges for packaged products that often include managed funds.

The 'mass affluent', it is argued, are hit in two ways, first by being overcharged and then by being steered in the name of safety into investments that produce poor returns.

OPEN-ENDED INVESTMENTS

Investment trusts are 'closed-ended' funds with a fixed number of shares in issue so the share price can be influenced by investor demand (see below). Unit trusts and open-ended investment companies (OEICs) are 'open-ended', with units or shares being newly created or cancelled whenever people invest or withdraw money, so the price of units is only influenced by the value of the total fund – the 'net asset value' (NAV).

UNIT TRUSTS

Before we look at what unit trusts are, you should be aware of these points:

- Unit trusts that are closely linked to stock market indices are one of the safest ways to invest in shares; the reasons for this are examined in detail below.
- Investment trusts frequently offer better value than unit trusts.
- Unit trusts are heavily marketed financial products aimed at the general public. Their literature and sales approach are designed to put fearful savers at their ease and are generally bland; the image projected is paternalistic and reassuring. You pay for all this 'service' in the charges.
- You hear a lot in financial advertising about how advantageous it is for you to put your money into the hands of the professional unit trust manager who will invest it so much better than you can. As will be discussed in Chapter 8, there is considerable evidence that this is not really the case.

Investment trusts frequently offer better value than unit trusts

Unit trusts were introduced into the UK from America, where they are known as 'mutual funds', in the 1930s. The fund is professionally managed and spread across a range of investments, including shares and bonds in the UK and in foreign markets. The value of the units fluctuates with the value of the investments of the funds. Since you pay charges to buy and hold units, they are medium- to long-term investments. In other words, you should expect to hold them for at least three years.

Traditionally, the main advantages of unit trusts are considered to be:

- Good diversification for the small investor – possibly better than you could do on your own.
- Less worry, and less work, than holding your own portfolio.
- At times it has been difficult for small investors to find brokers to handle their business. In such conditions, which do not exist currently, unit trusts were virtually the only way a small investor could get into the stock market.
- Unit trusts have been well regulated and far freer from scandal than other investments.

The money is held by a trustee, such as a bank or an insurance company, and not by the unit trust company itself. The trust is regulated by a Trust Deed, which lays down all the rules of how the money is to be handled.

Types of unit trust

There are various different categories of unit trusts, specializing in different kinds of investments. Here are the main ones:

- UK general trusts
- UK growth trusts
- UK equity income trusts
- gilt and fixed-interest trusts – these trusts invest in bonds, not shares, and are intended to provide safety, a higher income and low growth
- growth trusts spread across shares in particular countries or areas of the world, such as the Far East, Europe, Japan and the United States; they are designed to increase the capital value and are thus more risky than income-oriented funds
- financial trusts – these specialize in buying the shares of banks and insurance companies.

Offshore trusts

This is a British term meaning a trust that is not an 'authorized unit trust' in the UK. Many of them are run from places like the Channel Islands, Bermuda and the Cayman Islands, and are run on the same lines as 'onshore' unit trusts. They are harder to buy and sell in the UK, and are, in some cases, less well regulated, so you should check the companies out very carefully before investing. Their charges tend to be higher and there are no direct tax advantages for UK taxpayers.

Savings schemes

Many trusts allow you to pay in a monthly sum, and you can miss a few months, or reduce or increase your payment without any penalties. Such schemes should outperform financial products such as endowment and unit-linked insurance policies.

Managed unit trusts

The difference between an ordinary unit trust and a managed fund is that the latter uses an independent professional to decide how the money should be invested. The idea is that since the manager is independent and can be dismissed easily, he or she will have no motive to 'churn' (needlessly buy and sell) the investments held by the trust.

Umbrella funds

These are offshore trusts that have separate funds in different parts of the world, allowing you to switch from one fund to another at low cost.

Buying and selling unit trusts

There are many ways to buy unit trusts: you can buy through a newspaper advertisement, a bank, a solicitor, an accountant, a stockbroker or an insurance broker. If you buy through an intermediary, you will be expected to hand over a cheque once the units have been bought. You will then receive a contract note recording your purchase. Some weeks later you should receive a unit trust certificate which is your proof of ownership. As with all business documents, you should always check both the contract note and the certificate to see that the right type of unit trust is recorded, that the number of units are the same on the contract note and the certificate, and that your name and address appear correctly. If all is well, you should then store the documents somewhere safe where they will not be lost or destroyed.

When you come to sell, you contact the organization from whom you bought the units, and send them the certificate, having signed it first. Normally you should get the money within ten days. If you lose the certificate, you must apply for a new one, which will take several weeks. You can still sell units in the meantime, but you won't receive the money until you have surrendered the duplicate certificate.

Check newspapers for the bid and offer prices; remember that the higher one, the offer, is the one you must pay when buying, and the lower one, or bid, is the one you get when selling. Check the difference between the bid and offer prices; normally they are around 6 per cent, but they can be more than double this. The majority of unit trusts quote prices every day, but some may do so once a week or even only once a month. You may find that the trust has rounded up a buying price or rounded down a selling price by 1.25p or 1 per cent, whichever is the smaller; they are allowed to do this.

The charges

The two main charges are the 'front-end load' or fee that you pay when you buy, and an annual management fee. The front-end load is included in the published offer price. If you buy into a unit trust and sell soon after, you will probably lose 5 per cent or so. The idea is to hang on until the units grow enough to cover the front-end load. These charges are in addition to the bid/offer spread discussed above.

Check the annual management fee before you buy. It is usually 1 per cent or less, but VAT is added. This fee is usually taken from investment income automatically by the management.

Exchanges

If you have good-quality shares, you can exchange them for units in many unit trusts. The cost of doing this is usually lower than if you sold the shares in the normal way and then bought units, because the trusts want you to join their scheme. You can do such swaps if your shares are worth more than around £500.

Tax

Income tax is deducted from your dividends at the basic rate and you will have to pay capital gains tax (CGT) on profits over your annual exemption. However, there is no CGT on gains made within the fund, if, for instance, the manager switches investments.

Unit trust advisory services (UTAS)

There are over a thousand unit trusts available in the UK, managed by nearly 200 groups, and the trusts are in many categories. In order to expedite the process of picking the ones you want, there are unit trust advisory services (UTAS) available that monitor most or all of the trusts in the marketplace and will give detailed reports on them. Often the first report is free, after which, if you invest through a UTAS, you will continue to get advice for an annual fee of 0.75 per cent.

OPEN-ENDED INVESTMENT COMPANIES (OEICs)

OEICs and unit trusts are quite similar. They are both funds holding a large number of stocks and shares, divided into equal parts that are bought by many individual investors. The amount of capital they hold increases and decreases as investors buy and sell. If more investors want units or OEIC shares than want to sell, the manager will issue new units or shares, but if there are more sellers than buyers, the managers of OEICs may have to sell some of their underlying investments. Unlike unit trusts, OEICs are companies.

Suppose you invest £10,000 in a unit trust with a total of £10 million of assets. If you withdraw your investment, the fund's total assets would go down to £9,990,000. On the other hand, if you decided instead to add another £10,000 to your investment, the assets of the fund would rise to £10,010,000.

An OEIC quotes all its charges separately and lets you buy and sell shares in the OEIC at a single price. Unlike unit trusts, there is no 'bid/offer spread' – you know exactly what price you can buy and sell at. Unit trusts may now voluntarily move to single pricing, so this difference may disappear.

OEICs are being introduced to broaden the appeal of UK managed funds abroad. UK funds have been able to market throughout the EU for years but have not attracted much business because Continental investors aren't familiar with the pricing of unit trusts. Existing unit trusts are beginning to convert to OEICs.

THE CHARGING STRUCTURE OF OPEN-ENDED INVESTMENTS

As was noted earlier, there is a huge range of charges between different funds. Some will charge as much as 6 per cent at the outset with ongoing management fees of 1.5 per cent or more a year. Others have no initial charge and ongoing fees of 0.5 per cent or less. Some funds have 'exit charges' when you withdraw your money, usually within five years of investing.

In general, the cheapest funds are index tracking funds (see below), which tend to be cheaper because they are mechanical in nature and do not require the employment of expensive fund managers.

Open-ended funds have attracted the criticism that they prey on the naivety of inexperienced investors who are easily frightened by scare stories and are blinded by the mystique of stock market. Guerrilla investors never stop educating themselves about the market and have little need of this kind of investment product; occasionally, though, you may find a fund that is of interest.

INVESTMENT TRUSTS

Investment trusts are similar to unit trusts in that they are pooled funds which are professionally invested in a wide range of shares. They are not trusts, however, but companies whose shares are quoted on the stock market; you buy shares, rather than units, in an investment trust. They are taxed in much the same way, and offer a similar variety of categories, including monthly savings schemes. Generally, they are better value than unit trusts because the buying costs are often lower and the shares can often be bought at a discount to the value of the fund. The bid/offer spread is around 2 per cent, as opposed to 5 per cent in unit trusts, annual management fees are about half, and the initial charges are lower too. Another feature is that they are allowed to borrow money to invest; this makes them slightly riskier and more volatile than unit trusts. All this helps to boost their performance.

You buy the shares in the same way as you would those of any company listed on the stock market, through a stockbroker. Some large investment trusts also run schemes where you can invest small amounts on a regular monthly basis.

When you buy and sell, you pay the stockbroker's commission, plus stamp duty on purchases. Investment trust managers do make charges, which you can find in the accounts. These tend to be lower than the charges on unit trusts.

Net asset value (NAV)

All pooled investments are judged by their net asset value per share or unit. The net asset value per share is essentially the total value of the fund's portfolio of investments divided by the total number of its own shares.

Investment trusts are traded on the market like any other company, so their share price will fluctuate according to supply and demand. They calculate their net asset value per share at regular intervals, generally every three months. For a number of reasons investment trusts tend to trade at a discount to the NAV. Remember that while the published NAV is historical (recorded at the last valuation date), the share price is current, so you may not be able to calculate the precise difference between the two.

Fund raiders

With the growth of giant financial conglomerates, the industry is becoming 'vertically integrated', which means that a group may own banks, stockbrokers, unit trusts, investment trusts, bond traders and so on. This is not wildly good news for the guerrilla investor, but there are ways of exploiting it. There are a number of independently owned fund groups that buy control of investment trusts trading at a huge discount to NAV and 'crack them open' by converting them to unit trusts, a very profitable strategy for shareholders in the raiding company. Vertical integration has created huge conflicts of interest within financial groups, and raiders have many interesting opportunities to exploit inefficiencies among the giant financial institutions.

Individual Savings Accounts (ISAs)

The Individual Savings Account (ISA) is a new tax-free scheme designed by the government to encourage people to save. Like its predecessors, the PEP and the TESSA, it is likely to be tinkered with endlessly, so by the time you read this book, some of the rules and rates may have changed. The reason for the change of scheme? Politics, pure and simple – ISAs are intended to encourage a wider range of people to save while modestly reducing the benefits for those who already did so during the PEP era.

Since ISAs are a tax-sheltered scheme, if you don't pay tax in the UK, you don't need one. Most of us do pay tax, however, and despite the restrictions that ISAs impose, it will usually be worthwhile to have a scheme.

The principle of ISAs is simple – you put in your money, up to certain limits, and during its life it grows tax free, which makes it grow much faster. You can have an ISA for cash, shares, bonds or life insurance, subject to certain restrictions. ISAs were introduced in April 1999, and are guaranteed to run for at least ten years from that date.

You can invest less in an ISA than you could in the final version of the PEP scheme, but it is still attractive.

THE ISA COMPONENTS

ISAs categorize investments into three components:

- cash
- stocks and shares
- life assurance

and you can invest in any or all of these components. You can have three different managers for the three different components or one manager for all of them. You can also invest in certain unit trusts (see below). There are two sorts of ISAs, as follows:

- Maxi ISAs let you invest in one or more of the components with one manager.
- Mini ISAs are the separate components, held with different managers.

In any one tax year you can contribute to either one Maxi or up to three

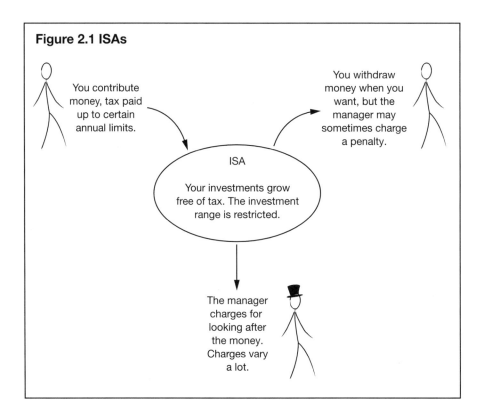

Figure 2.1 ISAs

You contribute money, tax paid up to certain annual limits.

You withdraw money when you want, but the manager may sometimes charge a penalty.

ISA

Your investments grow free of tax. The investment range is restricted.

The manager charges for looking after the money. Charges vary a lot.

different Mini ISAs, but you cannot contribute to both a Maxi and a Mini ISA in the same year.

INVESTMENT LIMITS

The annual contribution limits for Mini ISAs are:

- Cash – £3,000 maximum
- Stocks and shares – £3,000 maximum for 2000/2001
- Life assurance – £1,000 maximum

The annual contribution limits for Maxi ISAs are:

- Cash – £3,000 maximum in 2000/2001
- Stocks and shares – £7,000 maximum in 2000/2001
- Life assurance – £1,000 maximum.

The overall limit on the Maxi ISA is £7,000, but you can spread it across the three components subject to the limits listed above.

TAX BENEFITS

ISAs are free of both capital gains tax and income tax and a 10 per cent tax credit is paid for the first five years of the plan on dividends received from UK shares. You do not have to report or declare ISAs to the Inland Revenue. Losses within ISAs cannot be set against capital gains tax liabilities outside ISAs. To open an ISA you have to be aged 18 or over and resident and ordinarily resident (see Chapter 15 for definitions) in the UK for tax purposes. You cannot hold an ISA jointly.

COOLING-OFF PERIOD

Some kinds of ISA must give you a 'cooling-off' period (usually seven or 14 days) which allows you to withdraw from the deal. You are then free to start a different ISA scheme.

WITHDRAWALS

You can withdraw money at any time without losing the tax relief you have already enjoyed. Some fixed-term ISAs may impose a penalty for early withdrawal, as may some life assurance schemes.

PERMITTED INVESTMENTS

For the cash component, you can invest in:

- bank and building society accounts
- units in authorized unit trust money market funds ('cash funds')
- National Savings products, which are specifically designed for ISAs.

For the stocks and shares component, you can invest in:

- shares and company bonds listed on a recognized stock exchange anywhere in the world
- gilt-edged securities ('gilts') and similar securities issued by governments of other countries in the European Economic Area
- UK authorized unit trusts that invest in shares and securities
- shares in UK open-ended investment companies (OEICs)
- shares and securities in approved investment trusts (except for property investment trusts)
- units or shares in Undertakings for Collective Investment in Transferable Securities (UCITS) funds based elsewhere in the European Union (these are similar to the UK authorized unit trusts and OEICs listed above).

For the life insurance component, you can invest in:

- 'unit linked' or 'investment linked' policies
- 'with profits' policies, where you share in the profits the insurer makes from investing your premiums; if the insurer makes such profits, a bonus is paid, normally annually.

CAT STANDARDS

Following sharp practices in the design and selling of certain PEP products, the government has introduced CAT standards in the hope of preventing the same happening with ISAs. 'CAT' stands for reasonable **C**harges, easy **A**ccess, and fair **T**erms. CAT-standard ISA providers are committed to treating customers fairly. They must use plain English and avoid complex or misleading features.

CHOOSING A MANAGER

The trouble with consumerism and investment is that they don't mix well. Consumerism is about selling one-size-fits-all products to mass markets, while successful investing is about pursuing a highly individual strategy. As a state-sponsored scheme, ISAs present investment managers with the challenge of providing products that will appeal to large numbers of people who are not investment-literate, while making profits for both themselves and their clients. The clients' profits often suffer.

Check if the ISA manager will charge for running your ISA, including any charges for withdrawals and transfers. CAT standard ISAs have limits on charges. Some managers offer ISAs restricted to their company's own products while others offer a choice of their own and other companies' products.

When selecting an ISA, the two key points to remember are:

- Check all charges and penalties and seek to keep them as low as possible.
- Check all restrictions on transfers, choice of investment, withdrawals and so on. Ideally you should choose ISAs that give you the widest choices at the lowest cost.

ISAs cover a broad range of investments, not only shares, and are intended to provide something for everyone, but in the case of shares, self-select ISAs may be the most attractive.

Experienced investors tend to question the value of being charged fees by managers

As we will see later (page 150), there is evidence that investment managers are not superior in their ability to choose winning share portfolios, so experienced investors tend to question the value of being charged fees by managers to do something which they might do as well, or better, themselves.

TRANSFERS

Normally, you may transfer your ISA by applying to a new manager. The existing ISA manager may charge a penalty, or insist that you sell any existing ISA investments and transfer cash. ISA cash, savings and investments must always remain in the same component. For instance, you cannot move funds from a cash ISA with one manager to a stocks and shares ISA with another.

If you want to transfer the money you have put into your ISA in the current year, you must transfer all of it. Any extra money you contribute in the current year must go into the new ISA. You can also transfer some or all of the money you put into your ISA in earlier years, but some managers may not allow you to transfer only a part.

'SELF-SELECT' ISAs

'Self-select' ISAs are intended to give investors freedom from the restrictions imposed by providers' stock and share investments. This implies a degree of responsibility on the part of the investor, not least to trade judiciously, since every transaction on the stock market costs money. Some self-select ISAs have high charges, and all plans will have restrictions on the range of permitted investments. Self-select ISAs don't allow you to invest in life insurance, and most only offer the stocks and shares component.

You should check:

- The investment restrictions
- The charges
- The capacity of the manager to cope with clients' demands. There is no point in investing with the cheapest provider if it transpires that they cannot administer the scheme efficiently because they are swamped by demand. The most common problem is that the manager does not answer the telephone during busy periods, but it is more serious if the manager makes errors in your portfolio records. This can escalate into a time-consuming nightmare, and is definitely to be avoided if possible!

Few self-select ISAs make an initial charge but most plans have an annual charge, usually based on a percentage of the value of your portfolio, expressed as a percentage charged per quarter with a minimum sum. You can expect this charge to range from 0.5 per cent to 1.5 per cent a year with a minimum of £25 to £50. Charges, apart from dealing costs, attract 17.5 per cent VAT.

Dealing costs are the price you pay for buying or selling shares. You do this through the manager. Normally there will be a minimum dealing charge, which will have a disproportionately large effect on small deals. Minimum dealing costs range from around £9 to £45, with maximum rates of between 0.9 per cent and 2 per cent. ISAs are not really intended for the very active trader – if you want to buy and sell shares every day, don't do it through an ISA.

There may also be charges for ad hoc portfolio valuations, annual reports and accounts, attending meetings, dividend collection and transfers. In the case of annual reports, you can obtain them free from the relevant company's registrar, or, often, from the internet. You can value your portfolio yourself if you keep records of your holdings, and few people have the time to attend company meetings, so you should be able to avoid most of these charges.

Most self-select ISAs are provided by stockbrokers and the high street banks. Some managers offer both a maxi ISA with investment in stocks and shares and a cash component, and a mini ISA for stocks and shares only. They are generally designed to take lump-sum investments of between £250 and £3,000, but some allow monthly contributions of £50.

Any plan that shelters investments from tax is welcome

THE OUTLOOK FOR ISAs

Over the next few years the tax-free advantages of ISAs may be reduced, so they will not be as tax efficient as PEPs used to be, but any plan that shelters investments from tax is welcome. With very long-term growth of equity investments averaging less than 10 per cent annually, reducing the tax-bite will have a positive effect on your returns, even if you are being skinned alive by managers' charges. In the medium term (say, ten years), future governments may introduce better schemes or improve ISAs.

Use ISAs to save and to invest in blue chip companies that are unlikely to go bust. Don't expect to buy and sell shares within an ISA frequently – many people find that they only deal once or twice a year. As we will see later, there is substantial evidence that infrequent trading helps to improve your returns.

Investing in an ISA depends on how optimistic you are about the performance of your investments and how much you are investing. If you think that the annual capital gains tax exemption might not be enough to cover your capital gains, then you should make use of an ISA. For instance, if you are saving to repay a mortgage, it wouldn't do you much good if you had to pay CGT when cashing in your investments at the end of your 25-year term. However, this only helps if you would be liable for CGT outside the ISA. In general, basic rate and non-taxpayers currently pay CGT at 20 per cent on the gains that they make from selling shares. Higher-rate taxpayers pay CGT at 40 per cent. The CGT is reduced in a number of ways, including:

- **Taper relief** – the longer you hold an asset (up to ten years), the less capital gains tax you finally pay on it.
- **The annual exemption** – currently worth £7,200. You can make gains of up to £7,200 a year before you start to pay CGT, which is an excellent way of avoiding the tax. Broadly speaking, any losses you make on share sales can also be offset against CGT liability.

Buying and selling shares

Except for new issues, you must usually buy shares through a broker. Since the Big Bang, brokers have found that increased costs have made it difficult to offer an ideal service to everyone, so, unless you have £50,000 or more to invest, the cheapest deal available is the 'execution-only' service, which means that the broker just does what you ask, without offering any advice. Not all brokers offer this service, so you will have to shop around. If you are investing £7,000 or less each year, you should use an ISA scheme, which limits the field further (see above for how these work).

Judging shares – some commonly used terms

The following terms are commonly used in connection with the process of judging shares.

EARNINGS PER SHARE

Earnings per share (EPS) is simply the total dividends paid out by the company in a year, divided by the total number of ordinary shares. This is not the same as profits, since some profits are not paid out as dividends.

YIELDS AND PRICE/EARNINGS RATIOS

These are the two main ways that investors judge shares and both are published in the financial pages. The yield tells you the rate of income, as dividends, that you will get at the current share price. The p/e (price/earnings) ratio is the market price of the share divided by the company's earnings per share. It is a measure of how much the market is prepared to pay for the company, given the profits that it makes. It is often said that the actual number of a p/e ratio is irrelevant, and that it is whether that number is right that is important. For a more detailed discussion of p/e ratios, see Chapter 8.

FINDING BARGAINS THROUGH NET ASSET VALUE (NAV)

Unlike yields and p/e ratios, which can mislead those of us who are not maestros at the art of analysis, the net asset value of a share is a 'real' measurement. The NAV is calculated by adding up all the company's assets, subtracting all its liabilities, and dividing the result by the number of ordinary shares in the company. This gives you a number that is a theoretical value of a share in the company if it was broken up and sold off. The value is only theoretical because in practice the money that would be raised from selling assets is likely to be different from the valuation of those assets in the accounts. NAVs shed an interesting light on the stock market, though, because it is often the case that they are considerably lower than the market price of the shares. For instance, the NAV of a share might be $2 and its market price might be $6. If you are the kind of investor who is brave enough to buy shares during a crash and when there is 'blood in the streets', finding NAVs that were higher than the market price of the relevant shares could be a good guide to choosing which companies to invest in, the rationale being that you would be buying into the companies cheaply, and that their share prices would be likely to rise above their NAVs when times improved.

Investment strategies

Try this exercise when considering which shares to invest in. Obtain the prospectuses of a number of very successful investment and unit trusts that look for long-term growth and see which shares they hold. Make a list of these companies and organize them into their various industries. Now obtain annual reports for all these companies, and try to get to know them a little better. Look for companies that have good growth rates and a strong position in their own market and that sell something for which you believe there will be a continuing and growing demand. Now get in-depth studies for each of the companies on this shorter list – you may have to pay for these and do some detective work to find them, but they do exist. Increasingly, they are available on the internet. Try to understand these studies as fully as possible. Now list all the pros and cons for each of these companies and narrow down your list. Pretend to invest in each of the companies on your shortlist and watch what happens for a year. By the end of this process, you will not only be well acquainted with some of the best companies available, but you will also have learned a great deal about the interface between the stock market and business in general – you will be much better qualified to make your investment decisions.

Here are some strategies you may want to consider:

- If you have invested in a share that has increased dramatically, sell off enough to get back the original investment and hold on to the rest. This helps you to stay calm – losing a profit is not so bad as losing your capital.
- Look for companies that are worth a lot more than their share price. You can find this out by looking at their accounts and reading studies on them.
- Look for companies that have good growth potential but a share price that is still low.
- Look for companies that are likely to be taken over (see Chapter 5).
- If the market crashes in a big way, buy good-quality shares – they will probably go up again.

Here are my pet 'don'ts':

- Don't believe in technical analysis, which is the prediction of future prices on the basis of past patterns. It is supposed to work because of the 'psychology' of investors, but it has a rather less rational basis than astrology or the study of UFOs. See Chapter 8 for a more detailed discussion of this strange cult.
- Don't spread yourself too thin. Specialize in certain areas and get to know them well.
- Don't keep jumping in and out of shares in the hope of a quick buck. This will cost you money. Have the guts to hold on to companies that you believe in, having done the hard work of studying them before you buy.

Stock indices

A stock index is a mathematical measurement of the performance of a number of shares as a group.

Today, the most widely followed indices include:

- **The Standard and Poor's 500 Index** (S&P 500), which follows 500 shares quoted on the New York Stock Exchange, American Stock Exchange and the over-the-counter market in the United States. Dominated by stocks of large 'blue chip' companies, the S&P 500 Index accounts for roughly three-quarters of all US stock market value. It provides a solid foundation for investing in US stocks.
- **The Wilshire 5000 Total Market Index**, an index of all regularly traded US common stocks. The Wilshire 4500 Completion Index, a subset of the Wilshire 5000 Total Market Index, excludes the stocks in the S&P 500 Index.
- **The Russell 2000 Index**, which covers small-capitalization stocks in the USA.
- **The FTSE 100** (Financial Times Stock Exchange 100 Share Index), which measures 100 of the largest companies quoted in London and was introduced principally for options and futures trading.
- **The FT-30 Share Index** (also known as the Financial Times Ordinary Share Index), which measures 30 blue chip companies quoted on the London stock market.
- **The FT Actuaries Indices**, which examine the performances of different industrial sectors so you can judge the relative performance of, say, shipping and energy.
- **Morgan Stanley Capital International Europe, Australasia, Far East Index** (MSCI EAFE), which is the dominant standard for the major international markets.
- **The Morgan Stanley Capital International Select Emerging Markets Free Index**, which consists of stocks in 15 countries – Argentina, Brazil, the Czech Republic, Greece, Hong Kong, Hungary, Indonesia, Israel, Mexico, the Philippines, Poland, Singapore, South Africa, Thailand and Turkey.

There are many more indices, and they are a very helpful tool against which to compare the performance of individual companies. Anyone can run an index, and you may see obscure indices advertised by private investment firms.

In Chapter 8, stock market indices are shown to be extremely important in the analysis and measurement of the risks of investment. Indices provide strong evidence that shares are a good investment over the long term, and fund managers are always trying to get their funds to 'beat' the performance of the indices. There are even funds and portfolios that are tied to an index, and move up and down with it, the idea being to reduce risk. Investing in funds that 'track' the indices, by spreading money in the same proportions as the index uses to produce its measurements, is more popular in the United States than here, possibly because the realities of the risk/reward relationship are better understood there.

THE ROLE OF THE INSTITUTIONS

In important stock markets, such as those of New York and London, most of the investing is done by pension funds, unit and investment trusts and insurance companies. Along with banks and building societies, they are known as the 'institutions'. Most of the money in these funds is owned indirectly by ordinary people so, in effect, the institutions are middlemen. The funds are run by managers who decide how the money is invested. These managers are under enormous pressure to 'outperform' the averages of the market, as indicated by the market indices – this is principally because they want to do well in their personal careers, and the way to do well as a fund manager is to think in the short term and try to produce spectacular results. The net result is that most of these funds don't outperform the market. In fact, since they make up such a large proportion of the market's capital, one could say that they *are* the market, and can't outperform themselves – they are just too big.

DON'T BE MISLED BY THE INDEX

Indices are constructed to provide a measuring point for portfolio comparisons, but they are more useful for large funds than for private investors. For instance, the FTSE-100 is re-based (adjusted) every three months – companies that have fallen below the 100th place measured in market capitalization are dropped, while those rising into the top 100 UK companies replace them. If an investor does not sell a share because it has dropped out of the index, the value of his portfolio declines, while the index advances.

Index investing

Once available only to institutional investors, index investing has become an increasingly popular investment strategy, especially in America where more than $347 billion is invested in index funds. Indexing is an investment approach that seeks to match the investment returns of a specified stock or bond market index. When indexing, an investment manager attempts to mimic the investment results of the target index by holding all the securities in the index. The manager does not vary from this strategy, and does not buy other shares in an attempt to get better returns. Indexing is therefore a 'passive' investment approach emphasizing broad diversification and low trading activity. Index funds hold shares in all the companies of a given index in the same proportion as they are weighted in that index. In the case of very large indices covering many hundreds of companies, an index fund may only hold a representative sample in its portfolio.

Although indexing derives from the unproven theory that the markets operate efficiently (see page 152), its rationale is based on the undeniable statistical fact that it is impossible for the majority of investors to outperform the overall stock market at the same time.

The costs of fund management and of share dealing are high for the private investor, and by contrast index funds charge low fees, reflecting the low cost of administration. Since there is no active investment management, in theory the fund's overheads ought to be lower, which may result in lower charges to you, the investor. Indexing's main appeal is not to investors who want to make a 'killing'. It is attractive to long-term investors who seek a good long-term investment return through broadly diversified share investments.

When the overall stock market falls, you can expect the price of shares in an index fund to fall too. Indexing simply ensures that your returns will not stray far from the returns on the index that the fund tracks.

While the principle of index investing is simple, there are some points you should consider:

- Funds offering very low charges may raise their charges in the future and may suffer from increased dealing costs, which could, over the long term, cause their performance to diverge from the index (this divergence is called 'tracking error').
- Funds that track the large indices covering most or all of the market, such as the FTSE All Share Index in the UK, may not all use the same representative samples. Only time will tell just how 'representative' these samples really are.

- Funds with high charges may also suffer from tracking error because the charges reduce your returns.
- If index tracking becomes a major force in the markets and a particular index, such as the FTSE 100 or America's S&P 500, becomes very popular with index funds, large sums of money could drive it up to an unnaturally high level, followed by a sudden crash. If you are interested in indexing, you should monitor how much of the total market capitalization of the companies in an index comes from investment by the index tracking funds so you don't fall asleep at the wheel.

The world's stock markets

There are now more than 60 countries in the world with stock exchanges. The biggest one of all is the New York Stock Exchange (NYSE) where about a third of the total value of the world's shares are traded. Many of the newer stock exchanges are tiny, such as the one in Croatia which trades only a handful of stocks and shares. Some countries, such as Germany, finance their industries more by bank lending than through shares, and their stock markets are smaller than you might expect. Then there are the highly internationalized stock markets, such as London and Hong Kong, where the total value of shares far exceeds the country's gross domestic product (GDP). Different countries have different rules for managing their stock exchanges. Most of the big ones now allow unrestricted foreign investment. Dealing costs and tax arrangements vary considerably, and if you buy or sell shares worth less than £10,000 in some markets you may be hit with a wide bid/offer spread.

THE UNITED STATES

The most important stock exchanges in the United States are based in New York.

The New York Stock Exchange (NYSE)

The NYSE is the best known of the New York stock exchanges, trading tens of billions of shares in nearly 2,000 companies. It is well regulated by the Securities and Exchange Commission (SEC), and individual investors get preferential treatment over institutions when buying and selling thanks to the Individual Investor Express Delivery Service (IIEDS). The main index used is the Dow Jones Industrial Average, which is the arithmetic mean of the share price movements of 30 important companies listed on the NYSE.

The American Stock Exchange (AMEX)

Until 1921, brokers who didn't have a seat on the NYSE would trade in the street. Eventually, they were organized into a proper exchange where companies not large enough to qualify for listing on the NYSE are listed.

National Association of Securities Dealers Automated Quotations (NASDAQ)

NASDAQ began in 1971. It has no central dealing floor, but works as an international system of trading in shares and bonds via computer screens. It has information links with the London Stock Exchange and was the first foreign exchange to be recognized by the Department of Trade and Industry in the UK. In recent years, investors across the world have become very excited about NASDAQ because so many fast-growing high-tech companies, based both in the USA and abroad, are listed there. The wild booms in new sectors such as the dot com industry have made NASDAQ a hair-raising, speculative ride.

CONTINENTAL EUROPE

Shares have been traditionally regarded with some suspicion by continental Europeans, and not without reason. Nevertheless markets have existed for centuries in most countries. The world trend towards liberalization has encouraged European governments to reduce taxes on dealing and to move towards standardizing their regulations. EASDAQ, a new pan-European market, has been set up and is currently doing well (see page 93). The principal older markets are described below.

The Paris Bourse

The Paris Bourse is the largest Continental exchange after Germany's. It is highly advanced in its use of technology and there is virtually no floor trading. Trading is done through the 45 members of the exchange, some of whom are foreign-owned.

Germany

There are eight regional stock exchanges in Germany which together make Germany the next biggest market after New York, Tokyo and London. The biggest of these regional centres is Frankfurt. Only banks are allowed to deal in shares on behalf of investors – there are no brokers as there are elsewhere. German shares are usually issued in bearer form, meaning they can be passed around almost as easily as cash. Dealing commissions are comparable to those in the UK and United States.

THE FAR EAST

Eastern Asia is the fastest-growing area in the world and is likely to remain so for many decades despite the occasional crisis. Japan is the most powerful economy, but until the crisis of 1997, the 'Tigers' (Hong Kong, Taiwan, Singapore and South Korea) were catching up. Not far behind were the 'Dragons' (Thailand, the Philippines, Malaysia and Indonesia). Today, the 'Dragons' are troubled – Indonesia seems on the point of collapse at the time of writing – but the underlying promise remains strong.

People in these countries tend to save a large proportion of their incomes, which is one of the reasons why economists believe that their growth is sound and will continue. The Dragons are rapidly moving from being producers of commodities into heavy industries, such as car and machine manufacturing.

Most of the Far Eastern markets are 'thin', which is to say that shares are less frequently traded than those on, say, the NYSE. This has the effect of making the markets vulnerable to manipulation, and to financial shocks.

The Tokyo Stock Exchange (TSE)

There are eight stock exchanges in Japan but the TSE is the largest, rivalling the NYSE for the title of 'world's biggest'. Companies are listed in three sections, the first for over 1,000 of the biggest issues, the second for a few hundred smaller companies, and the third for non-Japanese companies. There is also an over-the-counter market which is separate from the TSE. The main Japanese index is the Nikkei Stock Average, which is price-weighted and includes over 200 Japanese companies from the first section of the TSE. Although there are still some limitations to foreign buying on the TSE, it is possible for a small investor to buy and sell quite freely.

The Stock Exchange of Hong Kong (SEHK)

Hong Kong has had a stock exchange since the last century but it wasn't until the 1970s that the market began its rapid expansion. It suffered badly in the 1987 crash and its regulation has subsequently been tightened. It has two main indexes, the famous Hang Seng Index and the broader Hong Kong Stock Index. Hong Kong was leased from China by the British in the imperial era and was handed back in 1997. While it seems that China will try to maintain Hong Kong as a world financial centre, long-term investment in the market looks risky. At present, though, there are no restrictions on foreign investment in shares.

Korea Stock Exchange (KSE)

South Korea's exchange is large and modern and is increasingly opening up to outsiders. Since the 1997 crash, the country has been mired in efforts to reform its banking and industrial sectors.

Stock Exchange of Singapore (SES)

This market is almost entirely open to foreign participation – only large stakes in certain important companies are prohibited. The SES has trading links with US dealers and many Malaysian companies are quoted on it.

Taiwan Stock Exchange

Trade in shares grew in Taiwan after a land reform in the 1950s gave owners stocks and shares in government-run companies. The market is very liquid and dominated by a few investors.

American Depositary Receipts (ADRs)

With the advent of the internet and the general liberalization of capital flows around the world, it is becoming increasingly easy for the private investor to purchase shares on foreign stock exchanges. Many excellent foreign companies choose to be quoted in the USA instead of, or as well as, on their home exchange. The reason is simple – America is where the big investment money is. A foreign company that is fully listed in the USA has to jump through the same hoops, and provide the same information, as a domestic American firm, which is reassuring to investors. There is also a class of security in the USA called the American Depositary Receipt, or ADR. Here is how ADRs work.

A major bank purchases shares in foreign markets which are kept on deposit by a custodian bank in the company's home country. The bank then sells ADRs which are evidence of the ownership of these shares. They are denominated in US dollars. In total there are over 1,600 companies listed in the USA under the ADR scheme from more than 60 countries. An ADR represents ownership in shares of a non-US company. The ADR holder usually receives the same benefits enjoyed by the ordinary shareholder in the company. Currently there are over 100 British companies with ADRs trading in the USA including SmithKline Beecham, GlaxoWellcome and Barclays Bank. ADRs may be listed on the NYSE, AMEX or NASDAQ.

The first ADR was created in 1927 by J.P. Morgan for Selfridges, the department store in London. Traditionally, the advantage of ADRs to Americans has been that they can purchase them on their home markets, rather than having to cope with the difficulties and uncertainties of opening accounts with foreign brokers. Until recently there were many foreign exchanges where outsiders were not allowed to invest, so ADRs were sometimes the only way for a private person to participate. Although today the trend is for stock exchanges across the world to abolish such barriers, there are still places, such as Russia and India, where it is simply too difficult, or too risky, to open a local account.

There are two main types of ADR:

- **Level I ADRs**, which are traded on the 'over-the-counter' market. These require only minimal US regulation and are to be avoided unless you are an expert.
- **Level II and III ADRs**, which are listed directly on the US securities exchanges and generally enjoy greater liquidity. Companies that have a listing for their ADRs must comply with the full registration and reporting requirements of the US Securities and Exchange Commission (SEC).

For investors in the UK, it can sometimes make sense to purchase a 'foreign' share – in other words, one that is not British or American – in its ADR form in the USA. There are a large number of ADRs available and there are now also newer variants, IDRs, EDRs and GDRs, which are sold on one or more international markets. Take a close look at the prices, though – ADRs and their variants often trade at a premium to the underlying share, which may be worthwhile because of their increased liquidity, or may simply reflect unwarranted investor enthusiasm.

You can find out more about ADRs at *adr.com*.

3

how online investing started
getting on the internet
the good news – more and better access to real research
the bad news – the temptation to trade wildly in thin or
volatile markets
online share dealing – so what?

Online investing

The internet is a boon to private investors.
It allows you to deal in securities via your
computer, check 'real-time' prices, and, most
importantly of all, do your own research.
In this chapter we will look in detail at how
guerrilla investors can take full advantage
of these new opportunities:

- *How online investing started*
- *Getting on the internet*
- *The good news – more and better access to real research*
- *Information overload – using agents*
- *The bad news – the temptation to trade wildly in thin, volatile markets*
- *Online share dealing*
- *Security issues – fraud and aggressive tactics by website operators*

How online investing started

When the internet started in the early 1990s, it was essentially the preserve of academics who were capable of using the convoluted codes that were then necessary to access data. It had had predecessors. In France, a system called Minitel had been introduced in the early 1980s that allowed ordinary people to access information interactively. Various telecom companies had tried to set up similar systems in their own countries, the essential idea being to increase revenues from telephone use. In the UK, Prestel was introduced, but flopped after a few years. In the USA, proprietary systems like Prodigy attempted to capture a non-existent market.

The internet is different from these earlier systems in one key respect – nobody controls all the information on it. The earlier systems all tried to own, or at least to control, the information that was made available and they tended to imitate the model of television, where programming is rammed down audiences' throats. The internet is different because it gives users choice – we don't all have to look at the same stuff. What's more, users can also be information providers. Anyone can publish on the web, and it is this facility that has driven the explosion in internet use.

There are currently attempts to take this consumer power away, and no doubt there will be more in the future. Internet 'portals', for example, are attempts to create centralized networks that are similar to the traditional media.

In the late 1990s, what had been the preserve of academics, hobbyists and the 'achingly cool' suddenly mushroomed into something everyone could have. With the advent of X-Mosaic, later renamed Netscape, the 'browser' was born, a computer program which enabled you to 'surf' the internet looking for web pages that might catch your interest. This made the internet much, much easier to use. Before there were browsers, you had to know some programming language, and there were no pretty graphics or buttons to point at and click on – all you usually saw was a screen of unattractive text.

With more users came real commercial possibilities, and a speculative boom began. Almost overnight, companies appeared that were attracting vast sums of investors' money on the dubious promise of 'first mover advantage'. 'First mover advantage' is the idea that if you are the first company to rush into a market and claim the territory, you'll be in a better position to defend it against competitors. Nobody seemed particularly worried that many of these firms did not make profits.

What bemused investors were witnessing was a real-life speculative boom, as wild and irrational as the legendary Klondike gold rush of the 19th century or the South Sea Bubble of the 18th. At the time of writing, the balloon has been punctured and values have plummeted. The market is licking its wounds and picking over the sector for those businesses, which were always in the minority, that may prosper in the long term. By the time you read this, new booms may well have occurred.

The internet looks as if it is here to stay, in one form or another. It is, I believe, a genuinely 'discontinuous' innovation, that is changing the way the world goes about its daily life. That was true, of course, of the introduction of cars, electricity and so on, so this is not to say, as some do, that the internet is the only important innovation in the last 100 years. Is it as important for communication as the invention of the printing press was? It's too early to tell – it's part of a nexus of innovations in information technology, such as the personal computer, that gives power to the people, just as the first printing presses did. Before printed books, remember, only the very wealthy could afford to own a few manuscripts, and few people could read. Printed books changed the intellectual life of the world. Perhaps information technology will eventually have an equally profound effect.

The world of investment relies on the rapid transfer of information, so the internet is a boon, allowing people to research and compare securities, sectors and markets more widely, more quickly and more cheaply than ever before – this is true for both finance professionals and private investors. As the internet grew, more and more financial services went 'online', and today the industry regards it as an essential part of its business – a far cry from the sneering dismissals of a few years ago.

Getting on the internet

Many readers will already use the internet. If you are not, you could be missing out. At present your basic investment will be:

- a personal computer (PC) with a modem
- an internet account with a service provider.

Your ongoing costs will be the cost of the telephone use and a regular charge from the service provider, unless you are with a free service (nothing is ever really free – most free services take their pound of flesh by making you plough through advertising, or limiting your use in ridiculous ways).

Don't stint on how much you spend on a PC – it's a false economy. Buy the best one, with the most data storage, that you can afford. Within a few years you'll be wanting a bigger one – and you should have easily recouped the purchase cost from the benefits of having a PC. No guerrilla investor should be without one.

At the time of writing, there are various other gadgets that give you internet access, but they tend to have small screens, so they are not really a good substitute for the PC's big screen and ample data storage. As an investor, you will want to save lots of information on to your computer for later perusal.

By the time you read this, the situation may have changed – perhaps there will be a fully integrated, all-in-one television/computer that lets you make video phone calls, surf the net, listen to music and watch TV, all at the same time. How marvellous that will be for people who don't have to work for a living! There will be gadgets you can stick on your fridge that will tell you that you're out of milk and let you access the internet to order some more, ones that will buzz in your pocket at work to tell you to take a risk on coffee futures, and so on. A lot of these gizmos will be useless and not work very well. They'll get better.

New users are often frustrated by the slowness of moving from one web page to another when you are online. We are in the Stone Age of internet development, and this problem will gradually be resolved.

Theorists (often called 'digerati') like to talk about the developing 'digital divide', which just means the difference between people who can use computers and the internet, and people who can't. This has nothing to do with intelligence or ability – there are plenty of incompetent idiots who use the internet, if their websites and newsgroup messages are anything to go by!

The 'digital divide' is taken very seriously in the USA. People agonize over whether it is fair for the 'haves' to enjoy such an enormous advantage in access to information over the 'have-nots'. It may turn out to be a non-problem, as developing countries seem to be latching on to information technology extremely quickly.

Having watched my own mother successfully learn how to use a computer at the age of 77, I don't believe that anybody should feel that they can't learn all these new things because of their age. It just takes some time getting used to it. Enjoy it!

The good news – more and better access to real research

For investors, the major benefit of the Internet is not the ability to deal in shares online, it's the access to an extremely wide range of research that hitherto only the very rich, or the professionals, could see.

Not everything that looks like research is good research, of course. Lots of people are trying to sell you reports on the internet. You can find a list of useful websites on page 293.

The guerrilla investor never pays for research

The guerrilla investor never pays for research. You don't need to – all the world's major stock markets have free websites. You can go and look at all the share prices in real time, or with a short delay, in most cases. Many stock market websites link you to the websites of their listed companies, where you will usually find several years' worth of annual reports, a huge file of press releases, gruesome photographs of the board of directors, charts, figures, product information, the works!

The SEC, the USA's market regulator, even gives you free access to EDGAR, its vast database of all the statutory filings and reports (not just the annual report) that any US listed company has to give them. You can find out about UK companies here too, if they have an ADR. In America, this kind of freely accessible information is regarded as a right – it puts the slimy, secretive public bodies in Europe to shame. EDGAR is pretty daunting unless you are searching for something very important, but it is important to know that it is there, and to use it from time to time to check out companies that you are following closely.

Of course, as a guerrilla, you don't merely rely on the official information, although it is remarkably reliable. There are also lots of respectable firms that run services that allow you to compare things like the performance of unit trusts. A very good UK service is run by Hemmington Scott (www.hemmscott.com), which allows you to check all sorts of useful things for free. It also tries to sell you things, like all commercial sites.

The online brokers, discussed below, generally have a lot of useful information on their websites as an inducement to encourage you to trade.

Be a hard-nosed researcher. Don't allow yourself to be babied by any one source of information. Check, check and check again. Most financial institutions want to keep certain things secret from you – for example, many of them don't want you to know how easy it is to buy US shares. As you move away from official sources, such as the stock markets themselves, and the SEC, the accuracy of the information becomes more doubtful, so be alert.

Next in the line of attack are the online magazines and commentary sites. There are ones for everything from the biotechnology sector to Brazilian commodity futures. Some of them are very professional and very good. Others are put up by crazy people. Guerrilla researchers have to learn to tell the difference – there is no one to hold your hand.

Then there are the 'search engines', such as AltaVista, Google and Excite. These tend to be much better than the proprietary ones on portal sites. A search engine looks for webpages that match your enquiry. Using one well is a skill that you simply have to learn. If you regularly get a million references as a result to an enquiry, it is your fault, not the search engine's! Practice the 'advanced search' techniques, and your results will improve.

Search engines are useful for trawling the net looking for things you haven't thought of. For instance, suppose the director of a public company was severely criticized for his actions at another company a few years ago. You aren't going to find out about this at the present company's website, nor, unless it was a criminal offence, are you likely to find out about it at a regulator's website. By trawling with a search engine, you may find articles that refer to it, sly remarks in analyst's reports, or even full-blown character assassinations put up by the director's enemies.

'Enemy' websites are a mixed bag, since many of them are cranky and deeply unreliable – they're often of the 'Company X eats babies and deliberately puts poison in cans of food' variety. A few of them, usually when large sums of money have been lost, are serious and professionally put together. A lot of them are in between – they look quite good at first glance, but as you dig deeper you start to find a lot of rubbish.

A specialized financial website that is currently interesting is run by Wit SoundView (www.witcapital.com), which was the first exclusively online share underwriter and investment bank. As well as good research, you can gain access to all kinds of placement deals that only insiders usually find out about. The venture capital world, where sophisticated investors finance private companies that may one day go public, is potentially much more profitable, and also much riskier, than the public stock markets, and Wit SoundView is a good place to start learning about this rarefied area.

Lastly, and to my mind, the least important of all, are the newsgroups, bulletin boards and chatrooms for private investors. The institutions hate them, of course, because the last thing they want is for investors to talk to each other, so they are always putting out dire warnings that false information is posted by unscrupulous investors who want to push up the price of shares they own, and then to dump their holdings once other private investors have bought in. This is called 'ramping', a time-hallowed practice that is illegal in many, but not all, markets. Guerrilla investors don't take tips and don't allow themselves to be influenced by other people's opinions but sometimes you can discover something interesting from chatrooms and the like.

Guerrilla investors don't take tips and don't allow themselves to be influenced by other people's opinions

The internet is transforming the investment world so rapidly that by the time you read this there may be new kinds of information services available in addition to those mentioned above. Research takes time, so try to pace yourself – a few hours every week spent on research is probably more useful than the occasional wild orgy of research followed by months of inactivity. Tailor your research to suit your own needs. One thing is for certain, though: there is no longer any excuse for not educating yourself about the markets. It is all out there, waiting for you.

INFORMATION OVERLOAD – USING AGENTS

The 'information highway' has caused an explosion in the number of computer-based tasks you have to do. There is no doubt that it is complicated, and getting more so. The human mind cannot cope with too much information being bombarded at it the whole time. One starts to suffer from 'information overload', and to develop wild, staring eyes. You may have noticed that computer games now come with warnings about epileptic fits … The screens we use today are bad for the eyes; people in the future will be horrified at how primitive they are.

So how can you take advantage of the internet without becoming a gibbering wreck? A new generation of 'interface agents' are being developed to help. Agents are computer programs that use artificial intelligence techniques to help you actively. The agent 'learns' from you as well as from other agents. Agents can:

- perform tasks on your behalf
- train or teach you
- help people to collaborate
- monitor events and procedures.

Agents will soon be able to do anything from filtering information and managing your e-mail to researching companies for you. Best of all, they are *your* agents, not somebody else's, so they do what you tell them to do. Web surfers may have encountered 'enemy' agents belonging to commercial sites that offer to think for you, which is a bit like an alcoholic offering to guard the key to your drinks cabinet.

Internet users are wasting many valuable hours in dealing with junk mail, changing the times of meetings, searching through trashy web pages for information, and so on. An electronic mail agent watches how you deal with your e-mail and learns your habits. For instance, if you save a particular e-mail, the agent remembers this and tries to predict what you will do the next time you get an e-mail. The agent may learn that the 'from' field of an e-mail message is highly correlated to whether you read it (in other words, that you read messages from your lover, but not from Wayne, the pub bore).

Gradually the agent learns how you behave. You can give it guidance, and override it. It can ask other agents (say, within a company's computer network) for advice. Eventually the agent becomes useful to you and you can rely on it to be your 'secretary' and tell you when you get an e-mail that you actually want to read.

A 'meeting scheduler' works in a similar way, by learning your personal behaviour patterns. Suppose you only make business phone calls after three o'clock – the agent will learn this and remind you. It can learn the priorities of different types of meetings (presumably, you would make an exception to your telephone rule if you had to call the queen). Think of this agent as a kind of living Filofax program.

Artificial intelligence is finally becoming impressive. Use it to fight through the information jungle and save yourself the modern world's most precious commodity: time.

The bad news – the temptation to trade wildly in thin or volatile markets

So, now that you can buy shares online in, say, Indonesia, the world is your oyster. Not so fast – markets are not all the same. The 'volume' of traded shares is very important. Many foreign markets are 'thin', meaning that there aren't many shareholders and they don't buy and sell very often. Thin markets are dangerous for the private investor because they are unpredictable and potentially illiquid. You could end up holding an investment that you can't sell.

High-volume markets, like the New York and London stock exchanges, are much safer in this respect. Large companies' shares are bought and sold in huge numbers every day. Your dealing is not going to make any difference to the market, and you are almost always going to be able to sell your shares when you feel like it. Stick to the large markets until you know what you are doing.

The NASDAQ is a special case. Volumes are generally high, but the industries that like to list there are mainly in high technology. High technology is a 'hot' area and things are changing very fast. There are lots of surprises, all the time, and this makes share prices lurch wildly. While well-chosen high-tech shares may ultimately make you very rich, they are not the place for money that you can't afford to lose, so be careful.

Online share dealing – so what?

Online share dealing gives private investors the opportunity to play stock market from their computer at home. This is not as wonderful as it sounds. Private investors are wise not to trade frequently. As we will see in Chapter 8, buying and holding shares for lengthy periods is likely to be more profitable. Frequent trading is what the professionals do, at a fraction of the cost to the private person, so you are starting at a disadvantage.

These are the alleged advantages of dealing online:

- **You can buy and sell in 'real' time, so you know the exact price at which you are dealing**. You check a share price and are given about 15 seconds to decide whether you want to buy or sell at the given price. Bad 'off-line' brokers may have busy phone lines much of the time, so you may not be able to get through to them while online brokers are supposed to be always accessible. A word of warning: when a market crashes, as it did in the UK in 1987, nobody could get through to their brokers because everyone wanted the same thing – to sell! There were not enough buyers, so prices kept on dropping and dropping. Brokers left their phones off the hook: what was the point in taking sell orders they couldn't fulfil at the price the customer demanded? If things get very bad, the bosses of an exchange will actually step in and suspend all trading for as long as it takes for things to settle down. Don't think that the same won't happen with the online brokers – in a true panic, they won't take your orders either.

- **Timing is said to be everything when buying and selling shares.**
  Grizzled veterans of the market know that this just isn't true. No one
  can 'time' the market successfully all the time. Anyone who tells you
  that they can is lying.
- **Great dealing rates when you go online**. This is true, relative to what
  they used to be. But it is not a reason to buy or sell unless you were
  going to do it anyway.
- **It is so popular! Literally millions of people are doing it**. This is a
  ridiculous reason for doing anything. You should never invest in
  something solely because it is popular. A biologist friend tells me that
  lemmings don't actually commit mass-suicide by jumping into the sea,
  so they are more sensible than the average private investor!

HOW ONLINE DEALING WORKS

Online brokers are discount brokers, so they don't give you advice. You must
set up an account with them, which may take anything from a few days to a
fortnight as documents need to be posted by 'snail mail'.

Once the account is open, you will normally be sent a user ID and
password or PIN number. You will only be able to trade on the website once
you have keyed in these codes. Much of the research information at the
website is only accessible via these codes.

Once you are in, you ask for the prices of the shares you want to buy or
sell. You then have to confirm online that you wish to purchase the number of
shares at the price they have been quoted.

The money to pay for the shares will either be taken from money you have
deposited in your brokerage account, or charged to your debit/credit card.

If you make a mistake after you have confirmed your deal online, many
brokers give you one last chance to cancel at the Order Status screen while it
is still pending. Once they have dealt for you, however, it is too late, so be
careful!

Crest

Crest is the UK computer system for the settlement of share transactions. As
an individual you can open a Crest personal account, or you can elect for your
shares to be held in a broker's nominee account. If you have a personal
account, your name stays on companies' share registers but the shares are
held electronically to your brokers' order, which means that you do not have
to deliver certificates and sign transfers when you make a sale. There is less
paper work, less risk of things being lost in the post and less risk of the missing
the settlement date.

SECURITY ISSUES

Online dealing is pretty safe, as is online banking. What is not safe is the howling wilderness of the internet outside the heavily protected broker's website. 'Data aggregation' is becoming a serious problem.

Online stockbrokers and banks use encryption (electronic scrambling) to change your personal account details into code which is sent across the internet. A computer hacker who was starting from scratch would have to try every possible combination of the 128-bit code, looking for one combination out of 3.4×10 to the power of 38 possibilities.

Banks and brokers are not all the same – so don't assume that some weird broker that you have never heard of is OK. They may be pirates. Take the trouble to check them out in the real world and make absolutely sure that they are authorized by the relevant market regulator. Another thing to watch out for is the dirty trick of making you think you are at your own broker's website when really you are at a hacker's – so keep an eye on the 'address' slot at the top of your browser to make sure that it is still displaying the right internet address.

Here are a few things you can do to minimize risks:

- **Don't e-mail account details to anyone outside a secure website** – a hacker may be able to get them.
- **Don't use obvious passwords**, like your birth date, your name or your partner's name. Hackers always try these first.
- **Do keep records**, both on paper and on your own computer.
- **Do think off-line before you act online**. There is no rush – the stock markets were there before you were born and they are going to be there after you are dead. Take a deep breath and relax.

Someone, somewhere, is getting rich fast. Market news invariably publicizes the stories of the big profits and the big losses. It is easy to start feeling that you are missing the boat, and yield to the temptation of doing something silly, risky, or both, when you are online. Don't get intoxicated by money – stock market news can be very deceiving. Concentrate on making steady, consistent profits over many years and you won't regret it.

It is easy to start feeling that you are missing the boat, and yield to the temptation of doing something silly, risky, or both, when you are online

COMMON SENSE AND ONLINE INVESTMENT

Technology has the strange property of causing some people to lose their heads completely while scaring others into their shells. I've been watching the process for decades, and there's no sign of this changing. The technologies have changed, but people's behaviour hasn't. (This is a clue to how to invest successfully, by the way.)

In the markets, and in business in general, what everybody knows isn't very valuable. What only some people know is far more valuable. Use the internet to search for the latter.

Little-known information isn't necessarily short-lived. The virtues of long-term direct equity investing are relatively little known, for instance – most amateurs either want to trade frenetically or buy an overpriced, locked-in savings plan that underperforms horribly. Many things are little known because it takes hard work and experience to get there, both qualities that are always in short supply. It may take wisdom to understand them – which is in even shorter supply!

Information technology has arrived. Investors cannot ignore it. Use it wisely, and prosper.

4

Bonds

A bond is an IOU issued by a government, local authority or a company in return for the loan of cash. In most cases, a fixed rate of interest is payable to the bond holder, and the bond issuer promises to pay back the amount borrowed (the face value of the bond) at a certain time in the future. Most bonds are registered, so if a bond is sold by one holder to another, legal title is only transferred when the ownership is re-registered. There is another kind of bond, the bearer bond, for which there is no register of ownership. Thus bearer bonds are similar to cash – whoever has physical possession of a bearer bond is its owner.

In the UK, bonds are traditionally called 'stocks' and equities are called 'shares'; in the United States, fixed-interest securities are called 'bonds' and equities, 'stocks'.

In this chapter we will look at:

- The price of bonds
- Understanding yields
- Gilts
- Auctioning new issues
- Buying and selling gilts

- *How gilts are taxed*
- *Futures and options*
- *Index-linked gilts*
- *Undated gilts*
- *The Barlow Clowes scandal*
- *Corporate bonds*
- *Convertible bonds*
- *Ex dividend and cum dividend bonds*
- *The US bond rating system*
- *The problem with investing for income*
- *Bonds and ISAs*
- *Sinking funds*
- *Bonds for the guerrilla investor*

The price of bonds

The price of a bond varies according to macro-economic factors, of which inflation is the most important. If the interest rate in the market goes higher than the interest rate payable on a bond, the price you can get if you sell the bond goes down. Conversely, if the market interests rates go below a bond's interest rate, you can sell the bond for more than its face value.

Every day information on bonds is published in the *Financial Times* and elsewhere; you are given the current market price of the bond (which is usually different from its face value), the high and low of the market price in the current year (which gives you an idea of its volatility), and then two figures for 'yields'. Market prices quoted are the middle of the bid/offer spread, as with shares. The 'interest yield' simply tells you what percentage of your money you would get if you bought the bonds at the current market price. It is a simple calculation.

EXAMPLE

Suppose the bond in question is 'Treasury 7¼ pc 2010': the 7¼ pc is the coupon rate for the bond, '2010' is the year when the government pays back the capital invested. Since you must buy the gilt for a price different from its face value, the 7¼ pc coupon does not tell you the interest rate you are getting. Let's say the market price is 102.88. You divide the coupon by the market price and multiply the result by 100:

$$(7.25 \div 102.188) \times 100 = 7.1 \text{ per cent}$$

7.1 per cent is the interest rate, or interest yield, that you will get at the moment. Since the market price is higher than the face value of the bond, its interest yield is lower than its coupon, and if the market price rises, the yield will go even lower.

UNDERSTANDING YIELDS

The yield is the crux of bond investing, because it is the tool you use to measure the return of one bond against another. It enables you to make informed decisions about which bond to buy.

As we have seen, the interest yield, or 'current' yield, is the rate of return on your bond investment but it is not fixed, like a bond's stated interest rate. It changes to reflect the price movements in a bond caused by fluctuating interest rates.

To pick the best deal available between comparable bonds (remember that company bonds are more risky than gilts, so you would expect a better rate on them in compensation) it is better to use the 'redemption yield', or 'yield to maturity', which is also given in the financial pages.

Redemption yield

The redemption yield tries to account for the difference between the price you pay for the bond and what you will get for it on redemption, plus any capital gain you will realize (if you purchase the bond below par) or minus any capital loss you will suffer (if you purchase the bond above par). It also includes all the interest you will earn. It's a complicated sum that in practice is not worth calculating yourself, so you can just look up the redemption yield in the *Financial Times*. In principle, it works as follows:

EXAMPLE

Annie buys a 10 per cent bond with a face value of £100 in the year 2005 for 111.11 because the current interest rate is 9 per cent. The term of the bond ends in four years' time in 2009 for £100.

Annie will make a capital loss of £11.11 if she holds the bond to redemption, which results from the difference between the price she paid (£111.11) and the face value (£100).

Step 1. Dividing the loss by the number of years left to run:

£11.11 ÷ 4 = £2.78

£2.78 is the amount of capital loss per year.

Step 2. Annie calculates what percentage £2.78 is of £111.11, the price she paid for the bond:

(2.78 ÷ 111.11) x 100 = 2.5 per cent

Step 3. At the time of purchase, interest rates were at 9 per cent, so the interest yield is:

Coupon ÷ market price x 100

$$(10 ÷ 111.11) \times 100 = 9$$

Step 4. Annie works out the approximate redemption yield by subtracting the annual percentage of capital loss (see Step 1) from the interest yield (see Step 3):

$$9 – 2.5 = 6.5$$

Annie now knows that the redemption yield is roughly 6.5 per cent. It is only approximate because it doesn't take compound interest into account, so Annie looks up the published redemption yield in the financial press to get an exact figure.

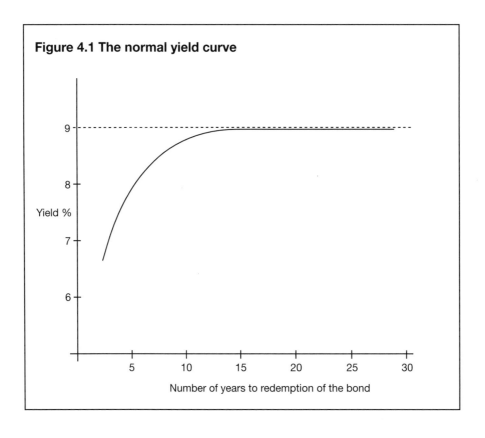

Figure 4.1 The normal yield curve

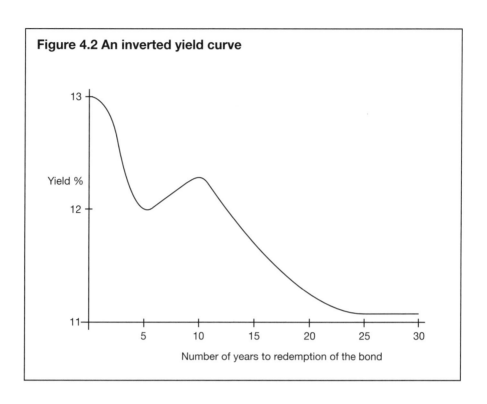

Redemption yields are useful for comparisons, but they don't remove all uncertainty, since the underlying market prices on which they are based will fluctuate, and the figures only tell you what return you would get if you held the bond to redemption, not what will happen if you sell before.

When comparing the redemption yields, say of different gilts, you will notice that some are higher than others. Usually, the longer that the gilt has to run, the higher the redemption yield because investors expect a reward for tying up their money for a longer time. This effect is called the 'normal yield curve'.

The normal yield curve happens when money lent for shorter periods of time earns less interest than money that is lent for longer.

When there is uncertainty about interest rates, the market distorts the normal yield curve both by trying to guess what long-term interest rates will be and also by moving in and out of bonds in response to changes in interest rates elsewhere. Banks mainly buy short-term bonds ('shorts'), while the institutions tend to buy long-term ones ('longs'), leaving medium-term bonds (5–15 years) out in the cold, which can cause them to have a better yield than longs. When short-term interest rates are up, yields on short-term bonds improve. Uncertainty about interest rates can cause longs to have lower yields than shorts, in which case the yield curve is inverted.

Figure 4.2 shows what can happen when there is uncertainty about interest rates. The hump in the curve over ten-year bonds indicates that they give a better yield than longs, reflecting their unpopularity.

Bond prices vary, so yield curves vary too – it is quite common for yields to fluctuate by 5 per cent over a 12-month period.

Gilts

'Gilts' or 'gilt-edged securities' are bonds issued by the British government. They get their name from their reputation for a very high degree of safety. It is thought, justifiably, that if you lend the British government money by buying gilts, it is extremely unlikely that it will default on the loan. The British government has issued gilts for hundreds of years without ever having failed to meet payments on the due dates. About two-thirds of the British National Debt is funded by the issuance of gilts; at times, it has been as high as 80 per cent.

It is thought, justifiably, that if you lend the British government money by buying gilts, it is extremely unlikely that it will default on the loan.

Gilts are issued either for a fixed length of time, such as five years, or, more unusually, for an indefinite period. They pay interest half-yearly, and repay the capital at the end of the bond's life.

The return on gilts is generally lower than you can get by investing in more risky propositions, such as shares, but is often better than the interest rate you can get by simply keeping your money in a bank or building society. It is also possible to make a capital gain on the sale of gilts that is currently tax free in the UK.

There are about 90 gilts in issue at the time of writing, of which 12 are index-linked. The interest payable (called 'the coupon') can be as little as 2 per cent on some bonds, and as high as 15 per cent on others. Most gilts are very liquid, meaning that they are easily bought and sold.

AUCTIONING NEW ISSUES

When a state body or a company wants to borrow money by selling bonds, it 'brings an issue'. In the United States, the government issues bonds to a regular timetable using the auction method. Individuals can obtain a tender form from a bank and apply for the bonds (usually Treasury bills which have a life of a year or less) at a set price, enclosing a cheque. Private individuals are classed as 'non-competitive bidders'. What happens is that institutions bid for large amounts of the bonds, at any price they choose, but usually quite close to the set price of $10,000 per bond. The US Treasury then accepts the highest bids to fulfil its quota and takes the average price of the accepted bids as the price to the non-competitive bidders, who are then refunded the difference between the average of the accepted bids and the price they paid when they applied for the bonds. In the UK, the practice of auctioning government securities has been adopted relatively recently, and purchasers don't know what kind of bond will be offered until about a week before the auction.

BUYING AND SELLING GILTS

Gilts are free of capital gains tax, so if higher-rate taxpayers expect the market price to improve they often invest in low coupon gilts, which may give a good capital gain. Since yields are constantly fluctuating in the opposite direction of the market prices, you are taking a risk in gilts if you don't keep them until redemption; making a gain or loss depends on when you buy.

The gilt-edged market makers (GEMMs) must quote bid and offer prices on demand for gilts at all times, thus ensuring that gilts are always liquid (i.e. that you can always buy or sell them). There are about 20 GEMMs, many of which are foreign-owned. The institutions can buy gilts directly from GEMMs; but many of them, like many private investors, buy gilts through a broker, who buys them from a GEMM. The GEMMs make their money on the 'spread' between their bid and offer prices, not by charging commission, except in certain special cases.

Brokers, known in the gilts market as 'broker/dealers' are regulated by the Securities and Futures Authority (SFA). They have a duty to get the best prices when buying and selling for a client. The broker charges the investor commission for this service. Brokers can also sell their clients gilts that they have bought themselves, but in this case the rules say that they must give as good a price as the best price currently being offered by a GEMM. As a private investor, you can also buy gilts through some accountants and solicitors, or through share shops. It is legal for you to sell a gilt to another private investor, provided that the transaction is properly registered.

The best way to buy gilts

By far and away the best way to buy and sell gilts if you are a small investor is at a Post Office. The commission is low – you only pay £1 commission if you buy up to £250's worth of gilts, and a further 50p for every £125 above this. Sales commissions are 10p for every £10's worth of gilts up to £100, £1 for sales of between £100 and £250, and a further 50p for every £125 over this. The interest is paid gross, but you must declare it to the Inland Revenue and pay tax on it later.

This system is run by the National Savings Stock Register (NSSR). You are allowed to buy up to £25,000's worth of any one gilt on any one day.

HOW GILTS ARE TAXED

UK taxpayers must pay tax on the interest they receive from a gilt at source (in other words, the tax is deducted from the interest before it is paid), unless they buy through the NSSR system, in which case it is paid gross and taxed later. Overseas investors should be careful to invest in those gilts that are defined as 'free of tax to residents abroad' (FOTRA) – this will enable them to receive the interest gross.

FUTURES AND OPTIONS

You can gamble on gilts by buying and selling futures and options on them on the London International Financial Futures and Options Exchange (LIFFE, pronounced 'life'). For a detailed explanation of how futures and options work, see Chapter 9.

INDEX-LINKED GILTS

These pay a rate of interest linked to the official inflation figures and the face value of the bond is adjusted for inflation when it is repaid. If you buy such a bond for its face value and keep it to redemption, you are therefore guaranteed to make a profit in real terms.

UNDATED GILTS

Some gilts have no redemption date; the government simply goes on paying the interest for ever, unless it chooses to redeem. Others have a range of years (e.g. 1995–1999) within which the government can decide to redeem the gilt at any point. Others give a redemption date followed by the words 'or after' (e.g. '1990 or after'), meaning that the government can choose when it wants to redeem the gilt at any time after the redemption date.

THE BARLOW CLOWES SCANDAL – HOW A CERTAIN KIND OF PUNTER IS EXPLOITED

If you've heard of the Barlow Clowes affair in the 1980s, you may be wondering why gilts are said to be so safe, when thousands of people who invested in gilts through Barlow Clowes narrowly escaped losing their life savings when the firm collapsed and two of its directors were jailed for theft. The point is that gilts are safe – it's the middlemen who may not be. Many of the victims of Barlow Clowes had invested through financial intermediaries, creating two unnecessary layers between themselves and the dealers. It is a classic example of how investors can get caught by believing printed lies: it seemed so unlikely that a company would actually dare to make false statements in their literature and on consumer radio programmes on the BBC that investors assumed that it must be all right. The Department of Trade and Industry's role in the affair was far from glorious – they knew about irregularities with Barlow Clowes for years before the collapse, and did nothing.

Low-risk, low-return investments have a great appeal to inexperienced investors who are afraid of losing money and are paralyzed by the apparent complexities of the investment world. This type of investor can be persuaded to purchase by emphasizing safety above all other qualities – but they may be paying too high a premium for this safety. Safety, like any other investment characteristic, has its fair price.

Dishonest firms can sell 'scaredy-cat' investors overpriced products by disguising the charges. After a while, the investors start to itch for better returns. This is what Barlow Clowes exploited: the desire of people to have their cake and eat it by having a low-risk/higher-return investment. There is rarely such a thing widely available in the markets, since risk is correlated to reward. The more risk you take, the more chance you have of a better return (see Chapter 8).

To paraphrase Gertrude Stein, 'a bond is a bond is a bond'. In current market conditions, and in the long term generally, you are not going to make a better return on them than you can on equities without taking on more risk, such as buying default grade corporate bonds (see page 79). There are going rates of return for bonds – if someone offers you a significantly better rate of return than is generally available elsewhere, be very, very sure that you understand exactly how they are able to achieve this. They may have no intention of keeping their promises!

Corporate bonds

Instead of buying a gilt and lending money to the government, you can buy a corporate bond and lend it to a company. Standard sterling corporate bonds are exempt from capital gains tax (CGT). However, more complex types of corporate bond (for example, convertibles) can attract capital gains tax. In this case, the arguments will be similar to those for shares.

CONVERTIBLE BONDS

Convertible bonds offer the investor the chance to exchange bonds at some pre-agreed time for shares in the issuing company. Whether this is worth doing depends upon the market value of the shares when you convert. Obviously, if the shares have gone up you will make a capital gain by converting to shares and then selling them. The price of these bonds usually rises and falls with the share price but at a lower rate. Usually the price at which you can convert to shares is set higher than the market price of the shares when the bonds are issued.

EX DIVIDEND AND CUM DIVIDEND BONDS

Interest on bonds is usually paid every six months, so when you buy a bond in the market you will want to know if a dividend is just about to be paid. Approximately five weeks before the interest is paid the bond is declared to be 'ex dividend', meaning that if you buy it, the seller keeps the imminent dividend and the first dividend that you receive will be the subsequent one – this is indicated in the financial pages by 'xd'. Ex dividend bonds are cheaper than 'cum dividend' (meaning 'with dividend') bonds to compensate for the longer wait for the first dividend. Cum dividend bonds require the purchaser to pay for the 'accrued interest' since the last time the interest was paid.

The US bond rating system

The main rating systems for US bonds are Moody's and Standard and Poor's. They are as follows:

Type of bonds	Standard and Poor's	Moody's
'Prime' quality bonds	AAA	Aaa
High quality bonds	AA+	Aa1
	AA	Aa2
	AA–	Aa3
Upper medium grade	A+	A1
	A	A2
	A–	A3
Lower medium grade bonds that may be insecure in the long term	BBB	Baa
Non-investment grade bonds	BB	Ba

The following categories are for bonds that are generally considered to be speculative and therefore bad investments for small investors:

	Standard and Poor's	Moody's
	B	B

The 'C' categories are for bonds issued by entities that have sometimes defaulted or are in danger of doing so:

	Standard and Poor's	Moody's
	CCC	Caa
	CC	Ca
	C	C
In default	D	–

The problem with investing for income

Many people, especially when they are retired, see the interest they receive from bonds as something separate from the capital, to be creamed off as a nice little earner. By all means use investment income for daily expenses if you must, or if you can afford to, but don't imagine that this is going to make you richer – it could make you a lot poorer. At the end of a bond's term, the capital sum is returned, but its buying power will have shrunk through inflation. As discussed earlier, perhaps the worst case of this in the 20th century was in the 1920s, when respectable German widows literally starved to death as the value of their bonds were inflated away during the galloping Weimar hyper-inflation, when cash became virtually worthless. In such circumstances, you need to move your wealth into a different asset class fast to stop any further loss.

Perhaps such horrors couldn't happen here, but spending the interest from a bond is a way to use the law of compound *depreciation*, causing your assets to dissolve over the long term.

Bonds and ISAs

Interest on bonds is taxed at 0 per cent for non-taxpayers, 20 per cent for basic-rate taxpayers and 40 per cent for higher-rate taxpayers. At current interest rate levels, this could be worth about 1.4 per cent at the 20 per cent rate and 2.8 per cent at the 40 per cent rate which is probably more than you will pay in ISA charges, so if you are committed to purchasing a bond, it is worth doing so through an ISA, assuming you pay tax.

Sinking funds

You can also use bonds as a tool for financial control, for instance by starting a sinking fund:

EXAMPLE

Suppose you own a beautiful thatched cottage that you let to summer visitors. One day, the thatch is going to have to be replaced, and it is going to be expensive. What's worse, although you know what the replacement cost is today, you have no certainty about what it will be in five years' time, since thatchers' prices may increase at a much greater rate than inflation. You make an educated guess that prices will rise at roughly the same rate as the coupon on medium-term bonds.

To avoid getting into a tight spot when the day comes when you cannot put off fixing the thatch any longer, you decide to start a sinking fund.

Today's thatch replacement cost = £20,000

Your spare cash today = £5,000

Estimated replacement date = 7 to 10 years

You buy bonds with your £5,000, taking professional advice on the best deal currently available.

You then decide to save the other £15,000 over the next seven years, which is £2,142.86 a year. You save this money out of the rent you get for letting the cottage, and each year you buy more bonds with it.

To make sure that you don't get a nasty shock at the thatcher's estimate in the future, you add a bit more to your annual saving. Let's say you round it up to £2,500 a year.

After three years you have:

- £5,000 plus 7 years' interest
- £17,500 plus varying amounts of interest.

If, at the end of seven years, the thatch is still in good condition and you estimate that it has a few years left in it, you might decide to stop saving within the fund, or even to draw some money out of the fund to invest more profitably elsewhere. The point is that by buying bonds with a life roughly equivalent to that of the roof, and giving you a return that protects you against price increases, you ensure that you will always have roughly the right money available to pay for the sudden huge bill that will inevitably come one day.

This is one of the main ways that large businesses use bonds – the numbers are bigger, but the principle is the same.

Bonds for the guerrilla investor

If you buy a bond just before market interest rates take a dive, you can make a substantial tax-free capital gain, as the market value of the bond will rise. Buying gilts through the Post Office will save you a fortune in broker's fees. Buying bonds outside your own country in other currencies can be a good bet if you think the value of your own currency is falling. For those who don't want to become specialists in the field, bonds are basically safe and boring. You will have to keep a weather eye on the economy at all times if you hold long bonds unless you hold them to redemption, and even then you may find that inflation has taken a bite out of them.

The main financial characteristics of high-quality bonds are:

- **High liquidity** – you can sell them very quickly, except for certain products.
- **A fixed interest rate** – useful in a world of fluctuating rates.
- **Low risk** – major governments pay their debts, mostly. The British government has never defaulted on gilts, although arguably it has pulled a few fast ones, like getting patriotic people to buy undated War Loans in World War 1. 'Undated' means 'I don't have to pay you back unless I feel like it, and if I ever do, it will be after inflation has made the bond worthless'.
- **Low returns** – you get the interest plus the chance of a small capital gain if you sell the bond in certain market conditions.
- **Inflation risk** – except for index-linked bonds, if you keep a bond to redemption, inflation may have reduced the value of the capital invested plus the interest earned. This risk is much greater on long-term bonds.

Personally, I find speculation on interest rates unappealing – it is so easy to get it wrong. Use bonds as a balancer to your other investments, rather than as a means of trying to accumulate wealth.

Use bonds as a balancer to your other investments, rather than as a means of trying to accumulate wealth

5

new issues
floating companies on the newer markets –
AIM, EASDAQ and OFEX
rights issues
biotechnology – thrills and spills in a new industry
scrip issues
takeover bids
Microsoft – folie de grandeur?
when companies go bust …

The life cycle of a company – from launches to liquidations

In this chapter we will look at:

- *New issues – how companies are floated on the stock market*
- *The offer for sale*
- *Stagging and application tactics*
- *Tenders*
- *Private placing*
- *Offers by subscription*

- *Introductions*
- *Floating companies on the newer markets – AIM, EASDAQ and OFEX*
- *Biotechnology – thrills and spills in a new industry*
- *Rights issues, calculating the value of rights and clawbacks*
- *Scrip issues*
- *Takeover bids*
- *The Monopolies and Mergers Commission*
- *Microsoft – folie de grandeur?*
- *When companies go bust …*
- *Gauging solvency*
- *Suspensions and liquidations*

New issues

Private companies seek to offer their shares through the stock market either to raise extra money cheaply, or so that the owners can get a lot of money out, or for a combination of both reasons. Doing this costs the company a fortune in fees to City professionals that you, the new investor, are ultimately paying for. This process is known as a 'new issue'. There are three main kinds:

- **The introduction**. This is where there are already many shareholders in the company. Additional money is not sought, and the company's shares simply become officially part of the stock market.
- **The private placing**. This is where shares are sold to big institutions without other investors getting a look-in, except in certain circumstances which are examined below.
- **The offer for sale**. This is where shares are offered to anyone who wants to buy them.

The company can choose which kind of issue it is going to offer, whether it wants to sell all or just some of its shares, and can also combine different kinds of issue at once. Because of the particularly high costs of an offer for sale, many smaller companies prefer a private placing, if they can find institutions to buy their shares. The rules for a new issue are stringent, and the company must conform to the Stock Exchange's standards for accounting methods, nature of the business, financing, and so on.

THE OFFER FOR SALE

This is the method used by the big privatization issues in the UK. The government decided to float on the stock market many of the big industries, state-owned since the post-war nationalizations, as private sector companies. Politically, it was a gamble that the public's desire for profit would overcome its outrage at having industries which, in theory, it already owned being sold back to itself. To make sure that the issues worked, the government had to try to arrange things so that investors who were new to the stock market would do well out of the issue and be encouraged to take more interest in shares. Here's how it was done:

- Investors were sold shares which they paid for in instalments, so they did not have to find all the money for the shares at once. This is called issuing 'partly-paid' shares.

- There was a huge advertising campaign, and several prospectuses were published to make it easier for the unsophisticated investor to understand what was going on.

- Existing customers of the industry to be privatized were given incentives to invest, such as free shares and priority share applications.

- People were generally given a longer time than usual to consider whether or not to invest, and the time between the closing date for the applications and the commencement of share dealing was extended.

- To reduce 'stagging' (see page 89), there were special rules to stop people trying to get more shares than they were supposed to by making multiple applications for shares.

- The share price was set at a level designed to ensure that successful share applicants would see a rise in the value of their investment as soon as market dealing began. This attracted a lot of criticism along the lines that this was a deliberate undervaluing of the company, which was unfair on those members of the public who did not, or could not, invest, since they were indirectly beneficiaries of the proceeds that the government would get from the sale. However, the howls of protest following a BP share issue, when the market share price went down, were for the opposite argument – that it was unfair for the government not to provide an instant profit for the investors.

- To improve the profits of investors who wanted to sell when dealing in the market began, dealing costs were greatly reduced for a period. In addition, as with all new issues, there were no brokers' fees or stamp duty when you bought the shares.

The principles behind all this are clear enough: the government wanted to widen the number of stock market investors in the UK, and to do this it made efforts to ensure that the new investors' first experiences were happy ones.

When an ordinary company makes a new issue, the situation is rather different in that investors cannot be so certain of doing well as they have been with the privatization issues. The first thing to check in the prospectus is what the company intends to spend your money on – how much of it is going to the people who presently own the company and how much of it is going to be spent on improving the company itself. Investors like to see their money being put to good use, rather than being siphoned off for someone else's benefit, so they generally don't like to see more than five per cent going to the original shareholders and another five per cent to the employees.

The next thing to look at is how much of the money raised is going on fees and expenses associated with the issue – these can be as high as ten per cent. You will hear all sorts of justifications for this but the fact remains that it is a lot to pay middlemen for bringing the company to market. Unless you feel that the fees are unusually high, even by City standards, then you have to live with it and invest anyway – you don't have to like it, though! As with privatizations, these new issues will get pre-publicity, though on a smaller scale, so you won't see huge posters on roadside hoardings, or nightly television commercials extolling the issue's virtues. The price of the share has to be set by the company. This is done in consultation with the banks and other institutions who have agreed to 'underwrite' the issue – this means that they have agreed to buy all the shares of the issue that the public don't want, thereby ensuring that all the shares in the issue will be taken up. Setting the price can be tricky; it is a fine balance between selling the company too cheaply by choosing a low price and the risk of the issue 'flopping' by setting the price so high that no one wants to invest. In the case of a flop, the underwriters must take up the shares and sell them off slowly into the market as opportunities arise. Naturally, underwriters hate flops, because they cost them money.

Once the price has been set, the prospectus is published, giving details of the business, its accounts, its future plans and so on. Past dividend yields and the p/e ratio of the offer price are given to help with rule-of-thumb calculations of whether the share price is good value. The time from the issue of the prospectus to the closing date for share applications can be surprisingly short, often a matter of days. Once the closing date has passed, all the applications are added up. If the number of shares applied for exceeds the total number of shares to be issued, the offer is said to be 'oversubscribed'. This means that the company has to decide who gets shares and how many they will get. Often there is no way of knowing for certain how the company will allocate the shares – will it make sure that the smaller investors get at least some of what they applied for, or will it favour the institutions who want to buy large quantities of shares? Oversubscription is moderately good news to the investor since the share price will usually rise when market dealing starts.

'Undersubscription' is bad news if you have invested. You'll get all the shares that you asked for, but the left-over shares are taken up by the underwriters who generally don't want to hold on to them and will keep the share price down as they dribble their shares into the market.

FOR GUERRILLA INVESTORS – STAGGING AND OTHER APPLICATION TACTICS

'Stagging' simply means applying for shares in a new issue in the hope that the price will go up quickly and you can sell out at a profit. Applications usually close at 10.01 am on the morning of the closing date. Long queues form outside the applications office – usually a bank in the City of London – waiting for the doors to open. Applicants crowd in, frantically thrusting their forms and cheques across the counters until a halt is called at 10.01 am, and anyone who has been unable to get his or her application in has missed the boat. Better to get your application in early, you might think, but there is a good reason for leaving things to the last minute – market sentiment. There is a 'grey market' in new issue shares that trades before the closing date, and everyone watches its prices to guess what the price will be when dealing the shares officially begins. Don't be tempted to deal in the grey market yourself, though – it's a game for professionals. Read the financial press and ask your broker for opinions on whether the issue will be a success.

Suppose you decide to apply for shares on the morning of the closing date. You apply for the maximum number of shares you are allowed, or can afford, and wait to see how many you get. Because you have to put up part or all of the cash when you apply, you may have paid out more money than the price of the shares you actually receive, and you may have quite a long wait before you are sent back the balance. Many stags are keen to borrow money in order to apply for shares, in the hope that the profit they make from selling will more than cover the cost of borrowing. This can be worth doing if you are pretty sure of success, since you are borrowing the money for a short period of time. Study the application form carefully. The rules are usually quite complicated and are strictly enforced.

For example, you may be allowed to apply for shares in amounts of 200 shares up to a total of 1,000 shares, then in amounts of 500 between 1,000 and 5,000 shares, and finally in amounts of 1,000 above 5,000 shares. If you apply for, say, 1,700 shares, you will get none at all – you would have had to apply for 1,500 or 1,000 to qualify.

Sometimes these cut-off points (the 1,000 and 5,000 limits in the example) are used in deciding on share allocations when an issue is oversubscribed. For example, those who applied for more than 5,000 shares may get allocated proportionately more shares than those who applied for between 1,000 and 5,000 shares, who, in turn, will get a bigger percentage of their application than people who asked for fewer than 1,000 shares. If the market price is higher than the issue price, you can sell at a profit, so the more shares you have the better, but naturally the more shares you have when an issue flops, the more money you will lose if you sell, so you may have to hang on to the shares for a long time before you can get your money back.

Multiple applications are not allowed – several apparently respectable people were prosecuted for making multiple applications in privatization issues. What some City folks do, though, is to get a large number of non-investors to apply for shares in their own names; all the shares ultimately go to the stag, who pays a small fee to his team of applicants. You can do this legally in a small way by getting your friends and relatives to apply, and giving them a piece of the action.

Clearly, if the City likes a new issue it is likely to do well. Look at the names of the brokers and banks who are sponsoring the issue. The top names, especially among the the banks, are generally thought more likely to have got the issue price right, to avoid a flop. If you are tempted to stag, watch the press, what the brokers say and the grey market. If you feel confident, take the gamble.

TENDERS

Some new issues set a minimum price at which you can apply for shares and invite you to tender a higher figure. Once all the applications are in, the sponsors then decide on the 'striking price'. This is the price that everyone will be asked to pay for the shares. If you tendered at a price lower than the striking price, you don't get any shares. You can make multiple applications as long as each application is at a different price.

Another variety of tender is called 'pay what you bid'. In this case you pay the price that you tendered for the shares if you have bid higher than the striking price. Usually you receive all the shares that you asked for.

PRIVATE PLACING

This method is popular with many companies as well as with City institutions. The private investor doesn't usually get the chance to buy shares since the sponsors place most of the shares with big fund managers, and any other shares tend to go to the favoured clients of a broker. Companies like placings because the costs are lower and the flotation happens with less risk and more quickly. If the money to be raised is between £15 and £30 million, the sponsoring broker must allow at least one other broker to sell shares, and if more than £30 million is being raised then part of the issue must be offered to the public.

OFFERS BY SUBSCRIPTION

Often used to introduce brand new investment trusts to the stock market, offers by subscription set a minimum price at which you can apply for shares. If there are not enough investors willing to apply, the issue is cancelled since it is not fully underwritten.

INTRODUCTIONS

This method is often used by foreign companies that are already quoted on another stock exchange. There is no chance of stagging since no new shares are issued. The company's shares must already be widely held in the UK.

Floating companies on the newer markets – AIM, EASDAQ and OFEX

The 'Official List' is the list of companies quoted on the main London Stock Exchange. The London Stock Exchange's Listing Rules, nicknamed the 'Yellow Book', have been relaxed to allow innovative high-growth companies to be quoted on the main exchange without a three year trading record, along with other concessions, but start-ups are often listed on the Alternative Investment Market (AIM), launched in 1995, which is the UK's second-tier market, succeeding the Unlisted Securities Market (USM) and the Rule 4.2 Market, which have now been closed.

In the last few years high-tech sectors have boomed in the USA, and 'initial public offerings' (IPOs) of new companies, often heavily loss-making, have been enthusiastically taken up by thousands of private investors. Some have done well, while others have gone belly-up embarrassingly fast. The advent of the internet has done much to increase private investor activity generally, and the fashion for floating new companies, especially in innovative high-tech fields, has spread to Europe and Asia.

While established 'old economy' companies have looked askance at these 'uppity' rivals, many pundits argue that all these developments are very healthy. The jury is still out, but it is certainly true that some high-tech companies have grown into profitable giants in a remarkably short space of time.

THE ALTERNATIVE INVESTMENT MARKET (AIM)

Shares traded on AIM are usually those of young companies with potential for high growth. AIM was started in 1995 and is run by the London Stock Exchange for companies that want to sell shares to the public but are too small to be listed on the main market. There are currently more than 300 companies traded. Some AIM companies have moved to the main stock exchange (the Official List).

The entry requirements and regulatory obligations for AIM companies are much lighter than for listing on the main exchange – this helps smaller, newer companies, and in certain new high-tech sectors, such as biotechnology (see below), it is probably the only way that these promising industries can find the capital they need to develop.

For investors who can afford to take speculative risks, AIM may be attractive because of its tax advantages

For investors who can afford to take speculative risks, AIM may be attractive because of its tax advantages. AIM securities are treated as 'unquoted' for tax purposes, giving investors various reliefs from CGT and income tax, subject to complex restrictions. Some observers argue that the tax benefits do not adequately compensate for the risks of investment in many of these companies.

EASDAQ

The European Association of Securities Dealers Automated Quotation (EASDAQ) is a European stock market for high-growth companies that operates across 14 countries in Europe. EASDAQ is regulated by the Belgian Banking and Finance Commission and is a Recognized Investment Exchange, and you can invest through an ISA. Shares are currently traded in three currencies, euro, sterling and US dollars, and you can buy EASDAQ shares through many UK stockbrokers.

You can research EASDAQ companies and follow prices at *www.easdaq.com*. At the time of writing, the EASDAQ index has been performing well, but like many of the newer markets that rely on investor excitement about new things, you can expect a lot of ups and downs over the years. No one knows quite how risky it is, but most people agree that it is risky! Dealing charges can be high; Barclays Stockbrokers, for instance, currently charges commission at 1.75 per cent on the first £10,000 (compared with 0.35 per cent for a trade on the London Stock Exchange), 1.125 per cent on the next £10,000, 0.50 per cent on the next £20,000 and 0.40 per cent on the next £40,000. Thereafter it is 0.3 per cent and there is a minimum commission of £100.

OFEX

OFEX was established in 1995 by the S. J. & S. group of companies to provide off-exchange share trading for unlisted and unquoted securities. One of the companies in the group, J. P. Jenkins Limited, a member of the London Stock Exchange, is the market maker, making a price in all OFEX securities during each trading day.

OFEX shares are high risk and may often be illiquid, which means you may not always be able to buy or sell your investment. The market is not a Recognized Investment Exchange (RIE) and is not directly regulated by the Financial Services Authority or the Securities and Futures Authority

Why do companies list on OFEX? New companies may use it as a way to raise money to get their business going, while other companies hope to move from OFEX to AIM or the Official List as they grow. A few companies use it as a way of obtaining an independent valuation of their shares, for example, when a major shareholder dies. You can track OFEX prices at their website, *www.ofex.co.uk*. You can buy OFEX shares through a number of major brokers, although you may have to place an order and wait for some time until it can be fulfilled. Some prices are published in the *Financial Times* and the *London Evening Standard*.

BIOTECHNOLOGY – THRILLS AND SPILLS IN A NEW INDUSTRY

Scientific discoveries in genetics have created an exciting new industry called biotechnology, which offers the promise of huge leaps forward in treating disease and improving crops. The first commercial successes came from the USA, where genetically engineered bacteria have been used to make vital substances, such as insulin and human growth hormone, much more cheaply and safely than was done in the past. The UK is a world leader in genetics, and is the leading country for commercial biotechnology outside the USA.

Despite all the optimism, biotechnology investors have had a rough ride, and this illustrates the risks involved in investing in very new things. One of the key stories in UK biotech investment was the dramatic sequence of events at British Biotech Plc, which, in 1992, was the first biotechnology company to receive a full listing on the London Stock Exchange, and was simultaneously quoted on Nasdaq in the USA.

In 1997 the market capitalization of British Biotech rose to nearly £2.5 billion and the company was on the verge of entering the FTSE 100, even though it had sales of only a few million pounds and was still loss making.

Dr Keith McCullagh, then Chief Executive, said in February 1997 that 'British Biotech has yet to sell any of the drugs it has been working on in the ten years since the company's foundation in 1986'. In May 1998 McCullagh resigned following allegations of impropriety and insider dealing made against the company after the sacking of its former Head of Clinical Trials, Dr Andrew Millar.

After a long enquiry, in June 1999 the London Stock Exchange issued a public censure of the company, the most severe punishment of a company other than delisting. The Quotations Committee said, 'A company should ensure that any information which emanates from it is neither inaccurate nor misleading.'

The company's alleged infringements took place between mid-1997 and early 1998, as the market waited for news on Zacutex, a treatment for pancreatitis that it was developing. The Stock Exchange said that a preliminary report by the EMEA, Europe's regulator of drugs,which ruled that Zacutex could not be approved on the information that had been submitted, should have been disclosed to shareholders. It also said that later press releases from the company gave a 'misleading impression'.

Rights issues

When a company whose shares are already listed on the Stock Exchange wants to raise more money, it can do so by a 'rights issue', offering new shares to the shareholders that it already has. In case not enough shareholders want to take up their rights, the company will often arrange for the issue to be underwritten by stockbrokers and banks who promise to buy shares in exchange for a commission. The problem is that if the rights issue flops, meaning that few shareholders want the new shares, the underwriters are stuck with them and have to dribble them out slowly on to the market; whenever the share price rises, the underwriters will sell more of the shares they are stuck with, and this will bring the price down again. 'Deep-discount' rights issues are when the issuing company offers the shares at well below the market price.

As a shareholder, you have the choice of whether to take up your rights or not. You have to come up with the money to pay for them, so you need to be confident that the company is conducting the rights issue for a good reason (e.g. expansion), rather than to pay off debt. You will receive an 'offer document' explaining why the company wants to raise the money and giving its accounts so you will be able to make a judgement. However, even a 'rescue rights issue' by a company in trouble can sometimes result in an increase in the subsequent market price. If you decide not to exercise your rights, you may still be able to make a profit by selling the rights themselves. Once dealing begins after the issue, the price will, in theory, be between the old market price and the amount of discount on the issue price, so the effect for the shareholders is that their old shares will come down a little and the new shares will go up. If you sell your rights for more than the amount your original shares drop to, you make a profit.

You can estimate the price of the shares after the rights issue by multiplying the number of shares you are being offered by the offer price, adding the result to the total market value of the shares you already own, and dividing by the total number of shares. This figure represents the expected movement down from the old market price after the issue because of the discount on the new shares. It is called the 'ex-rights' price since it is, in theory, the price that the share will settle down to after the issue is over, when the shares will be sold in the market without the rights. The ex-rights price is used to work out the price you should get for selling your rights. You can do this either by not responding to the offer document, in which case the company will sell the rights for you and send you the money, or selling them in the stock market 'nil paid'.

EXAMPLE

Working out rights values

Suppose you own 22 shares in a company with a market value of 300p each, and a rights issue offers you the chance to buy one share for every 11 shares you already own at a price of 250p each. You can calculate the ex-rights price as follows:

> 2 new shares x 250p = 500p
> 500p + (22 old shares x 300p) = 500p + 6600p = 7100p
> 7100p ÷ 24 shares = 296p per share

Thus, you estimate that by buying the two new shares at the discounted offer price, you will see the market price drop from the 300p of the old, 'rights-on' shares to the 296p of the ex-rights price. The value of the two new shares that you bought for 250p each will have gone up, however.

During the rights issue, there is a period between the time when you are notified of how many new shares you are being offered and the deadline for acceptance during which the old shares are traded in the market ex-rights. This means that the person selling them is keeping the rights and the rights are traded separately as 'nil paid' shares. In our example, the ex-rights price during this period should in theory be around 296p and the nil paid share price should be about 46p (the difference between the ex-rights price and the exercise price). In practice, though, the nil paid value will fluctuate.

Suppose you want to exercise your rights, but you don't have enough cash to do so. You could try to sell some of your rights and use the cash to exercise the rights you have left. You can work this out by multiplying the number of new shares you have been offered by the price you can get for the rights and then dividing the result by the actual ex-rights price.

EXAMPLE

Suppose you owned 220 shares originally and have been offered the right to buy 20 shares:

$$(20 \times 46p) \div 296p = 920p \div 296p = 3.1$$

This tells you that you can sell 17 shares nil paid (17 x 46 = 782p) and use the cash to buy three new shares (3 x 250 = 750p).

CLAWBACKS

Clawbacks are becoming more popular than rights issues. The company issues new shares to one or more institutions, but allows existing shareholders to buy some shares at the issue price, thus 'clawing back' the shares. The big difference for the shareholders is that if you don't want to exercise your clawback rights, you can't sell them in the market.

Scrip issues

'Free' scrip issues, also called capitalization issues or bonus issues, are when a company offers new shares to shareholders in proportion to the number that they already own, but without asking for more money. This is done in order to make the total number of shares in the company larger, so that there are more shares in the market and they can be bought and sold more easily, and also so that the company can transfer some of its reserves into capital on its balance sheet, giving it various business advantages. The company needs the approval of its shareholders to conduct a scrip issue. The result will be that the company has more capital, though it is not worth more, and there are more shares, but with a lower nominal value to reflect the scrip issue. Generally, shareholders like scrip issues and share prices often increase at the announcement of one.

A similar method is 'share splitting', where a company splits each share into several more with lower nominal values that add up in total to the nominal value of the original share. Both these methods are often thought to make shares more attractive because investors don't like to buy shares that have a high market price; it is considered that it somehow 'feels' better to buy 800 shares for £1 each than 200 shares at £4 each.

Some companies have annual scrip issues and increase the amount they distribute in dividends by keeping the dividend rate the same as before. They can also pay 'scrip dividends', which means that they pay you a dividend on your shares or free scrip shares. A variation on this is 'enhanced scrip dividends', which offer scrip shares of a considerably higher value than the alternative of a cash dividend.

Takeover bids

While rights issues are generally regarded as a mixed blessing for shareholders, the news that a company is trying to take over your company by buying its shares is almost always good news. Often companies compete to take over a target, so its shareholders find themselves the focus of a stream of letters urging them to accept or reject increasingly higher bids for their shares. There then follows the enjoyable task of deciding which bid to accept, and when.

The news that a company is trying to take over your company by buying its shares is almost always good news

You usually have 60 days in which to decide whether to accept a bid. Once the bid has expired, if the bidding company has succeeded in buying over 90 per cent of the total number of shares in the target company, it can then force you to accept a price for your shares that is lower than the successful bid price. The bids for your shares may offer shares in the acquiring company, or a combination of such shares, fixed-interest securities and cash in exchange. These shares must be examined carefully – you may not feel that they represent a profitable exchange. Sometimes a company does not want to be taken over and decides to fight the bids; it will produce strong arguments for rejecting the offer.

As we have seen, if you own shares in a company that is the subject of a bidding war, you are likely to gain substantial profits, as long as you sell out to a bidder before your company is bought. The rules for takeovers say that bids cannot be called 'final' until very near the end of the war, so if you receive a bid that is not described as final you should wait for a better offer. The target company may try to find a 'white knight' investor to counter-bid in the hope that life under the white knight will be better than under the predator. Bidders can improve their offers up to the 46th day of the bid, and the defending company has until the 39th day to produce key financial arguments against the bids.

A bidding company doesn't have to own any shares in a company to bid for it, but often it tries to build up a stake in advance of bidding. The rules say that shareholdings of over 3 per cent in a company must be declared publicly so that people can have some warning of what may happen. Once a bidder controls over 50 per cent of the shares, he effectively controls the company. Predators sometimes buy up to 15 per cent of a company in a 'dawn raid' on the stock market, after which they may not buy any more shares for a week. They can then build their holdings to 25 per cent before waiting again. Once the shareholding has passed 30 per cent, they must bid for the company. If they can persuade people to sell them 20 per cent more of the company's shares, they can then announce that the bid is 'unconditional as to acceptances', which means that the rest of the shareholders have two weeks in which to make up their minds. If these shareholders refuse the offer, which is unusual, they keep their shares in the company, but it is now under the bidder's control (as mentioned earlier, if bidders manage to get 90 per cent of the shares, they can forcibly buy the remaining 10 per cent).

Once a bidder is in control of the company, it remains to be seen whether the predator has gauged its value correctly: companies engaging in a series of takeovers during a boom, doing their sums on the assumption of ever-increasing values, can be very badly caught out in a crash. Just because an acquiring company is willing to pay a high price for your shares does not necessarily mean that it is cannier than you are, so if you think that the cash you are being offered is a lot, take it – you may be glad that you did! Sometimes people prefer to take some shares in lieu of cash because there is no capital gains tax to pay when you receive the shares. If you decide to do this, don't assume that these shares will rise, and consider when you want to dispose of them and what they will really be worth then. If you want to take the cash, check how much time you have in which to accept – sometimes you are only given 21 days from the date of the bid in which to decide on cash.

The financial press, in particular the *Investors Chronicle*, covers takeover bids and often offers useful advice on whether or not to accept what is currently on offer. If you use an advisory broker, you should also ask for his or her opinion.

BUYING AFTER A WINNING BID

This is often speculative. If you really think that the takeover is sound and you expect improved business results, then it may be worth investing after a takeover. However, make sure that other speculators haven't pushed the share so high that you are paying too much.

The internet boom in the USA during the late 1990s threw up many companies that were able to acquire others very rapidly, using their own soaring shares as payment. An acquisitive company may actively pursue many targets in the hope of obtaining a near-monopoly of a market – but it is not always certain that they will succeed. Instead a rapid expansion may ultimately result in total collapse.

During stock market booms, mergers and acquisitions become fashionable because there is plenty of money around and buying another company can be a way of making a quick buck, rather than a soundly planned step towards long-term expansion. It's often hard to tell, especially when bankers and analysts are all singing the praises of a predatory company. Be cautious!

HOW TO CHOOSE COMPANIES THAT MAY BE SUBJECT TO TAKEOVER BIDS

Some companies get a reputation for being likely to attract bids that lasts for decades without a bid ever actually emerging, so it is difficult to spot winners with certainty. The profile of a likely candidate for a takeover bid is a company with a large amount of assets, a broad shareholder base and a good underlying business. Sometimes they are found in the following situations:

- Companies that have been controlled by families for decades, if not for generations, may be amenable to takeover bids; it all turns on whether the major shareholders want to sell, perhaps in order to retire, or whether they are determined to hang on.
- Companies that produce a lower return on the capital employed than is normal in their industry can be the target of takeover bids from other more competitive companies in the same industry, the idea being that the acquirer will be able to make the company more profitable than it is at present. The same goes for trading profits: sometimes a famous name is going downhill, and is taken over by a company in the same business which hopes to increase margins through the power of the combined turnover.
- Companies in which a possible predator has bought a large number of shares can be the target of takeover bids. The share price will rise on this news, but if you feel that the target company is an attractive one, it can be worth buying now and waiting for the bid. Sometimes the stakeholder sells the shares on to another bidder, so you must play a waiting game. The danger is that the stakeholder may simply withdraw.

- Although it is now illegal in the UK to buy shares because you have inside information, share prices have a curious tendency to rise before any news of the acquisition of a large stake appears. Company employees, their relatives and people in the City who know about the planned bid may buy shares without realizing that it is illegal to do so – but even if the insider trading is deliberate, it is very hard to prove (see Chapter 12). Thus, some people invest on unexplained share price rises on the assumption that the insider traders know that a bid is the air. This may work sometimes, but it is a puny strategy, rather like being a builder who undercuts his competitors' quotations for work and finds himself making a loss because he hasn't done his own budgeting – after all, the share price increase may simply be the result of false rumours, so look at the company carefully to see if you think that a takeover is credible.

THE MONOPOLIES AND MERGERS COMMISSION AND OTHER AUTHORITIES

There are laws to prevent companies buying up their competitors in order to create a monopoly, so there is a chance that a UK takeover bid may be referred to the Monopolies and Mergers Commission. Sell your shares if you think that the bid will be referred, as a failure can mean a large fall in the price. Although companies take a lot of advice to ensure that their bids will not be referred, some bids do fail. The British Takeover Panel is a City organization which oversees the takeover process and tries to make sure that everybody plays by the rules. It is not a state-controlled body, and has attracted criticism from outsiders who feel that it does not have enough power to force people to play fair. The European Commission is also sticking its finger in the pie with the job of overseeing big European takeovers. The European Commission is expected to try to change the way that takeovers are conducted in the UK in the future.

In the United States the rules are different. The 'anti-trust' laws make it illegal for companies not only to monopolize markets, but also to 'tend' to create a monopoly, use unfair methods of competition or attempt to 'unreasonably' restrain trade. In practice, the bigger the companies, the more likely it is that a takeover bid will provoke anti-trust lawsuits. Such lawsuits have a political dimension. Under President Reagan, corporate America was given clear signals that there would be fewer government lawsuits against them and a greater freedom to seek profits wherever they could be found. In Chapter 12, we will look at some of the scandals that emerged during a frenzy of takeovers (known as 'mergers' in the United States) in the 1980s. More recently, the computer software giant Microsoft has been under pressure from anti-trust suits. One way of interpreting this event is to say that while you are allowed to get very rich indeed in the USA, there are limits – too much financial power has to be curbed, and anti-trust legislation is a relatively civilized way of doing this.

MICROSOFT – FOLIE DE GRANDEUR?

Who would have thought, back in 1970, that an unprepossessing computer nerd could build his tiny software firm into one of the world's most important corporations, and become the world's richest man in the process? Yet that is exactly what Bill Gates has done with Microsoft.

In April 2000 a US judge found Microsoft guilty of breaking America's anti-monopoly laws, enshrined in the 1890 Sherman Act, which prohibits powerful companies from using their dominance to damage the competition and limit customer choice. The judge ruled that the company should be broken in two, one to own the best-selling Windows computer operating system and the other to own programs such as Word. At the time of writing, the appeals process is dragging on, and Microsoft appears to hope for leniency from the new president, George W. Bush.

Microsoft controls 90 per cent of the market for computer operating systems, and the judge accepted that it had used its power to prevent certain competitors from thriving. From an investor's point of view, a break up may present opportunities. When AT&T, a telephone company, was broken up in the 1980s, the new, smaller firm became stronger, and the entire telecommunications industry has been revolutionized by lower costs and better technology as a result, argue pundits, of the increased competition.

Many computer buffs will not be sorry to see Microsoft broken up if, as many hope, it will result in even better and more powerful software products in the break-neck information technology race. New developments, such as the internet, are transforming the way the world works and plays, and many feel that while Microsoft did the public a great service by creating a near-universal software standard that made personal computers useful and affordable, the time is ripe for unleashing a new wave of software competitors for a new generation of computer-based products.
Watch this space!

CYCLES OF TAKEOVERS

Takeovers seem to come in waves. Around 1900 there was a flurry of takeovers, then another one in the boom of the 1920s, and others in the late 1960s and the 1980s. Today we are seeing merger mania in certain sectors, such as pharmaceuticals, as industries reorganize in response to changing conditions.

Merger waves are associated with bull markets (periods of generally rising share prices), although one would expect to see takeovers in bear markets too (periods of generally falling share prices), if the real motive was to pick up a bargain. Since many eager predators have come a cropper over the years, there is a general feeling that there is often something wrong about takeovers, and that they may be bad for the economy as a whole. As far as the private investor is concerned, they represent an exciting and profitable process if you are fortunate enough to own shares in a target company.

THE REASONS WHY COMPANIES BID

Takeovers can be divided into three kinds: 'horizontal', which is where both companies are in the same business; 'vertical', where the companies are in associated businesses at different points on the route from the production point to the point of sale; and 'conglomerate', where the companies are in unrelated businesses. The acquiring company may have sound business reasons for making the offer, such as the following:

- **Economies of scale**, where the combined buying power of the two companies can improve research and development and reduce costs. Horizontal takeovers are very often for reasons of economy of scale, but the same motive is sometimes claimed for conglomerate mergers. This is less convincing, because conglomerates tend to breed large bureaucracies which can outweigh the benefits of the takeover.
- **Vertical integration economies**. Taking over a supplier or a customer can help a company to become more powerful in the marketplace while substantially reducing costs. Sometimes a new method or product can be made more profitable in this way.
- **Improving efficiency**. If the target company is peopled by bad managers who are firmly entrenched, a takeover by a dynamic company which will sack the old regime and increase efficiency is sometimes the only practical way to save the company.
- **Tax losses and pension funds**. A company may have made substantial tax losses that it cannot use. If it takes over another company, it can benefit by setting off the tax losses against the other company's profits. Some companies hold large pension funds for their employees, which have been known to be an attraction to predators.
- **Taking over a smaller specialist company to market their products better** can often be cheaper for a big business than setting up competing products from scratch.

Here are some less convincing reasons for takeovers:

- **Diversification**, or the conglomerate-style takeover, is not thought to increase the value of the companies concerned. Buying a number of unrelated companies does not seem to be very good business in the long run, and often shares in diversified groups of companies fall lower than their book value.
- **The 'chain letter' effect**. This is when a company with low earnings and high growth conducts a series of takeovers of high-earning, low-growth companies, financing the offers mainly with its own 'paper' (e.g. offering its own shares to shareholders in the target companies). There is nothing wrong about this in principle, but if the acquiring company fools the market into thinking that its rapid growth is for sound business reasons, rather than simply growth through acquisition, it must continue with the same rate of growth if it is to keep its share price up. The temptation is to find more acquisition targets that may not be good bargains. In the end there will be no more companies to buy, its growth will slow and its share price will collapse. Here's how it works:

EXAMPLE

Suppose that Company A, the acquiring company, has total earnings of £300,000 and 1,000,000 shares, making its earnings per share 30p. Its p/e ratio is, say, 20, so its share price will be 600p. Now suppose that Company B, the target company, also has earnings of £300,000, 1,000,000 shares and earnings per share of 30p, but the lower p/e ratio of 10, making its share price 300p. Company A's market value is thus twice that of Company B's; if Company A can buy Company B by offering half of its own shares, it will then have total earnings of £600,000 and 1,500,000 shares, making the earnings per share 40p. If its share price stays the same, its p/e ratio falls to 15. If investors think that the increase in earnings per share is 'real' growth, they may invest, pushing up the p/e ratio as the share price rises.

- Reduced borrowing costs. This doesn't mean the genuine saving a company can get by making fewer and larger rights issues in the future after the takeover; it refers to the notion that corporate bonds can be issued at lower rates of interest because the increased value of the company gives lenders (bond buyers) more security. This may be true, but it is essentially an adjustment of risk rather than a real gain to the company.

When companies go bust …

If you invest in a company that is not listed on the stock market, you either know what you are doing or you are a brave soul indeed. In comparison with unquoted companies, the ones in the stock market don't go into liquidation very often. When they do, though, they often go in large numbers, as happened after the stock market crash of 1929, so one can never be complacent. We all hear about recessions causing companies to go under, but this doesn't mean much. A company that is going to survive will survive a recession, and one that is unsound can collapse even in times of prosperity.

If you invest in a company that is not listed on the stock market, you either know what you are doing or you are a brave soul indeed

Nevertheless, even top companies that are included in market indices have gone bust in the past, and will do so in the future. When this happens, you have to assume the worst. A liquidator is appointed to sell the company's assets in order to pay off its debts, and while you may have done sums to show that you will get back, say, 40p in the pound, in practice the insolvent company's assets tend to be sold off at rock bottom prices. The proceeds go to the 'secured creditors', and the shareholder, who is at the back of the queue, often gets nothing. The cautious investors will get out when danger signals appear, before the collapse happens. One way of watching out for trouble is regularly to check your investments' business ratios.

USING BUSINESS RATIOS TO GAUGE SOLVENCY

The 'gearing' or 'leverage' of a company is an important test. What you are looking at is how much the company is borrowing as a proportion of its own capital. To understand its significance, imagine you had friends who bought a house for £300,000 with £50,000 of their own money and borrowing the rest as a mortgage. Would you think they were wise? They might be able to service the debt on their current salaries, but what if one of them got ill, or lost their job, or if the property market went down, or interest rates doubled? What if all these things happened at once? We know from experience that bad things can happen to people; obviously, the same is true for companies too.

While it is true that some industries are more dangerous than others, any company which borrows more than £1 for every pound of its capital should be treated with caution. A high-borrowing company is called 'highly geared'. Companies can become highly geared when they expand very fast and borrow money to do so. In all the excitement the company's overheads have a tendency to grow very quickly too, and if the business subsequently gets into trouble, high overheads and interest payments can sink it like a stone.

From a conservative point of view, companies that borrow the equivalent of less than half of their capital are pretty stable, and ones that borrow the equivalent of between a half and all of their capital are usually OK. Another way of measuring a company's ability to pay its debts is to look at the proportion of trading profit that is being spent on paying the interest on loans. There is something wrong if most of the money is going in this way – after all, a company is supposed to be making money for you, not for the banks!

The next thing to do is to look at the company's 'liquidity'. In this context, liquidity means the ability of the company to pay off its current creditors, such as suppliers, the Inland Revenue and short-term lenders, with its current assets, such as its stock, the money owed by customers and its money in the bank. If the proportion of current debt to current assets is more than 2:3, it is a bad sign. Remember that current assets are sometimes valued rather optimistically, and may be worth far less than their book value if they have to be sold in an emergency. There are, however, vast, well-established companies that allow their current liabilities to exceed their current assets by a wide margin, confident in their power to keep their suppliers waiting for payment should the need arise. Indeed, quite a number of large companies are well known for taking many months of credit from their smaller suppliers as a matter of course.

All kinds of things can kill a company, including regulatory changes, changes in the market and losing big court cases. Accountants know that something is wrong, after it has happened, by looking at the books, although the published accounts may not reveal the whole story. In published accounts, accountants use certain stock phrases to signal that they are unhappy; large 'extraordinary items' and a change in accounting practice should alert you to possible problems. The reason why you cannot take published accounts as the absolute truth is that it is very difficult to value things correctly, given the complexity of modern business and also that it is often in the directors' interests to distort the accounts in some way. Directors want to improve the look of profit figures for such motives as improving the chances of a sale of all or part of the company, to put off unwelcome bidders, or even to ensure their own bonuses, and they may try to lessen profit figures for reasons such as reducing the tax bill, avoiding public criticism and defending attacks from trade unions. When a company gets into trouble some directors react by trying to fight their way out by fair means or foul, and may juggle the accounts to put off the evil day when they must declare insolvency. Although the external accountants must, by law, audit the books each year, and will do their best to present an accurate picture, it is not impossible for directors to pull the wool over their eyes, for a few years at least.

Interestingly, accountants feel happier about low valuations and profit estimates than high ones because they know that there may be unintentional overvaluations elsewhere, and also because they are far less likely to be sued if it turns out that the company is worth more than was thought, than if it emerges that the company was grossly overvalued.

SUSPENSIONS AND LIQUIDATIONS

Suppose you wake up one morning to find that the shares in your favourite stock have been suspended. This does not necessarily spell disaster. 'Suspension' means that the trading of the shares in the market is stopped. The idea is that suspending shares when there is uncertainty about a company levels the playing field, giving time for all the investors to find out what is going on. The danger is that the suspension can last for years, which means that you are stuck with a dodgy shareholding that you cannot sell and that you cannot claim as a loss against capital gains tax. However, suspensions are sometimes used in happy circumstances too, such as when a bid is in the air, to allow time for all the information to reach the investors.

Despite their comparative lack of access to information, small investors will usually get plenty of warning when a company gets into trouble. The actions of its directors have a great bearing on what happens to a company once it starts to sink. In many circumstances they can put the company into 'administration' before a creditor, or the law, forces them to relinquish control. An independent accountant is appointed by a court to manage the company for three months or more before creditors can take any action to recover their debts. This gives time for re-financing, cutting losses and raising cash by selling off businesses and assets. It is a courageous thing for the directors to do, since, as mentioned earlier, the money raised may not be enough to cover the debts, so the temptation is to go on trying to keep the company going, ignoring its slide into ruin. Creditors may object to an application to put the company into administration, and they can themselves apply to put the company into 'receivership'. This effectively takes all control out of the directors' hands. The 'official receiver' appoints a 'liquidator' to sell off what he can.

GUERRILLA INVESTORS AND INSOLVENT COMPANIES

People who have had no experience of insolvent companies have a tendency to remain hopeful long after disaster has struck. It is a matter of judgement, but if you feel that a company is getting into trouble, get out while you still can. Once a company goes into administration or receivership you haven't really got a prayer.

6

Banks

Many people think that anything to do with banking is deadly dull, but any subject that has such a direct effect on one's life as the banking system does has to be of interest to the guerrilla investor. In this chapter we will look at:

- *Money – why and how it works*
- *The money stock and the money supply*

- *The role of central banks*
- *The Bank of England*
- *UK monetary policy*
- *The Federal Reserve*
- *Types of bank*
- *Interest rates*
- *The BCCI story*
- *How banks lend to individuals*
- *Guerrilla borrowing tactics*
- *Banking and Big Brother*
- *The future of the banking industry – merger mania and the advent of electronic banking*

Money

There is an alternative to money. If you live an isolated life and can obtain all that you need through your own physical work, you don't require money. This is the kind of life lived by most people in the distant past. Money is an invention, like writing, which grew out of the increasingly complex needs of settled societies.

In essence, money is a solution to the problems of barter. If I spend a week making a chair and I want to give it to you in exchange for your grapes, how many grapes should you give me? Perhaps I don't want very many grapes, because I don't want to spend time converting them into a form that won't spoil, so I ask you for 'change' – a few grapes and some other items in return for the chair – but all you want to give is grapes … You can see how cumbersome bartering is! Anyone who has spent time in less developed countries can testify to the awkwardness and inefficiency of non-money economies. Money makes exchange easier. It is a token that can be passed from hand to hand, and which most people will accept as payment. It doesn't have to be in the form of coins and notes – even highly civilized nations have occasionally reverted to using other objects for money during periods of collapse, for instance when cigarettes were widely used for money in Europe at the end of World War 2.

The main characteristics of money are:

- It is generally accepted as payment for other things.
- It is a way of measuring the prices of other things.
- It can be stored, so you can keep the value it represents until later.
- It is relatively easy to transport.
- The units of money are, or should be, standard and easy to recognize.
- The supply of money must be controlled.

GOLD AND MONEY

Gold and silver coins were once popular as money, since they had an intrinsic value to which their monetary value was related. However, they are vulnerable to tampering: people would clip off tiny bits of the metal before spending the coins, which were then worth slightly less than they were supposed to be. It was also possible to forge coins using a lower content of precious metal. This activity was popular with kings and governments who controlled the coinage. If a king minted coins with, say two-thirds of the official gold content, he could buy a third more goods and services with the coins. Eventually people would discover the trick and adjust prices accordingly (an inflationary process), but in the meantime the king had benefited by cheating his subjects.

Nowadays governments are supposed to be more responsible and protective of their currencies, but this kind of thing still happens. For example, the horrific inflation in Germany during the inter-war years is thought to have been, in part, a tactic to reduce the unjust burden of war reparations imposed by the victorious Allies: Germany paid part of the huge debt in devalued currency while ordinary people saw their savings evaporate.

Because of the problems with coins, bank notes were introduced. These have no intrinsic value, but are guaranteed by the government that issues them. To operate such a system you need stable, organized bodies to run it, which is where banks come in. Banks developed from trusted groups, such as goldsmiths, who were able to issue receipts for money that they held in safekeeping for other people, and thus bank notes were born. In the 19th century British currency was tied to the gold standard. This meant that coins and notes could be exchanged for gold at the Bank of England on demand. The gold standard was abandoned during the upheavals of the two world wars, and the international system which replaced it is discussed in Chapter 10.

THE MONEY IN CIRCULATION

We hear a great deal about the importance of the money supply: different political forces and economic theorists hold conflicting ideas about how, and how much, the money supply should be controlled, but it is clear that some degree of control is necessary. If, for example, anyone could print as much money as they liked, people would soon become very wary of accepting it as payment. Thus, it is in everyone's interest for the creation and movement of money to be regulated.

The world has become so complicated that it is actually quite difficult to keep tabs on the movement of money, even within a country, so in order to make analysis easier, various definitions of different parts of the total supply of money have been invented. In the UK they are as follows:

- M0 (pronounced 'M nought') is the notes and coins in circulation, the notes and coins kept in banks for their daily operations, and the banks' balances at the Bank of England.
- M1 is the notes and coins in circulation, and non-interest-bearing bank deposits made by private sector companies and individuals repayable on demand (excluding deposits made by government-owned bodies).
- M2 is the notes and coins in circulation, and non-interest-bearing bank deposits made by private sector companies and individuals repayable on demand and certain interest-bearing private sector deposits.
- M3 includes the money defined in M1, plus all private sector deposits held by UK residents, including certificates of deposit, building society deposits and National Savings.

The amount of money in M1 is roughly ten times the amount of notes and coins in circulation, and the amount of money in M3 is about 20 times the amount of notes and coins in circulation. So where does all the extra money come from? Part of it is created by banks in the following way.

UK banks are allowed to lend around three-quarters of the total amount of the money that has been deposited with them for safekeeping. Suppose you borrow £1,000 from Bank X to buy a cheap car. You pay the money to the vendor, who deposits the £1,000 in Bank B; Bank B lends £750 of it to another customer, who pays it to Company A. Company A deposits the £750 in Bank C, who lends £537 of it to another customer, and on it goes. This process actually increases the amount of money in the banks' accounting systems several times over. In effect, they are creating extra money by giving credit, relying on the fact that not all their customers will want to withdraw their deposits at the same time. When this happens, there is a 'run on the banks', which we will examine later. The 25 per cent that the banks don't lend is called their 'reserves', and can vary, which leads directly to changes in the total amount of money in the system.

GOVERNMENT BORROWING

In Chapter 4 we saw how governments borrow long-term money by issuing bonds. They also borrow funds in the short term, often using the banking system and the money markets (see Chapter 7), and this has a great affect on the money supply. If the total amount of money the government earns (mainly tax revenue) is less than the amount it spends in a certain period, the difference is called the Public Sector Borrowing Requirement (PSBR). The PSBR can be covered either by borrowing, or by selling assets. If the government borrows from banks by issuing Treasury bills in the Discount Market (see Chapter 7), the money supply is increased, which may have inflationary consequences, but if it borrows from the public, by issuing National Savings securities, it is thought that there is no effect on the money supply, since the money is raised to be spent, and thus returns to the banking system.

Central banks

Most countries have one central bank which acts on behalf of the government to control the banking system. In the UK, this role is performed by the Bank of England. Like most central banks, it is owned by its government and it acts as a state instrument rather than as a business undertaken for the profit of its shareholders. The main jobs of central banks are:

- To be the 'lender of last resort' for other banks in the country. This helps to give stability to the banking system and offers a limited guarantee to people using banks that they will not lose their money in a banking collapse.
- To oversee the activities of the other banks in the country.
- To exercise a degree of control on the money supply by regulating the amount of credit that the other banks are giving.
- To control the issue and circulation of notes and coins.
- To act as bankers to the state in the same way that other banks service their customers.
- To administer bonds issued by the government.

Every central bank has its own peculiarities, according to the character of its own country's system.

THE BANK OF ENGLAND

As well as being the banker to the government, the Bank of England also provides banking services for a few private sector companies and individuals, the other banks and financial institutions in the UK, a few central banks from Commonwealth countries, the International Monetary Fund (IMF), the World Bank, the Bank for International Settlements, and members of its own staff.

The government holds many accounts with other banks, but by far its biggest ones are at the Bank of England. Taxes and other moneys go into the government's Exchequer account, and all the money that the government spends comes out of it. Other UK government accounts at the Bank of England include those necessary for the payment of interest on gilts. The Bank of England borrows money on behalf of the government by issuing bonds and Treasury bills (see Chapter 4), but only lends for very short periods (e.g. overnight). It also advises the government on what is happening in the market. Most banks operating in the UK have to keep deposits of 0.45 per cent of their liabilities at the Bank of England. These earn no interest, and are called 'cash ratio deposits'. They also have accounts called 'operational balances' which are used for clearing all cheques through the system.

The Bank of England is the only bank allowed to issue bank notes in England and Wales. Bank notes get dirty and torn quite quickly, so the old ones have to be burned and millions of new ones are printed daily to replace them. As well as being the registrar for gilts, the Bank of England also handles bonds issued by some Commonwealth countries, UK local authorities and nationalized bodies. In Chapter 10 we will see how the Bank of England can act to influence the rate of exchange between sterling and other currencies. This is done through the 'Exchange Equalization Account', which holds the government's gold reserves, special drawing rights (see Chapter 10) and foreign currency. If banks get into trouble, they can come to the Bank of

England for a loan; this will cost more than the money market rates (see Chapter 7) and will be on terms that make sure that banks will only seek the loan if they have no other way of obtaining the money.

UK monetary policy

The Bank of England acts on behalf of the government to control bank lending in the following ways:

- **Interest rates**. The Bank of England can affect UK interest rates by setting its own rate of lending to the discount houses (see page 30). The idea is that if the Bank of England raises its interest rates, people will borrow less, but this does not always happen.
- **Special deposits**. The Bank of England can raise the amount of money that financial institutions must deposit with it. This reduces the amount of money in the system and forces banks to lend less.
- **Directives**. The Bank of England can tell banks what category of customer to lend to in order to influence the economy in different sectors. In the past it would also issue directives specifying that banks could lend up to a certain amount during a certain period. These are called quantitative directives, but they are not used at present.
- **Open market operations**. This is when the Bank of England buys or sells already issued gilts and Treasury bills in the marketplace, thereby reducing or increasing the money available to banks for lending.

THE FEDERAL RESERVE: THE CENTRAL BANK OF THE UNITED STATES

The Federal Reserve, or the Fed, is actually 12 banks with 25 branches across the United States. Founded in 1913, it is run by a board of governors appointed by the president for 14-year terms to protect them against political vagaries. Like all central banks, its job is to oversee and stabilize the banking system. It is owned not by the government but by other banks. Apart from this important difference, the Fed operates on very similar lines to the Bank of England. Under the chairmanship of Alan Greenspan, it is generally agreed that the Fed managed the exuberant growth of America's economy during the 1990s wisely and well.

Types of bank

You are probably aware that there is more than one kind of bank; in this section we will look at the various kinds of bank to be found in the UK.

The banks that people are most familiar with are the *'retail' banks*, which have branches all over the UK, and clear people's cheques through the system. Until recently, the most important of these were the 'big four' clearing banks, the three Scottish banks (the Bank of Scotland, the Clydesdale Bank and the Royal Bank of Scotland, all three of which have the power to issue Scottish bank notes), and four banks in Northern Ireland. Since regulations were relaxed, merger activity has increased and building societies are merging with, or becoming like, traditional banks, while large foreign banks are increasing their presence in the UK.

The next category is that of the *merchant banks*, a variety that is peculiar to the UK – the nearest equivalent in the USA are called 'investment' banks. Merchant banks arrange finance for companies, by issues of shares and bonds, and manage large investment portfolios, principally for institutional funds. They also accept interest-bearing deposits from companies, are involved in factoring (giving cash advances to companies secured on money owed them by their customers), leasing and insurance for companies, and are very active in the 'Euromarkets' (see Chapter 7). They can be thought of as the wholesalers of banking services, operating higher up the chain of the banking system. They have only a few branches and rarely deal with private individuals.

There are also banks that are owned jointly by a group of other banks, often from different countries, and are not controlled by any one bank. These *'consortium' banks* are involved in making large loans, too big for one bank to take the whole risk, to companies and state organizations internationally, and are active in the Euromarkets.

There are several hundred *foreign-owned banks* that have branches in the UK. United States banks are keen to take part of the British retail market as well as to benefit from differences between the regulatory controls of the United States and the UK, while others concentrate on serving businesses and consumers connected with their own countries. They sometimes offer advantages to the guerrilla investor, mainly in lower costs and improved services when conducting international transactions. Occasionally you can find a foreign bank in the City that will change major currencies without commission, which is worth the effort if you are going on holiday.

British overseas banks are the remnants of the imperial banking system, the owners of banks in foreign countries, mainly in the Third World. Due to nationalizations and the blocking of funds by the host countries, the overseas banks have become progressively less profitable as Britain divested itself of its imperial territories during the last 60 years or so. New markets have been sought, including retail banking in the United States and Canada, the currency markets and the money markets (see Chapter 7).

The *National Savings Bank* used to be part of the Post Office but is now administered by the Department of National Savings. Its purpose is to offer facilities for saving to the public and it is similar to a building society.

Finance houses are banks that specialize in lending money to companies and individuals for the purchase of large items on hire-purchase schemes. They also offer factoring and leasing services. More recently, they have opened retail outlets known as 'money shops'. The big banks have interests in the finance houses and they are carefully regulated to protect the consumer.

UK RETAIL BANKING FOR GUERRILLAS

In the 'good old days' the bank manager was a paternalistic friend to his customers: he was sometimes allowed to sell them insurance and take the commission personally, but in general he was able to offer relatively sound and independent advice to customers on their affairs and investments. The emphasis was on building long-term relationships, trust and integrity. The situation has changed. Bank customers are now bombarded with sales pitches for insurance and other financial products, their 'personal banking officers' change every six months, such advice as they get is far from impartial, and they are generally treated in an adversarial manner. Minimize the business that you do with banks and don't inform them of your affairs unless it is absolutely necessary.

Minimize the business that you do with banks and don't inform them of your affairs unless it is absolutely necessary

Interest rates

Interest rates vary, as most of us know, and the variations are caused by a number of factors:

- **Supply and demand**. If the public is saving a lot by depositing money in banks, the banks will have more to lend. Since they are in competition with one another, the interest rate they demand will tend to drop to attract borrowers. The amount that the government borrows or lends has a similar effect on the total supply of money available.

- **Risk**. Borrowers who are regarded as good risks can generally borrow money at a lower rate of interest than a 'bad risk' borrower.
- **Inflation**. As money becomes worth less through inflation, so lenders ask for higher interest rates to compensate. You can compare rates by subtracting the inflation component from the interest rates, but since the rate of inflation can only ever be an estimate, the figures will never be exact.

These factors affect all lenders and borrowers, however large the sum involved. In addition, rates vary according to your own position in the marketplace. Banks set a 'base rate' which represents the minimum interest it is prepared to charge to the majority of its consumer and commercial customers. The base rate is set higher than LIBOR, the London Inter-Bank Offered Rate (see page 132), which is what banks charge each other for loans. Most consumers borrow from their banks at rates much higher than the base rate.

In the longer term, the interest rates in any particular country are affected by the exchange rate of its currency against the currencies of other countries, and by interest rates in the world's biggest economies. UK interest rates tend to follow US rates quite closely.

NOT ALL BANKS ARE LILY-WHITE — BCCI AND OTHERS

Where there is money, there is fraud, and the banking community has its fair share of villains. What many people do not realize is that banks are, by their nature, involved in the grey world that lies between politics and commerce.

When Iraq invaded Kuwait its forces seized a vast amount of Kuwaiti dinars held in cash by Kuwaiti banks. After the liberation of Kuwait, its government changed the currency in order to prevent the looted currency being spent; anyone holding the old currency legitimately could apply to change it for the new money. To my personal knowledge, at least one London branch of a foreign-owned bank assisted in the changing of old money captured by Iraqis, using Kuwaiti middlemen as a cover. Was a crime committed? Presumably some Kuwaiti laws were broken, though, perhaps, British ones weren't. This kind of thing goes on all the time, but is very rarely reported.

The collapse of BCCI, the Bank of Credit and Commerce International, brought to light examples of fraud and of what might be called 'political crime'.

BCCI had knowingly operated accounts for terrorist organizations, laundered drug money on a large scale and also, it was claimed, had assisted the CIA, Britain's secret services, and those of several Islamic countries in covert operations. It has even been suggested that civil servants in the regulatory bodies were actually afraid to do anything about BCCI because of its intelligence connections. The bank was started in the late 1960s by Pakistani bankers using oil money from the Gulf. Its operational headquarters were in London, though it was legally based in Luxembourg and the Cayman Islands, and it had branches all over the world. In the early 1970s it opened more than 40 retail branches in the UK, mainly serving customers who had recently emigrated to Britain. By the late 1970s, the Bank of America, which had increased its shareholding in BCCI from 25 per cent to almost 50 per cent in 1973, was eager to sell out, which it managed to do in 1980. In 1979, the Banking Act in the UK tightened the rules on what kind of bodies could call themselves banks, and BCCI found itself awarded the lowly status of 'licensed deposit taker'. Because it had overseas branches, it could still use the word 'bank' in its name, but it had to display a sign reading 'licensed deposit taker' at its branches to tell customers that it was not as safe as a bank. In fact, ill-informed customers were told that this meant that BCCI was a more stable and important bank than the others with high street branches. Major losses followed, and BCCI began to pay out old depositors with the new ones' money.

In 1985 the Bank of England forced BCCI to move its money market operations to Abu Dhabi, and soon afterwards the authorities in Luxembourg asked the Bank of England to take over the supervision of the bank, which it refused to do. In 1987 a compromise was reached in which the central banks of several countries, including the Bank of England, formed a 'College of Regulators' to supervise BCCI. The following year several senior BCCI employees were arrested for drug money laundering in Florida. While banks acted to reduce their exposure to BCCI, customers kept on coming, in the touching belief that an international bank of its size (it had assets of $20 billion) would be properly controlled by the governments in whose countries it operated.

In 1991 the Bank of England finally made its move, leading some 69 regulators across the world in closing down BCCI. Unhappy customers mobbed its branches and a succession of court cases followed. Perhaps the whole story of what happened, and why the regulatory authorities took so long to act, will never emerge.

How banks lend to individuals

Most people don't really understand how banks think, which leads to a lot of public resentment. The first thing to appreciate is that in the UK, as well as in most other developed countries, banks are heavily regulated by the government.

The kind of borrowing we are considering at the moment is called the 'consumer loan'. The key word is 'consumer'. Banks behave very differently towards consumers than they do towards commercial customers. By law, and inclination, banks 'baby' consumers. If you want a loan, the banker will want to know several things:

- How much?
- What for?
- How long for?
- What is the repayment schedule?

In asking how much you want to borrow, the banker really wants to know how much you have got in assets and how much you earn. If, say, you have a house worth £100,000, no mortgage and no other debts, banks will be happy to lend you a smallish proportion of your £100,000 net worth without too much difficulty. If you have no assets and no income, the bank will be much less happy with a request for an overdraft. This is obvious once you understand it, but many people don't: they think that banks are being unfair, and are discriminating against people with no money.

In asking what the money is for, the bank wants to be sure that the amount borrowed will actually be enough to cover the proposed expenditure. No banker wants you to come back later and ask for more because you didn't get enough the first time. The length of the loan is important for accounting and regulatory reasons – the bank wants to control the proportions of money it lends for different periods and it must, by law, not lend more in total than certain limits, based on the size of its own assets.

The repayment schedule may come as more of a surprise: surely, you think, it doesn't make any difference to the bank how the money is repaid as long as it gets it back with interest at the end of the loan term? It does matter, though, because the banker looks upon you as a unit capable of producing a stream of future earnings (your wages). The banker wants to take regular sums out of your wages towards the repayment of the loan – he or she may suspect, perhaps rightly, that you hope to find a lump sum for repayment by borrowing elsewhere, which may not be as easy as you think.

SECURITY

The next thing the banker thinks about is security for the loan. This is not because the bank wants to sell your property in order to recover the money lent (this is considered bad for business, particularly where consumers are concerned), but because he wants to be able to do so if he has to. Bonds and shares are acceptable as security since they are easy to value and to transfer from one owner to another. Shares in unquoted companies are generally unacceptable because they will be difficult to sell. Bankers keep a close eye on the market price of shares that they hold as security to make sure that their value still covers the loan.

Banks are stickier about life policies. They want to read all the fine print to make sure that the insurance company isn't going to wriggle out of paying. Nevertheless, whole life and endowment policies are generally acceptable.

UK banks hate to repossess which is worth bearing in mind if you ever have to negotiate an extension of the repayment schedule

Houses and land are also often used as security, usually by the banks taking a charge on the equity in the property. UK banks hate to repossess – it makes them look very bad when they throw people out on the street – which is worth bearing in mind if you ever have to negotiate an extension of the repayment schedule.

FOR GUERRILLA BORROWERS – DON'T BE A NICE GUY

Suppose there are two businesspeople, Sally and Jane. They both borrow from banks to acquire investment property, using the buildings as security. Sally has £3 million's worth of property and bank loans of £2,400,000. Jane was advised that she should keep her gearing low, so she owns £140,000's worth of property and owes banks £70,000. In both cases, income from rents service the loans. Suddenly the property market crashes by 50 per cent and rents drop too. Sally's properties are now worth only £1.5 million but she still owes £2.4 million, while Jane's properties are worth £70,000, which is what she owes. Neither of them can service their loans fully, so they go to their bank to ask for a change in the terms of the loan.

Guess what? Sally gets terms she can live with, and stays in business, but the bank re-possesses Jane's property, giving her a bad credit record. After a few years property values creep up again and Sally is back in profit. Jane was wiped out and stays out of the business. This happens because the bank doesn't want to make a huge loss by repossessing Sally's properties, so, believing that she is a competent businesswoman and that the market will bounce back, it gives her a chance to keep going. The bank may believe that Jane is equally competent, but it doesn't have to give her a chance because it can get all its money back right away.

The moral of the story is not to be nice to banks. Work out your own defensive strategies in case everything goes wrong, and be tough – you can be sure that banks won't listen to reason if they have you over a barrel, so make sure that you hold the aces!

Banking and Big Brother

In recent years a disturbing pattern has emerged of increasing state interference with banking privacy. Like most modern tyrannies masquerading as a moral crusade, this started in the United States, a country where ordinary people are prosecuted under anti-racketeering laws and innocent individuals have their property seized in the 'war on drugs'. Many so-called democratic countries are following suit. This catch-all legislation is being used by tax authorities to conduct 'fishing expeditions' in search of possible wrong-doers. Almost every financial organization must report 'unusual' transactions, the registry of safe-deposit boxes and so on. The justification is that if you have done nothing wrong, then you have nothing to hide, but in a world where government departments exceed their briefs, break the law, and deceive and pressurize the innocent, this argument does not hold water. Chapter 13 on overseas investing suggests a strategy for countering this trend, but realistically you need a net worth of £200,000 or more before it can be effective.

The future of the banking industry

Following the Asian crisis of 1997 and increased efforts to raise financial standards globally, optimists have said that, in future, the world may not have to suffer so much from dodgy banks propped up by Second and Third World regimes – now all we have to worry about are the dodgy banks propped up by First World regimes!

Banking customers are becoming disloyal, and banks are having to change the way they present themselves

Banking is in turmoil. New technologies are making them more efficient, but at the price of sacking vast numbers of staff. The internet allows customers to compare services offered by banks more easily, and as their clients become better informed, banks must become more competitive. Banking customers are becoming disloyal, and banks are having to change the way they present themselves. Financial content sites on the internet are winning away customers from retail banks as well as other financial institutions, and stakes are high.

MERGER MANIA

All this change has stimulated merger activity among banks as the big fish swallow up smaller ones in an attempt to become global players – with the trend towards less regulation and freer capital flows between countries, banks that have relied on regulatory barriers to keep their markets 'captive' must now either eat or be eaten. How effective the new merged mega-banks will be in retaining their customers and making profits remains to be seen.

Another factor encouraging mergers in Europe is the introduction of the euro, the EC's single currency. Cosy local oligopolies held by local banks across Europe are being thrown into disarray as it becomes plain that customers are prepared to switch banks when they are offered better choices. On the Continent, American-style aggressive business tactics have shaken up the banking world, hitherto steeped in a tradition of government-sponsored cartels. The advent of the euro has increased competition by eliminating currency risk for investors, so, for instance French fund managers can more easily invest in German companies. The concept of 'shareholder value' – running companies for the benefit of the shareholders – is gaining ground, overthrowing the clubby relationships between banks and companies in much of continental Europe.

NEW PRODUCTS FOR A DIGITAL AGE

Many electronic payment products have come on to the world market, such as VisaCash, Digicash, Proton, eMoneyMail, BillPoint and Payme.com. Most have only had limited success so far. So why have things moved so slowly? One reason is that both businesses and consumers don't want to change the way they do things unless there is a compelling reason to do so, and another is that they don't want to risk their money on what might be a fad. Another problem is that for such systems to take off, there need to be universal standards among the computers that are used to operate them.

If the new electronic payment systems are to succeed, they must save money and reduce the costs. In theory, they should do this – a cash machine transaction may cost a bank around 20p, compared with around 80p for a clerk to do the same job. 'Swiping' credit cards in a shop costs a bank pennies.

Most industry observers believe that eventually electronic banking will be widely accepted, especially as more and more businesses use the internet to deal with their own customers and suppliers.

Electronic banking isn't just a marketing problem, though. One unresolved question is whether electronic payment affects the money supply – it is conceivable that vast sums of electronic cash surging through the system could destabilize it. And should ordinary companies be allowed to create electronic money anyway? Governments do not usually allow anyone except themselves to create money. Suppose a company running a widely used smart card got into trouble – it could cause the equivalent of a run on a bank but, unlike conventional bank failures, there could be huge knock-on effects to other businesses. It is small wonder that bankers and civil servants across the world are wrestling with the question of how to move into the cyber age in an orderly fashion.

SCREEN SCRAPING — HOW TO PROTECT CONSUMERS AGAINST DATA AGGREGATION

'Screen scraping' means taking account information from internet websites using an account holder's PIN numbers and posting it on a website for easy access by the account holder. Screen scrapers could be anyone from a financial institution or a stockbroker to a frequent flyer scheme run by an airline.

The supposed benefit to users is that they can access the aggregated information with one master PIN number and then see all the PIN numbers, codes, share portfolios, bank accounts and so on in one place. The main problem is, of course, that the screen scraper could build up a very detailed financial profile of a user which could be abused. If that sounds far fetched, you should know that in January 2000, the internet auctioneer eBay sued ReverseAuction.com and Biddersedge.com, claiming that they had copied auction seller details from the eBay website. eBay also claimed that the two companies had sent eBay customers e-mails fraudulently saying that their eBay identification codes were about to expire, and asking users to start using the companies' own websites.

In late 1999, the American bank, First Union, sued a company called Secure Commerce Services, claiming unauthorized access to a computer and that it had misrepresented its relationship with First Union to retail customers. Later, First Union dropped the action after the defendant agreed to comply with the bank's data aggregation rules.

As electronic money matters become increasingly complex, there will be many nefarious attempts to trick the unsuspecting. Personal data is extremely valuable, and there are many ways it can be abused. The best way to protect yourself is to keep yourself informed of developments, to be reluctant to send key financial information about yourself over the internet, and to keep paper records.

bills of exchange
certificates of deposit
the discount market
the local authority market
the inter-bank market
the finance house, inter-company and
commercial paper markets
the certificate of deposit market
the Euromarkets

The money markets

The money markets are not physical locations. It is simply the name for the 'wholesale' trade in large sums of money that are lent and borrowed for short periods of time. It is important to understand something about them, but only investors with large amounts of cash can participate in them directly.

In this chapter we will look at:

- *Bills of exchange*
- *Certificates of deposit*
- *The discount market*
- *The local authority market*
- *The inter-bank market*
- *The finance house, inter-company and commercial paper markets*
- *The certificate of deposit market*
- *The Euromarkets – Eurodeposits and Eurobonds*
- *Interest rate and currency swaps*

In order to understand how the money markets work we should first examine two financial instruments which are used to move money around – 'bills of exchange' and 'certificates of deposit'.

Bills of exchange

There is one kind of bill of exchange that is familiar to all of us – the cheque – but there are others too. In essence, they are written IOUs promising payment at a future date. Bills of exchange are negotiable, so the recipient can sell them on to someone else who can claim payment on the due date. The issuer of the bill of exchange either promises to pay the bill himself, noting this on the bill, or addresses it to a bank, which will provide the money. The origins of these bills were in the 18th century when businesses frequently settled debts with one another by the use of bills, usually dated for payment in three months' time. If the recipient wanted to be paid sooner, he could present it to a bill broker, who would pay the face value of the bill less a certain percentage and then re-sell the bill to a bank that wanted to invest money for a short period. The brokers began to hold bills themselves and developed into the 'discount houses' that are discussed below.

When a bill is issued, it has to be sent to the bank on which the money is to be drawn for 'acceptance'. This means that the bank signs the bill and agrees to pay the money on the due date. The law says that anyone signing a bill can be sued if it is not paid, so the safety of a bill of exchange depends upon who has 'accepted' it. For this reason certain banks, called 'accepting houses', specialize in accepting bills, and such bills are generally recognized as secure instruments.

Certificates of deposit

Certificates of deposit, or CDs, are issued by banks and other financial organizations as evidence that a deposit has been made with them for a fixed period of time at a fixed interest rate. Like bills of exchange, they are negotiable, so a company can deposit money, receiving a CD in return, which they can sell to another party. The life of a CD varies between three months and five years. If they are issued for less than a year, the interest is paid on the expiry of the CD, and if they are for more than a year the interest is paid annually. CDs are popular with organizations with large amounts of money to be invested for short periods because they give flexibility. If you simply make a fixed-term deposit, you cannot get your money out before the end of the term, but with a CD you can sell at any time. For CDs denominated in sterling, the smallest sum of money you can deposit is £50,000.

CDs are popular with organizations with large amounts of money to be invested for short periods because they give flexibility

The discount market

Many organizations have large sums of cash which they want to lend for a very short time (as short as overnight), but still earn interest. The discount houses and discount brokers, members of the London Discount Market Association (LDMA), are the middlemen between borrowers and lenders. The main instruments that they deal in are bills of exchange, certificates of deposits, gilts and bonds. One of the most important of these are Treasury bills, which are issued every week by the British government and have a life of 91 days. They don't carry interest, but are instead issued and traded at a discount to their face value. The discount houses have a deal with the government to buy all the Treasury bills it issues and in return the Bank of England agrees to act as the lender of last resort to the discount houses. Other bills of exchange fall into two categories: 'eligible' and 'non-eligible' bills. These are a measure of how sure one can be that the bill will be paid, as the Bank of England will only take eligible bills as security for loans. Eligible bills are ones that have been 'accepted' by big banks in good standing, while non-eligible bills have been accepted by smaller banks. Bills are used by large businesses that borrow money from banks and financial institutions, issuing a bill in return which promises to repay the money. The rate of interest is usually better than they can get elsewhere. Gilts with a maturity date within five years are also held by discount houses, as are bonds and bills issued by local authorities in the UK, and certificates of deposit issued by banks. Discount houses are institutions that are unique to Britain, and exist for historical reasons. Their relationship with the Bank of England enables the government to tinker with the money supply by varying the amount of Treasury bills that are issued each week; the discount of the Treasury bills are a good predictor of short-term interest rates generally available in the UK. If the discount houses cannot borrow money elsewhere, they can borrow from the Bank of England, which will set a rate higher than those prevailing in the market and take Treasury bills and eligible bills from the discount houses as security. This mechanism ensures that the discount houses only borrow from the Bank of England as a last resort and, when they do, it has the effect of driving up the market interest rates. If the Bank of England wants to lower the rates of interest in the market, it buys Treasury bills from the discount houses, thus releasing more money into the system and causing the cost of money (interest rates) to become cheaper.

Surrounding the discount market interface between government and banking are all the other banks and financial institutions, all eager to borrow and lend large sums for short periods. This is done in various ways which are collectively described as the 'parallel money markets', meaning that they work in parallel to the discount market and one another. An important difference between the discount market and the parallel markets is that the parallel markets have no lender of last resort, and so are less stable, although they are supervised by the Bank of England. Deals are done either directly between the banks and other organizations in the market, or through money brokers who act as middlemen.

The local authority market

It is cheaper for a local authority to borrow through the government than directly from the markets but, because of financial restrictions that the government places on them, local authorities are often driven to borrow money elsewhere. Generally they borrow for two or seven days, but they can borrow for three months or more in amounts of £25,000 upwards. Lenders include big companies as well as banks and other financial institutions.

The inter-bank market

This market grew up as banks started to lend to each other instead of through the discount market. Most of the money is lent overnight, but loan periods can be for up to five years. The interest rates fluctuate according to supply and demand; the going market rate at any particular time is called the London

Inter-Bank Offered Rate (LIBOR). The amounts lent are always over £250,000 and no security is requested – the banks rely on one another's good faith and ability to repay. The LIBOR rate is usually the cheapest short-term rate to be had outside the discount market, and thus other rates are linked to it.

The finance house, inter-company and commercial paper markets

Finance houses, which provide money for hire-purchase and leasing, borrow their funds from banks, usually via the inter-bank market. Large companies sometimes lend directly to one another, cutting out the banks – the sums involved start at £50,000, and are lent through money brokers. Security is required, usually taking the form of a bank guarantee, and the sums are lent for between three months and five years.

A newer option for larger companies is to use the commercial paper market, in which they exchange promissory notes ('paper') for money. The minimum amount borrowed is £500,000. The paper is owned by the bearer and is sold at a discount in the same way as Treasury bills.

The certificate of deposit market

We saw earlier that certificates of deposit (CDs) are issued by banks and other financial organizations and that they are negotiable bearer securities. Companies, and even individuals, can invest in CDs, which are more flexible than a fixed-term deposit because they can be sold in the market if required.

All the parallel markets are inter-linked and a transaction in one market leads to more transactions in the others. The liquidity of the money markets allows large sums to flow freely around the system to wherever they are needed without delay. The money that is borrowed and lent by ordinary people ultimately goes through the money markets, but in between are the retail banks, insurance companies and building societies.

The Euromarkets

For historical reasons large amounts of the major currencies are held outside the jurisdiction of their home country. The prefix 'Euro' does not mean that they are all European currencies, nor that they are held in Europe.

THE EURODEPOSIT MARKET

Companies and private individuals are able to hold foreign Eurocurrencies on deposit in British banks, each currency earning interest at a rate related to those prevailing in its home country. Originally looked down upon by traditionalists, the relaxation of exchange controls has caused this market to mushroom, and it has become so respectable that even countries borrow in the market.

THE EUROBOND MARKET

Despite its name, the market for Eurobonds is truly international; both issuers of the bonds and investors can come from any country, and while most of the banks involved in the market base their Eurobond offices in London, they, too, are from all over the world. Some $7 billion's worth of Eurobonds are traded every day over the telephone across the world. Eurobonds can be denominated in any currency and are usually issued outside the country of the borrower (issuer). An important feature is that they are issued in 'bearer form'. This means that whoever is holding the bond owns it, giving a great degree of discretion and anonymity to the investor. If Eurobonds ever lose their bearer status, the market is likely to shrink dramatically.

How Eurobonds started

After World War 2, the United States poured dollars into Europe to assist reconstruction. These dollars came to be known as 'Eurodollars'. In the 1960s, US legislation made it increasingly difficult for American lenders to provide dollars for foreign borrowers. The Eurodollar pool of capital, which was outside US control, then became the obvious place to go to borrow dollars. Banks in London jumped at the chance of earning fees and had a more sophisticated infrastructure than elsewhere in Europe at the time. Thus, London became the focus of the Eurobond market. The market has now grown to include all currencies, not just dollars.

The Eurobond market really came into its own in the late 1960s, with the introduction of a clearing system. In fact, there are two: Euroclear in Belgium and Cedel in Luxembourg. Euroclear is the bigger system, having an annual turnover of trillions of dollars' worth of bonds and holding hundreds of billions of dollars' worth of bonds for their owners.

Who issues Eurobonds?

Banks, large companies, governments, quasi-governmental bodies and organizations such as the EC (European Community) all issue Eurobonds. Banks are the most active issuers.

Who invests in Eurobonds?

Banks, insurance companies, pension funds, government organizations and large companies all invest in Eurobonds, as can private investors. Unsurprisingly, most investment is done by institutions.

Interest and the credit rating of Eurobonds

Interest is paid gross, with no withholding tax deducted. Common maturity dates are 5, 7, 10 and 12 years. Like other bonds, most Eurobonds are rated by Moody's and Standard and Poor's, the best quality being rated as 'triple A' (see page 79). Curiously, corporate bond issuers with household names are often more popular with investors, and can thus offer a lower rate of interest than obscure companies with higher credit ratings, the latter type being the better bargain.

Corporate bond issuers with household names are often more popular with investors, and can thus offer a lower rate of interest than obscure companies with higher credit ratings, the latter type being the better bargain

Fixed-rate bonds

This is the most common kind of Eurobond, having a final maturity date and paying a fixed rate of interest. As with other kinds of bonds (see Chapter 4), if interest rates elsewhere rise above the fixed rate of the bond at some time during its life, the re-sale value of the bond goes down, and if rates fall, the bond's value will rise.

Floating-rate bonds

This variety ties the rate of interest to LIBOR (see page 132) or some other short-term interest rate by means of a stated formula.

Convertible bonds

An investor can exchange a convertible bond for shares in the issuing company at a predetermined price.

Interest rate and currency swaps

As with other bonds, it is possible for two Eurobond issuers to 'swap' (exchange) interest rates on their bonds, or even to swap the principal from one currency to another. The exchange is usually between a fixed-rate bond and a floating-rate bond, and gives both issuers an 'arbitrage' benefit (see page 199). Local authorities in the UK got into this in a big way in the 1980s and some began to speculate wildly on interest rates. Hammersmith and Fulham were the worst culprits with Hammersmith swapping interest on some £7 billion which it didn't have. When interest rates doubled it was in serious trouble, but after the courts ruled that local authorities were not allowed to make swaps and that the deals were invalid, the financial institutions who had dealt with Hammersmith had to take the losses. If only private investors could get off so lightly!

Investment theories

Some people have very odd ideas about how the stock market works and still make money from their investments, while others have beautifully rational theories but lose money. The reason for this is the extraordinary complexity and mutability of the markets. As yet there is no complete, all-encompassing model to explain how all the mechanisms of the market intermesh, but this does not mean that we must resort to superstition, since there is sound evidence that certain strategies will produce a good return over the long term. Millions are spent on predicting stock movements, yet as soon as a method seems to be working the market seems to adjust itself back to unpredictability. In this chapter, we look at the methods used by professionals:

- Probability, and why some people are just lucky
- The Kondratiev Wave, an unproven economic cycle lasting 60 years or so
- Technical analysis, or 'chartism', for the fortune-tellers of the stock market
- Fundamental analysis, the science of evaluating companies, and why it tends

to cancel itself out

- *The efficient market theory, which explains why most strategies don't work for long, and why 'buy and hold' does*
- *Risk – shares did better than other financial investments during the 20th century*
- *MPT (modern portfolio theory), which describes the virtues of diversification*
- *CAPM (capital-asset pricing theory), which gives a measurement of risk, called 'beta', and APT (arbitrage pricing theory)*
- *GARCH, chaos theory and computer models, which are newer ways of trying to predict price movements*

Introduction

Mathematically speaking, the stock market is, as yet, full of unsolved problems. Many attempts have been made to describe and predict the market, but none have been completely successful. In this chapter we will review some of these theories and examine ways in which they are unsatisfactory. Much of the mathematics is too complicated to be dealt with in this book, but we will be able to cover some of the basic calculations. Before we look at some of the techniques and theories used by market players, it's worth considering two general points: first, that even in a completely random stock market there will be some winners; second, it is always possible for the unscrupulous to look as though they are winners even when they produce mediocre returns.

It is always possible for the unscrupulous to look as though they are winners even when they produce mediocre returns.

Winners

We all hear the stories and meet the people – they can't do anything wrong, they always make money, they have the Midas touch. Naturally, we want to know what they've got that we don't. How is it that they have become 'winners'? We should be aware that it may simply be a function of probability; in any race, someone has to 'win'.

Suppose you eat out regularly with a colleague for many years, and always flip a coin at the end of the meal to see who will pay. After you've done it thousands of times, one of you is going to be seriously out of pocket, despite the fact that overall, the ratio of heads to tails gets closer and closer to 1:1 the more often you do it. This is because the monetary value of the difference between your wins and your colleague's wins is likely to be greater the more you play, even if the difference itself is getting smaller as a proportion of the total cost of all the meals. In addition, the person who gets ahead is quite likely to stay ahead for a very long time – it might take a lifetime for the lead to swap to the other person. Thus, if you've played the game for ten years, the winner at the end is quite likely to have been ahead 90 per cent of the time – is this person a 'winner' who has special knowledge, or a magic touch?

Obviously not. The winner is simply benefiting from chance. In the stock market, there may be individuals who are highly successful simply because of random events – no special significance should be attached to their success.

A SIMPLE CONFIDENCE TRICK

EXAMPLE

Here's an example of an illegal confidence trick that illustrates the need for scepticism in following the advice of a successful predictor. Suppose you are an investment adviser and you write to 100,000 investors predicting the change in the value of a stock index. You tell 50,000 investors that the value will rise in a month, and the other 50,000 that it will fall. A month later, you write to the 50,000 who received the correct prediction, making a further prediction, again telling 25,000 the value will rise and the other 25,000 that it will fall. In the third month you have 25,000 people to whom you have made two correct predictions. Apply the same technique three more times, and you will have 3,250 people to whom you have given six correct predictions. Now you write to them asking for money, say £800, to continue sending them your information which has 'proven' its value. If half of them pay up, you've just made £1,300,000. Naturally, you will have supported your predictions with spurious claims about the techniques and theories you have employed. It is now time to disappear with the loot before you are caught.

Let's examine some of the techniques that are really used by stock market professionals. The rationale behind some of them contradicts that behind others, and one or two seem quite unreasonable, but they have all been used to invest large sums in the markets.

The Kondratiev Wave

Also known as the 'long wave', this is, on the face of it, an implausible idea – that there are recurring cycles of boom and slump in the world economy. It has also been an unpopular idea, because it is so directly opposed to the grand vision of an ever-growing world economy upon which so much policy has been based.

The long wave is said to take between 45 and 60 years to go from peak to peak. The post-war economic boom from 1948 to 1973 is considered to be the 'upswing' of a wave that was going down during the depression of the 1930s. We are now considered to be approaching the end of a 'downswing', implying a gradual period of deflation until around 2025.

The existence of the long wave has not been proved. It is difficult to prove that any economic cycle exists without showing that it has repeated itself many times. If you go back four long waves (say 200 years) from the present, you get to the beginning of the Industrial Revolution, which is arguably the starting point of modern economies, and four waves is a small sample. Another difficulty is the lack of trustworthy data before about 1870. Figure 8.1 shows one view of the Kondratiev cycle.

Kondratiev was a Russian economist who gave his name to this cycle. Western economists became interested in his work after he successfully predicted the depression of the 1930s and the subsequent boom. His ideas cost him his life – he died in a Stalinist labour camp in the late 1920s.

More than one explanation has been offered for how the long wave might work. Briefly, Kondratiev himself thought that during the upswing industrial economies expanded as fast as they could until the primary producing countries were unable to keep up with the demand for raw materials. The downswing then began, driving capital and labour abroad to 'new' countries (e.g. Australia and America), and stimulating inventions and discoveries which would be exploited in the next upswing as the 'new' countries increased their supply of raw materials.

Remember that the long wave wasn't intended to be applied to shares – it is about the economy as a whole.

Whether or not you choose to believe the predictions made by adherents of the long wave theory, it is a useful counterbalance to the 'short termism' inherent in so much business activity. The idea that there are long-term 'pulses' in economic activity is very intriguing, but the problem for investors is how to apply this view in their investment practice.

'Short termism' is what most trading in the stock market is all about, since many investors want to make money quickly. Let's look at the well-known, though controversial, method known as 'technical analysis', which promises a way to beat the market in the short term.

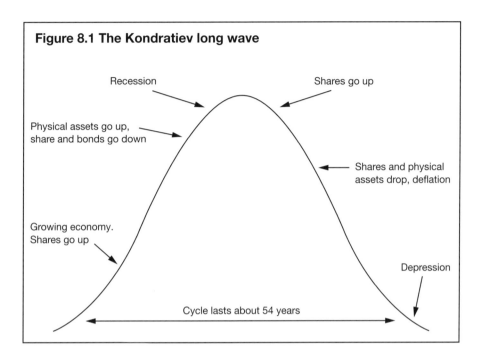

Figure 8.1 The Kondratiev long wave

Recession

Shares go up

Physical assets go up,
share and bonds go down

Shares and physical
assets drop, deflation

Growing economy.
Shares go up

Depression

Cycle lasts about 54 years

Technical analysis

Technical analysts, some of whom are called 'chartists', try to predict future stock trends by analyzing past movements. The purists don't ever look at any other information, such as political events or industrial data; they concentrate on studying the changes in stock values alone, believing that it is unnecessary to know why the changes have occurred.

Most of us know intuitively that human beings are subject to a herd instinct. If you opened two identical restaurants in two equally attractive locations and you paid actors to fill one of them every day, pretending to be customers, which restaurant do you think would attract the most customers? It would be an interesting experiment to try. My bet is that the one that looked full would attract more customers. 'Ah,' you might say, 'But that's only because people like to be in a happy atmosphere when they eat, and if lots of people look as if they are enjoying the food, others will think that the food must be OK.' That's the point about herd instinct, though; every individual makes their own individual decisions, but taken as a whole you see that they are all doing the same thing, without really judging the quality for themselves. It's all based on appearances – it looks good, so they try it.

This phenomenon plainly happens in the stock market. In 1998/99, dot com companies looked good, so everyone piled in. Later their share prices dropped by staggering amounts – as much as 85 per cent even for huge, well-funded firms – and everyone howled in anguish. What had really changed? Many dot com companies were not profitable before the boom and were equally unprofitable afterwards. The only thing that had really changed was 'investor sentiment'. If you could predict investor sentiment accurately, you could jump in and out of shares at the right moments and clean up. This is what technical analysis tries to do.

Technical analysis makes three main assumptions:

1. That patterns identified in charts of stock movements recur.
2. That stock price changes move in trends, and are predictable.
3. That all the factors that influence stock prices are immediately reflected in the price, and so do not need to be considered separately.

PATTERNS IN CHARTS

Figure 8.2 shows an example of one of the best-known patterns used by technical analysts, called the 'head and shoulders reversal pattern'. Points A and E are called the 'left and right shoulders', respectively, points B and D the 'neckline', and point C is called the 'head'. The idea is that if you see a head and shoulders pattern forming, prices have reached a ' top' and will start declining.

Figure 8.3 shows a 'flag'; this is supposed to be a reliable sign that an upward price trend will continue.

There are many other patterns recognized by technical analysts, and each analyst seems to have his own particular favourites. Many technical analysts believe that it is the psychology of investors *en masse* that are the cause of these patterns.

THE DOW THEORY

Charles Dow published the first stock market average in 1884 and was the father of technical analysis. His theory is based on the following principles:

1. There are three kinds of trends in the market, primary, secondary and minor. To explain them, Dow used the simile of the movements of the sea: a primary trend is like the tide, a secondary trend is like the waves in the tide; and a minor trend is like the ripples on the waves.
2. There are three phases to major trends. Dow said that there is an 'accumulation phase', when the smart money spots the right moment to buy, a second phase when the technical analysts jump on the bandwagon and a final 'distributive' phase when the public starts

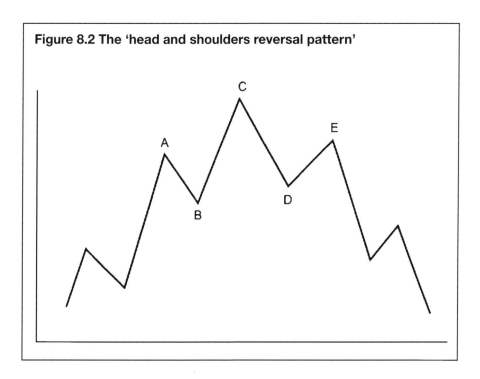

Figure 8.2 The 'head and shoulders reversal pattern'

buying as the news gets out, and the smart money starts selling, or 'distributing'.

3. All the averages – in Dow's time, the Industrial and Rail averages – must confirm each other for a trend to exist.

4. A trend continues until signals (the patterns that technical analysts think are important) appear in the charts that it has reversed.

There are lots of other versions and theories of technical analysis. These days, the 'Elliott Wave' is more often used than the Dow theory.

THE ELLIOTT WAVE

The Elliott Wave theory was invented by an American accountant named Ralph Elliott who, like all good technical analysts, believed that you could spot recurring patterns in the stock market. Figure 8.4 shows a simplified Elliott Wave.

The idea is that the stock market has a 'supercycle', as depicted in Figure 8.4, which is rather like the Kondratiev Wave. The Elliott Wave is a pattern of three steps forward and two steps back, or as some put it, two and a half cycles on the way up, followed by one and a half on the way down. The same

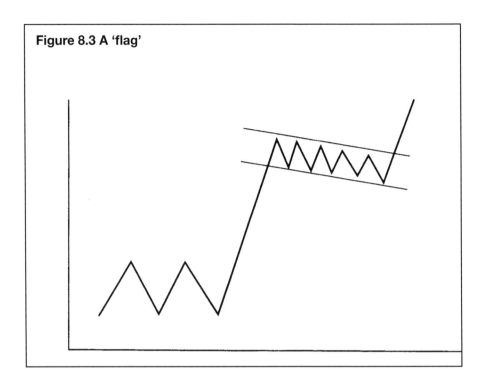

Figure 8.3 A 'flag'

pattern is supposed to exist over any length of time, from millennia and centuries down to annual, monthly and daily patterns, and even over a few minutes.

Elliott also used the Fibonacci numbers. Fibonacci was a mathematician in the Middle Ages who discovered a numerical sequence that appears widely in nature. It is formed by adding the two preceding numbers in the sequence to get the next one, so it starts:

1, 1, 2, 3, 5, 8, 13, 21 ...

Elliott tried to find the Fibonacci sequence in share price movements.

The Elliott Wave 'Grand Supercycle', lasting centuries, is now supposed to be contracting, and a bull market that began in 1784 has now ended. Elliott Wave fans predict a sort of gradual descent into financial collapse and barbarism from now on.

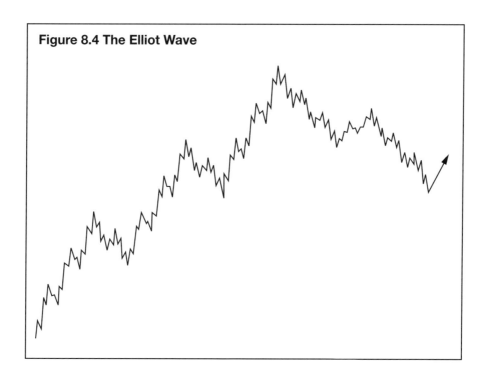

Figure 8.4 The Elliot Wave

COULD THE DOOMSAYERS BE RIGHT?

You might laugh at all this 'doomsaying', but consider this: if you could have invested £10,000 at a real return (i.e. inflation-adjusted) of 5 per cent for 2000 years, today your descendants would theoretically be worth more than the value of entire world's GDP, yet a 5 per cent return is not generally considered to be particularly good.

Over the course of history, many financial markets have flourished and withered away, as have many nations and cultures. From time to time there have been massive upheavals that have utterly destroyed capital. Where has all the wealth of the Roman senators gone? Horrific upheavals have occurred within living memory. Before the 1917 Russian revolution, Russia was the favourite investment destination of the French, but in 1917 their investments were completely wiped out. Shanghai and Manchuria once enjoyed 90 per cent of all the foreign investment into China; in 1949 they went to zero. In 1945, Egypt had the third largest stock market in the world, but in 1956 Nasser nationalized everything, and all shares became worthless. Which were two of the top five most economically important cities in the USA 250 years ago? Charleston and Savannah. The third largest city of the Roman Empire, Antioch, is today a sleepy provincial town in Turkey, close to the Syrian border.

Other once-great cities have disappeared altogether, or have decayed into villages.

Nothing, it seems, offers us a truly permanent store of value. In this sense, 'doom' is guaranteed. Cities and civilizations seem to have their life cycles, just like people and companies. Eventually they cease to exist.

What is a guerrilla investor to make of these slightly spooky facts? My view is that we should remember that most of the time fundamental changes happen very slowly, so the thought that one day there will probably be no 'Western civilization' shouldn't really bother us. Doomsayers tend to mix up important things – like how to protect your money during a war – with irrelevant things, such as the near-certainty that Wall Street will one day (it might take a thousand years!) be worthless. Asset protection in times of crisis is very, very important, so every so often you should consider how you would move your assets in a worst-case scenario – one day it just might happen.

SHOULD PRIVATE INVESTORS AVOID TECHNICAL ANALYSIS?

Private investors must use brokers to buy and sell, and brokers take a commission for each transaction. Technical analysis encourages trading – you are supposed to respond to the 'buy' and 'sell' signals indicated in the charts in order to make your money. This means that your brokerage charges are going to be far higher than those of a long-term investor who holds on to stocks for years, so the system must do better than simply holding what you have bought in order to cover the trading costs. A private investor would do well to reflect on the fact that it is in a broker's interest to have clients trade frequently, and that a client who believes in technical analysis is going to make the broker more money in commissions than one who rarely buys and sells.

When brokers themselves persuade clients to switch investments unnecessarily in order to earn fees, it is known as 'churning' – and is certainly not confined to followers of technical analysis.

DOES TECHNICAL ANALYSIS WORK?

Batteries of mathematical tests on a century of stock prices in London and New York seem to have shown that such correlations as exist between past and future prices are too small to beat trading costs. Essentially, there is no evidence to support the idea that trends in stock movements are other than random, except for an overall trend of growth across the entire market. Randomly selecting stocks and holding them produces results that are just as good, if not better. Flipping a coin many times will produce long runs of just heads or just tails, and when plotted on a chart will produce patterns of the kind that technical analysts like. However, we know from probability theory that each flip of the coin is independent of the previous flips, and that long runs are simply chance, not trends. Nevertheless, large banks and other financial institutions continue to pay large salaries to technical analysts, some of whom presumably do make good predictions. The point about this phenomenon is that, from a mathematical point of view, success does not in itself prove anything. A Cambridge mathematics professor says, 'There are traders who may be successful due to intuition and specialized knowledge who honestly ascribe their success to a baseless technique.' In other words, it is very human to try to explain good results, but the explanation may simply be wrong.

Alternatively, it may be that if there are enough technical analysts engaged in advisory positions, they somehow unintentionally combine together to produce a self-fulfilling prophecy. Things can't be quite as simple as this, however. There is another group of analysts, the 'counter-cyclical analysts', who believe that the best strategy is to do exactly the opposite of what technical analysts and others are recommending. This view is called 'contrarian'.

So, if we don't believe in technical analysis, is there any other way to make money from the market in the short term? The theory of fundamental analysis says that there is.

Fundamental analysis

Fundamental analysts attempt to predict future prices by finding out what a stock is really worth – its intrinsic value – which may have little to do with its current quoted price. First, the prospects for the industry as a whole are examined, and then the records, plans and management of individual companies within the industry are subjected to a thorough scrutiny. An estimate of the company's future earnings is then made, incorporating estimates of future sales, overheads, accounting policies and a host of other factors that might affect profit. Broadly speaking, stock market professionals tend to have a lot more faith in fundamental analysis than technical analysis, because it is dealing with the nuts and bolts of real companies. Professional fundamental analysts, so the argument goes, will achieve better returns than the small investor because they are better informed.

PRICE/EARNINGS (P/E) RATIOS

As we saw in Chapter 2, the p/e ratio is a key analytical tool, and we can get an insight into how analysts work by looking at what they do with them. Having estimated what a particular company will earn in the future, the analyst then looks at its current share price and calculates the ratio of price to earnings. If you look at the stock market pages of the *Financial Times*, you will find that the p/e ratio is listed for you. If the p/e is 6, it means that the price of the share is six times the share's proportion of the annual profit stated in the most recently published accounts of the company.

A big, well-established company may have a fairly low p/e ratio, because it is thought that its prospects for growth are low, while a small company in a high technology industry may have a very high p/e, say 40 or more, because it is thought likely that its earnings will sky-rocket in a few years' time. P/e ratios are also affected by factors such as recessions, when they tend to go up in anticipation that a recovery will increase future earnings.

What the fundamental analysts do is to decide whether the current p/e ratio is right, based on their own detailed examinations of the company. They are comparing the p/e ratio with their own estimate of what it should be.

INTEREST RATES

When interest rates are high, an investor can make a high return by keeping money in safe, stable bonds and other interest-bearing instruments outside the market. Fundamentalists, therefore, compare interest rates with returns from stocks. Low interest rates are seen to make the market more attractive because of their potential for higher returns, so when interest rates are low, the 'intrinsic value' of stocks is thought to be higher.

DOES FUNDAMENTAL ANALYSIS WORK?

Fundamentalists believe that past earnings can be a good indicator of future growth; if the management of a company is very good, so the thinking goes, then it will continue to be good in the future. Five years is a long time in the stock market, and most fundamental analysts hope to make good predictions for shorter periods than this.

Many studies have shown, however, that the analysts' predictions show massive errors and are, if anything, worse for short-term predictions than for five-yearly ones. Two reasons why this may be so are randomness and the variety of different accounting methods in use. The effects of random events in the real world, such as natural disasters and political events, can throw out the most sound estimates of a company's future earnings for obvious reasons; as yet there is no way of predicting them. Accounting methods (particularly the so-called 'creative' accounting methods) can distort profits hugely – the special accounting methods for depreciation, land, leasing, insurance and conglomerates, to name but a few, can confuse even the most sharp-eyed analyst.

SELLING A GOOD STORY

Another major factor, especially during booming times when more and more people across the world are buying shares, is that analysts are generally paid employees of institutions that want to encourage customers to buy and sell shares. Customers want happy stories – it makes them feel more enthusiastic about buying and selling. Listed companies want happy stories, and they can make life very difficult for analysts who are 'against' them. A bouncy young analyst, fresh from academia, wants to make a name; going around pointing at grossly overpriced shares is not the cleverest way to claw your way up the corporate ladder. Analysts may be paid substantial performance bonuses, in which case they, too, may be highly motivated to persuade customers to trade.

It's not quite that institutional analysts are dishonest – it's more that they know what the 'right' answer is, and are under pressure to draw conclusions that head in that direction. Some time ago I talked to a whiz-kid analyst for a major institution who had just been given an important job covering a booming new industry. He raved about a certain company, and demonstrated how, if its share of the market continued to grow, it would be worth billions soon. Today it is worth about 10 per cent of its value then. Was the whiz kid being dishonest? Not really – he plainly stated his assumptions ('if X happens, then Y could happen'). The trouble was that X didn't happen. I didn't think it would, so I didn't invest in the company. The whiz kid still has his job, and life goes on. Perhaps now that the company is so cheap, it is worth buying …

MISINTERPRETING FINANCIAL DATA

It is very easy to confuse coincidence with cause and effect. They are not the same. If interest rates go one way, for instance, the market doesn't always go the other way.

Many professionals like 'clean' data that is complete and neatly arranged. Real raw data is 'dirty' – what has just happened will never happen again in exactly the same way, and there are always ifs and buts. Cleaning up data to fit into a fancy computer model takes time, which often does more harm than good in a business when a delay of a few minutes can make or break a transaction. Clean data tends to remove the odd, unusual measurements that may actually be the clue to a big score.

Good research often produces surprises – if you massage data and pat yourself on the back for getting answers that confirm your suspicions, you may be kidding yourself. A famous study in the 1920s set out to prove that the more light there was in a certain factory, the more products were produced. Researchers in white coats patrolled the factory with clipboards, and came up with a result that seemed to confirm the prediction. A young statistician, F.J. Roethlisberger, wanted to make sure, so he turned all the lights down, expecting output to fall. Output increased. He turned the lights down even lower, and output soared. There are numerous cases like this where a study fails to confirm what seemed 'obvious', yet often stock market pros don't want to listen.

So, if the theories used by market professionals don't always hold water, how does the market really work? In the 1960s, academics developed the idea that there was absolutely no way to beat the market other than by getting information more quickly than anyone else. Since all the highly competitive analysts were getting information at the same time, the market must be 'efficient'.

The efficient market theory

Whenever there is news affecting a stock, fundamental analysts will react immediately, and the stock price will adjust very fast as they trade. The efficient market theory says that it is precisely because fundamentalists are good at their job that their predictions don't work – the prices of stocks and shares are immediately adjusted as the professionals buy what they think is undervalued and sell what they think is overvalued, leaving the smaller investor as well off by selecting a portfolio by throwing darts at the financial pages as by following the advice of the professionals.

Like most stock market theories, there is some truth in it, but it is not true all of the time, or in all markets. It is certainly true that large well-regulated markets, like the New York Stock Exchange, are more 'efficient' at pricing than obscure stock markets in developing countries where there are few share investors. All markets and industrial sectors occasionally 'overshoot', meaning a sudden change in prices to reflect changing economic circumstances that 'overdoes' the adjustment and goes too far. Some highly successful investors, such as George Soros, the man who 'forced' the UK out of the ERM a few years ago, is interested in overshooting as a way of making unusually good returns. He doesn't always get it right, though.

In essence, what the efficient market theory says is that fundamental analysis is no more helpful at improving investors' returns than if they simply bought shares and held them for a long time.

But if examining companies in detail in order to value shares has become too efficient for investors to beat the market, is there no other way to value them? Efficient marketeers think that there is, by looking at shares in terms of their risk.

Risk

It has been argued that risk is the only characteristic of a stock that is worth measuring. The idea is that 'blue chip' stocks – the shares of certain vast and stable corporations – are safer, or less volatile, than other stocks, and that it is therefore worth paying more for them. In other words, the price/earnings ratios of blue chip stocks should be higher. Investors endeavour to spread their risk by investing in a number of shares (a portfolio), hoping that while some of the shares may go down, others will go up. An investor who wants to do better than the market average may well be able to do so by investing in riskier shares, but is taking the chance that the shares may do worse than, for example, an index tracker fund.

There is no evidence that the past performance of a unit trust is a guide to the future

There is a vast amount of literature on the performance of unit trusts, which many private investors choose as their vehicle for playing the market. From it, one might be led to believe that a particular unit trust has 'got it right', and will perform as well as it has done in the past. Statistical studies tell us that this is not the case, since there is no evidence that the past performance of a unit trust is a guide to the future.

So how can you measure risk? One way is to measure the swings of a stock price over a year against the changes in the market overall. A blue chip company does not swing much. If the market goes down by 15 per cent, it may only go down by 7 per cent, and if the market shoots up, it will lag behind.

RISK OVER THE LONG TERM

During the last twenty five years or so, the stock market has been good to investors, but if you look back over the 20th century, you see that there have been many occasions when investors have lost their shirts, such as the hyper-inflation in Germany in the 1920s, when it took a suitcase-full of bank notes to buy an egg, the Wall Street Crash of 1929 and the 1973 oil crisis.

Some people say that US investors are keen on shares because the USA has grown and prospered during the last century, while countries like the UK have dwindled in economic power. Let's look at the facts:

In spite of all the wars and crises, and adjusting for the effects of inflation, both the UK and the USA have achieved investment profits over the 20th century. What about Germany and Japan, who suffered even more damage during war? The same is true for them too! The following information is reproduced from Elroy Dimson, Paul Marsh and Mike Staunton, *The Millennium Book: A Century of Investment Returns* (ABN AMRO/LBS 2000).

Average inflation-adjusted annual return on shares, 1900–2000

Britain	5.9%
USA	6.9%
Japan	4.2%
Germany	4.5%

Copyright © Dimson, Marsh & Staunton (ABN AMRO/LBS 2000)

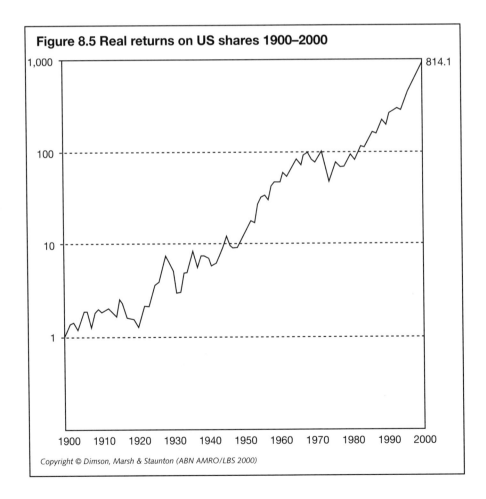

Figure 8.5 Real returns on US shares 1900–2000

Copyright © Dimson, Marsh & Staunton (ABN AMRO/LBS 2000)

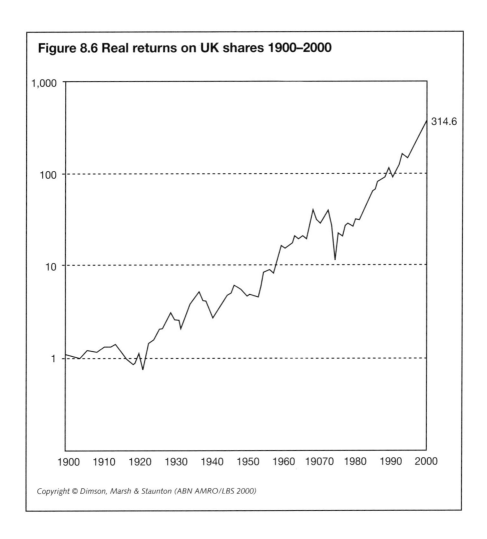

Figure 8.6 Real returns on UK shares 1900–2000

314.6

Copyright © Dimson, Marsh & Staunton (ABN AMRO/LBS 2000)

Does an annual return of 4.2 per cent–6.9 per cent sound miserably low? It's not so bad if you consider that if you'd invested over the whole of the 20th century, your end result would be the equivalent of your money doubling every 15 years or so, despite wars, plagues, mass murder and everything else that went on.

If you are old enough to remember the 1973/74 oil crisis, you may recall that the total value of shares quoted on the UK stock market dropped to US$50 billion, a fraction of what it had been worth, and that shares produced an average annual loss of 1.4 per cent between 1970 and 1980. The good news is that if you had bought shares in 1970 and held on to them until 2000, you would have seen the market's average annual return become 8.1 per cent over the 30-year period. Japanese shares were virtually worthless in 1945, but by 2000, in spite of the collapse of the bubble economy in the 1990s, they were worth over ten times their 1945 value.

In any given year, the returns on shares will usually be far wider than for bonds. That's because share prices are more volatile, or risky. The returns on shares have been much higher in the long run, however. This is what people mean when they talk about risk and reward – you get 'get what you pay for' in terms of risk. Shares are more risky than bonds but produce a higher rate of return over the long term. An investor who is prepared to buy and hold shares for several decades is likely to do better than one who holds bonds for the same length of time.

Modern portfolio theory

Modern portfolio theory (MPT) assumes that investors want the least possible risk for a given return, and offers a way of investing in a portfolio of shares that is less risky than investing in any of the particular stocks within it.

Imagine you are investing in a tiny country that has only two industries and two seasons. It has an alpine resort and a beach club. When the weather is good, the beach club does well, and when the weather is bad, the alpine resort booms. The returns for the two resorts are:

	Alpine resort	Beach club
Good weather	–30%	60%
Bad weather	60%	–30%

If the probability of a particular season having good or bad weather is one in two, investing in the alpine resort would produce returns of 60 per cent half the time, and –30 per cent half the time, giving an average, or expected return, of 15 per cent; the same is true for investing in the beach club. It would be risky, though, to invest in only one of the resorts because there might be many seasons one after the other with the same weather, just as you might get a long row of heads when flipping a coin.

If you invested £100 in each of the resorts, your results over five seasons might be as follows:

	Alpine resort	Beach club
Good	−30%	60%
Bad	60%	−30%
Bad	60%	−30%
Bad	60%	−30%
Bad	60%	−30%
Total at end	440.20	48.20

You have lost £51.80 on the beach club, but made £340.20 on the alpine resort, giving you an overall return on your £200 investment of £288.40.

If you had invested all of your £200 in the alpine resort, you would have made £680.40. If you had invested the whole £200 in the beach club you would have lost £96.40 of your capital, leaving you with only £103.60 to re-invest – it would take time to get your money back to its original level, and if you attempted to do so by investing again in only one of the two resorts, you might well make a further substantial loss. Thus, the argument for spreading the risk is very strong.

The two resorts have negative covariance. Here is the formula for calculating covariance:

Let A_g and A_B be the actual return from the alpine resort in good and bad weather respectively, and A be the expected return (average), B_g and B_B be the actual returns from the beach club and B the expected return:

The covariance between A and B =

COV_{AB} = Probability of good weather $(A_g - A)(B_g - B)$ + probability of bad weather $(A_B - A)(B_B - B)$

In our example, the probability of good or bad weather are both 0.5, so:

$$
\begin{aligned}
COV_{AB} &= [0.5(-30 - 15)(60 - 15)] + [0.5(60 - 15)(-30 - 15)] \\
&= 0.5(-45 \times 45) + 0.5(45 \times -45) \\
&= -0.10125 + -0.10125 \\
&= -0.2025
\end{aligned}
$$

In real life, however, shares tend to move up and down together, so it is rare to find a perfect opportunity to eliminate risk. It is possible, though, to reduce risk by investing in shares with a low covariance or, better still, a negative covariance. This is called diversification, and can be achieved by investing across a wide number of industries and countries.

The capital-asset pricing model (CAPM)

The variability of the stock market as a whole, known as market risk, is different from the variability of individual stocks. Fundamental analysis may discover influences on a particular company that cause it to rise or fall, such as labour problems or a new patent, but all stocks tend to rise and fall with the market overall. The market risk prevents investors from being able to eliminate completely their risk of making a loss by diversifying in companies with negative covariance. In our example of the tiny country, we could think of the market risk as being the possibility of, say, fewer tourists coming to the country because of economic or political problems elsewhere. Fewer tourists would reduce the profit potential for both resorts, whatever the season.

To compare the movements of a particular share against the market overall, we say that the 'beta' (ß, the Greek letter b) of the market risk is 1. A share with a beta of 3 will swing three times as much as the market does in either direction, and a share with a beta of 1.5 will swing only one and a half times as far. Thus, the higher the beta of a portfolio or individual share, the more risky it is.

Because, as we have seen, diversifying cannot reduce the investor's exposure to market risk, what it can do, however, is bring the risk of a portfolio down to a beta of 1, the same as the market risk beta. This is a refinement of fundamental analysis (see page 149), which can be extended to value stocks in terms of the total risk. CAPM says that it is only the overall market risk that is relevant for valuation of a stock, since the part of the risk that is peculiar to an individual stock, the 'unsystematic risk', can be eliminated by diversification, just as we did in our hypothetical country. As a rule of thumb, CAPM says that a portfolio of as few as 20 diversified stocks should be enough to eliminate almost all of the unsystematic risk.

Giving the overall market risk a beta value of 1, and a 'risk-free' investment, such as a bank deposit, a beta value of 0, CAPM uses the following formula to work out the expected return on a diversified portfolio:

Expected return on a share = 'Risk-free' interest rate + [Beta of the share x
(Expected return on the market – 'Risk-free' interest rate)]
The reason for calculating the expected return is that CAPM states that if,
in the long term, you want to get a higher rate of return than the market
average, all you have to do is to increase the beta value of your portfolio.

EXAMPLE

You have £100,000 to invest and you decide to work out the expected return
from four choices:

1. A 'risk-free' investment in a bank deposit.
2. An investment of half your money in the stock market and the other
   half 'risk-free'.
3. Investing the whole sum in a portfolio with a beta in line with that of the
   market average.
4. Investing in a high risk portfolio.

You find that you can get 5 per cent interest from the bank deposit, and
that the market average return is 8 per cent.

Choice 1 – Your expected return is the interest rate the bank gives you, i.e.
5 per cent, or £5,000. Remember that no investment is completely 'risk-free';
in the UK, for example, only 75 per cent of a deposit at a major bank is
protected if the bank collapses. Short of a major crisis, however, it is argued
that it is reasonable to describe such an investment as 'risk-free', although
inflation may eat into the capital and the interest.

Choice 2 – You decide to put £50,000 in a portfolio with a beta of 1, and
the rest in a bank. Using the expected return formula, the expected rate of
return = 5% + 0.5(8% – 5%) = 6.5%. Note that although the portfolio has a
beta of 1, you have only invested 50 per cent of your money, so you must
halve the beta value.

Choice 3 – You invest all the money in a portfolio with a beta of 1; your
expected rate of return will therefore be in line with the market average, 8 per
cent.

Choice 4 – You invest in a portfolio with a beta of 2.5, which should
generate higher returns; expected rate of return = 5% + 2.5(8% – 5%) =
12.5%.

Beta has been an officially approved way of measuring risk, and you can obtain estimates of the beta of a stock from brokers and investment advisers.

CRITICISMS OF CAPM

A portfolio with a beta of 0 should, according to CAPM, produce the same return as a risk-free investment outside the market which also, by definition, has a beta of 0. Studies have shown, however, that over the long term stock portfolios with a beta of 0 have done better than risk-free investments, contradicting the theory. In addition, in the 1980s mutual funds in the United States produced returns that had no correlation to their beta values. There have been objections to the way that beta values are measured, and it has been shown that betas for individual shares fluctuate significantly over time.

Perhaps the most serious criticism of CAPM, though, is the argument that none of the market indices are a perfect reflection of the overall market risk. In fact, calculating beta using different indices has produced widely differing beta values for stocks. It has been said that you cannot measure the overall market risk accurately; if this is so, then CAPM is untestable, and therefore useless. Many traders do continue to use CAPM, and claim that they have good results and are refining their techniques.

Arbitrage pricing theory (APT)

Like CAPM, APT says that it is the overall market risk element of the total risk of a stock that should be measured. To do this, a number of risk factors have been identified to be used in addition to beta. These include inflation rates, interest rates, company size and price/earnings ratios.

CAPM and APT are perhaps the nearest thing to a mathematically sound analytical approach to the stock market. We should look briefly at two more theories that have been applied recently, and upon which the jury is still out: the GARCH and chaos theories.

The GARCH theory

GARCH, or Generalized Auto-Regressive Conditional Heteroskedasticity (you can see why people prefer to call it GARCH!), predicts that there are trends in volatility – if a stock price has had a large swing on one day, then it will have a large swing on the next. Trends were identified by squaring the returns, which produced an apparent correlation over time. The investment strategy suggested is to purchase options to buy and to sell, thus betting that the stock price would move one way or the other. You would only lose if the stock price remained the same. Other studies, however, have contradicted the GARCH theory – the trends only seem to appear when the market is not very volatile. Thus, GARCH may work but not all the time.

Chaos theory

The chaos theory has been devised to explain the discovery that some apparently complex and random patterns have simple underlying causes, and can be predicted in the short term even though prediction accuracy decreases over time. The spread of disease epidemics and growth patterns of micro-organisms, for example, have been successfully modelled using chaos theory.

Attempts to apply chaos mathematics to the stock market have so far met with only limited success. The idea is to identify periods when the 'Lyapunov time horizon' (the point in the future when a predictable trend disappears) is high, allowing predictions to be made for longer periods than normal. The techniques employ staggeringly large amounts of trading data on computer, and the companies using them are secretive. So far the consensus is that there may be 'pockets of predictability' that chaos theory can predict, but that the market undergoes frequent changes that disrupt the predictions generated by chaos theory.

Neural networks

Computer programs that are able to spot patterns in the data are increasingly being used in market forecasting. These programmes, known as 'neural networks', are a tool in the never-ending trawl of market data in search of relationships and trends. Their popularity has made them affordable – you can now buy neural network software that will run on a personal computer at home.

Neural networks are simply tools. You still need to use judgement to know when and if to exploit the patterns they throw up. For example, they tend to 'overfit', which means that they often identify patterns that are purely coincidental. It is then up to the operator to weed out such spurious patterns. As computer technology improves, so will the usefulness of neural networks, but the complexity of their operation may keep them in the hands of the biggest traders.

Conclusion – long-term investing is not a zero sum game

Many brokers will tell you that new techniques for predicting the market may work for some time, but as more and more people catch on to them they will become less effective. Most of the theories that we have looked at in this chapter have probably been effective at one time or another in the history of the stock market. The paradox is that the market seems to be protected against the monopoly of one method in the long term by its own nature – if it works, everyone will start doing it, and it will stop working.

The market seems to be protected against the monopoly of one method in the long term by its own nature – if it works, everyone will start doing it, and it will stop working

Given this state of affairs, index investing for the long term has a lot going for it. It is certainly a way of reducing your effort and is superior to purchasing most unit trusts, since the majority underperform the market averages. No guerrilla investor need be ashamed of taking this route.

Many investors, however, enjoy the thrills and spills of choosing equities for themselves. If you find direct investment fun and you are prepared to learn how to avoid making silly mistakes, like buying the wrong share because it has a similar name to the one you intended to buy, then it could ultimately be very rewarding.

There is an old joke about the host of a poker game who says, 'Let's play carefully, boys, and we can all win a little.' In poker it is impossible for everyone to win, because poker is a 'zero-sum' game, meaning that the total amount of money in the game comes solely from what the players have brought with them, so the game is simply a process of this money moving around between the players. In poker, there has to be winners and losers, unless by chance everyone ends up with what they began with.

The stock market is not a 'zero-sum' game. It waxes and wanes, but it grows over the long term as long as the economy it represents grows too. During the 20th century, the world grew. Overall, the world's population increased, life expectancy increased, productivity increased, standards of living generally increased, body size increased, education improved and so on. If the world continues to grow during the 21st century, we can expect the stock markets of economically powerful countries to grow too. If the polar icecaps melt, or there is a mass die-off because of a plague, or a giant asteroid crashes into the earth, then the situation might be not be so promising – but you cannot be certain even of that. As we've seen, despite all the awful things that happened in the last century, wealth increased. There is a lot to be said for being, in this sense, an optimist as an investor; in any case, what is the alternative? Is it really wise to put all your money into canned food and fallout shelters? By all means take steps to protect yourself and your assets, but don't deny yourself the chance of prospering if things don't go too badly after all!

9

commodities
futures
financial futures
LTCM – even the 'rocket scientists' can get it wrong
the London International Financial Futures and
Options Exchange (LIFFE)
US futures
Japanese futures
futures in the main commodity-producing countries
continental europe
other Far Eastern markets
smaller futures markets
options
traded options – a private investor's view

Commodities, futures and options – for gamblers only

In this chapter we will examine 'derivatives' (futures and options), which are financial instruments that are related to the prices of 'real' securities such as shares and bonds, and commodities, which are basic standardized products such as oil, tin and wheat. Apart from traded options (examined below), they are no place for the smaller investor, but it is important to have an understanding of how they work since they have a bearing on other financial markets and the world economy generally. Essentially, these markets are systems for the reduction of risk in trade between large companies and institutions, overlaid with a large number of speculators who hope to make profits from price fluctuations. They have a reputation for being highly volatile and dangerous, but this is true only for the speculators. The underlying business is an essential part of the world's economy.

The topics covered in this chapter are:

- Commodities – what they are and how they work
- Futures – how they developed

- *The difference between hedgers and speculators*
- *Financial futures – how money is treated as a commodity*
- *LTCM – even the 'rocket scientists' can get it wrong*
- *The London International Financial Futures and Options Exchange (LIFFE)*
- *Chicago and other US futures markets*
- *Japanese futures*
- *Futures in the main commodity-producing countries*
- *Continental Europe*
- *Other Far Eastern futures markets*
- *The smaller futures markets*
- *Options and traded options*
- *Calls, puts, hedging and option writing*

Commodities

Commodities are the basic raw materials that the world needs in order to function – they are the fruits of the earth. They include wheat, coffee, oil, sugar, livestock and precious metals such as gold and platinum. People who are in the business of producing or processing these commodities are performing a vital function for which we should all be grateful. Many of these businesses trade in their commodities on a cash basis; prices fluctuate according to supply and demand, often in seasonal cycles. For instance, the cash price for wheat is lowest at harvest time, when there is plenty of it about. Precious metals have seasonal cycles too – prices usually increase in the autumn as jewellers begin to prepare their products for sale at Christmas and need more raw materials.

Commodity prices are unpredictable – all kinds of events can affect prices

Commodity prices are unpredictable – all kinds of events can affect prices, including wars, political unrest, strikes, extremes of weather, changes in consumer buying patterns, plagues of insects, plant and animal diseases, and the activities of financial interests who wish to influence the market. This has been the case for hundreds, if not thousands, of years. It makes life difficult for producers and users alike, since it is very hard to run a business if you don't know how much you can buy and sell your goods for. For this reason, a market has grown up in 'commodity futures'.

Futures

Buyers and sellers of commodities can make a contract to deliver a product at some time in the future at an agreed price, thus taking the uncertainty out of their operations. They can agree on the amounts, quality and date of delivery, and both parties will put down deposits to protect each other from one side defaulting on the deal. This is known as a 'futures contract'. Futures are a kind of insurance policy, or 'hedge', against the risks of price volatility – businesses can simultaneously trade in futures and in the cash market. In fact, most futures contracts are cancelled before the delivery period.

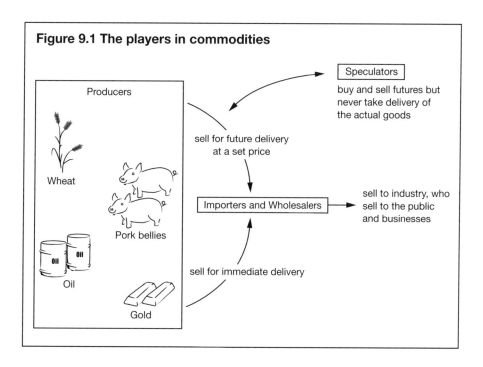

Figure 9.1 The players in commodities

Producers

Wheat

Pork bellies

Oil

Gold

Speculators

buy and sell futures but
never take delivery of
the actual goods

sell for future delivery
at a set price

Importers and Wholesalers

sell to industry, who
sell to the public
and businesses

sell for immediate delivery

This is where the speculators come in. It is argued that speculators are a vital part of the futures market, because they provide it with greatly improved liquidity. Speculators aren't interested in using the commodities themselves; they are gambling on the difference between the price of a futures contract and the actual delivery price. Thus the commodities businesses, or 'hedgers', and the speculators behave differently in the market. The hedgers are able to offset, roughly, gains or losses in the cash market by an opposite effect in the futures market, and are thus able to run their businesses more steadily. The speculators have to watch the fluctuations of futures contracts every day, and get out on top when they can.

COMMODITY SWAPS

Suppose you are an aluminium company who agrees to protect a customer against a rise in price over a fixed amount. In return, the customer agrees to compensate the company if the price falls below a certain level. This is known as a 'swap', though it is related to options (see page 181). Swaps generally last for two or three years, though some can be for as long as fifteen. Oil is the most actively swapped commodity, and there are even bonds available with redemption values stated in terms of an amount of oil, thus tying themselves to future oil prices.

BUYING ON MARGIN

Hedgers have never liked to pay the full price for their purchases long before the goods are delivered. Traditionally, when you purchase a futures contract, you only pay a small percentage of its value as a deposit. This is the main attraction for speculators, since it means that you trade futures 'on margin'.

EXAMPLE

If you buy £200,000's worth of a futures contract, you only have to pay, say, £20,000 as an up-front deposit. If the gamble pays off and the value of the contract goes up to £280,000, you can sell, making a profit of £80,000 on a deposit of £20,000, an increase of 400 per cent rather than the 40 per cent increase you would have made if you had paid out £200,000. If the deal goes against you, you could end up owing much more money than you originally deposited.

It is the fact that you buy on margin that makes futures risky for the speculators, since the margin means that prices are around ten times more volatile for speculators than they are for the hedgers, who actually trade in commodities themselves and do not use the margin to buy more than they otherwise would. The futures markets have grown massively as more and more speculators have become involved, and this has increased short-term volatility.

Financial futures

Shares, bonds and currencies can be treated as commodities and futures contracts can be made on them. There is a wide range of financial futures and new ones are being invented all the time. Most futures are tied to important currencies or widely followed indices, such as the FTSE 100, the Standard and Poor's 500, sterling, yen, US Treasury issues, Eurodollars, and so on. They are also tied to interest rates and bonds. Margins on financial futures can be considerably less than the 10 per cent or so required as a deposit on commodity futures, and this increases the risk unless you are using financial futures to hedge against changes to large liquid investments you have elsewhere, in which case you are behaving in the same way that a hedger in the commodities business does.

EXAMPLE

Suppose you are dealing in futures based on 'long gilts' (e.g. long-term gilts). In this case, the contract size is £50,000. Suppose that the price when you buy is 100–28 (this means $100^{28/32}$). Gilts move in 32nds of 1 per cent; each 32nd is called a 'tick'. The margin you must deposit is £500. If you are certain that gilts are going to go up and you want to buy gilts at a future date when money becomes available, you might buy the futures contract now to hedge against the expected higher cost of the gilts when you have the cash to buy them. If you are wrong, all is not lost, because the lower cost of gilts will roughly balance the loss you make on the futures contract. You can close out a futures contract either by delivering the gilts on the due date or by selling an identical contract. Most people do the latter.

If you are speculating, however, the situation is rather different.

EXAMPLE

Suppose the underlying value of your gilts contract dropped by 50 per cent; you would not have lost £250, but £25,000, all on your £500 initial deposit. The rules of the system say that investors' contracts have to be checked daily for losses and profits; if you are losing, you will get a 'margin call' for more money to cover the losses, and you can close out the contract to stop any further losses.

PLAYERS IN FINANCIAL FUTURES

Owners of very large share portfolios, such as brokers, unit and investment trust fund managers, pension funds and other institutions, trade in financial futures to hedge against the chance that share prices will fall. Anyone can speculate by taking a buy or sell position on a futures contract, betting that shares will either rise or fall. Futures are either traded on exchanges using the 'open outcry' system, where traders shout at each other over the din of the 'pit' where they trade, communicating using a system of hand signals, or using linked computers. Futures prices generally keep in step with cash prices, but are adjusted to account for interest rate differences. Occasionally futures prices can become much more expensive due to activity in the market; then the arbitrageurs step in to profit from the difference, pulling futures prices back to normality in the process.

TRADING IN FUTURES FOR GUERRILLAS

The majority of players in commodity futures are speculators. Each year, they leave billions of pounds' worth of commissions with the brokers. It's a casino with the odds firmly rigged against the smaller investor. It may seem exciting, but it's not a good investment – almost everyone gets wiped out within a few years. To win as a speculator, you have to possess an enormous amount of knowledge and huge amounts of cash to get any kind of an edge. The only people who really know what is going on are the commodities businesses themselves – so don't expect your broker to have any special expertise. Stay out of commodities. The same goes for financial futures, unless you are hedging.

To win as a speculator, you have to possess an enormous amount of knowledge and huge amounts of cash to get any kind of an edge

LTCM – EVEN THE 'ROCKET SCIENTISTS' CAN GET IT WRONG

In 1998, Long Term Capital Management (LTCM), a so-called hedge fund, suffered such great losses trading in derivatives that it had to be rescued by a consortium of 14 major US securities firms and commercial banks. At the time of the collapse, LTCM was said to have a potential loss of some $80 billion, a staggering sum that might have sparked off a worldwide financial panic had it not been for prompt action by Alan Greenspan, Chairman of the Federal Reserve Board.

Prior to the collapse, LTCM had been regarded as one of the top American hedge funds. The term 'hedge fund', incidentally, is misleading. Hedge funds are not generally conservative operations intended to reduce their clients' risks – they are intended to achieve good returns, and are designed to avoid regulation, only admitting financial institutions and rich, financially sophisticated people as customers.

LTCM was started in 1994 with $1 billion of its investors' money. It was the creation of John Meriwether, former vice chairman of Salomon Brothers, who was immortalized in the excellent book about Salomon Brothers in the 1980s, *Liar's Poker* by Michael Lewis. LTCM boasted two Nobel Prize-winning economists, Robert Merton and Myron Scholes among its employees.

LTCM had a lot of prestige because of its talented team and the large amount of money it has raised as its initial capital stake. In its first few years, it achieved above-average for its investors. In 1995 and 1996 it produced net annual profits of over 40 per cent. In 1997, the profit fell to 17 per cent.

The main way LTCM made profits was by exploiting temporary valuation differences between similar types of financial securities, increasing the potential profit or loss by highly geared bets in the futures markets. The idea is that varieties of, say, foreign bonds, are similar enough to be comparable, so you buy a bond that looks cheap and simultaneously sell an equal amount of another bond that looks expensive.

To get a clearer idea of the complexities involved, imagine that a fund manager thinks, before the days of the euro, that the European Community is moving ever closer towards a common currency. He decides that this implies that yields on European government bonds will move more closely together than before. He notices that, say, Spanish government bonds are yielding a lot more that German government bonds, so he buys Spanish bonds while selling an equal amount of German bonds short in the futures markets.

This kind of activity is supposed to be a kind of arbitrage and is often claimed to be 'market neutral', meaning that the fund wins a profit whether or not interest rates go up or down, since it is long on one bond and short on the other one. That's the theory – but the fund is still relying on the assumption that the yield 'spread' between the two bonds will get closer together.

So, how do you get from a measly 1 per cent or 2 per cent profit on a transaction like this to the lofty 40 per cent plus annual return that LTCM was making early on? You do that by doing lots and lots of deals across the world's derivatives markets, using as much margin as possible. LTCM relied on sophisticated mathematical models of price behaviour to decide exactly how to construct their deals. These models were based, by definition, on assumptions about the market, but they used vast amounts of historical data, so they were quite good at predicting the future under 'normal' market conditions. LTCM could use the models to detect short-term price anomalies and pounce on them.

One thing is certain about the stock market. If someone comes up with a good wheeze that makes money, a crowd of other people will start copying the technique. Once everyone is doing it, the opportunity for profit vanishes. By 1997, LTCM saw that the opportunities were drying up, and started to take more risks.

It was bad timing. Around the world, financial uncertainty was increasing. The Asian currency crisis of 1997 was succeeded by the Russian government's decision to default on its bonds (yes, governments *do* default) and to devalue its currency. A large number of foreign institutional investors who had charged into Russia earlier got badly burned. LTCM's sophisticated financial models were suddenly all wrong, because the markets were behaving in a different way from how they 'normally' behave.

When there is a panic in the financial markets, lots of pin-striped young professionals are the first to lose their heads – their main thought is how not to lose their jobs if they are hauled up in front of their bosses to explain why they have made losses. To forestall this, they tend to sell everything that could be perceived as risky, irrespective of whether or not it is a valuable bargain, and buy the safest, most unexceptionable assets they can find. You can imagine the scene – the boss berates Jenkins for his idiocy in having invested in Ruritanian longs, while praising Fisher for having had the prescience of moving out of Ruritanian securities altogether and into US Treasury bills, even though the boss had been encouraging them both to fill their boots with Ruritania for weeks. In the nasty world of corporate politics, someone generally has to get the blame, however unfairly.

Fear drives professionals to make unprofessional mistakes, and good assets get dumped indiscriminately. The market overall stops being the marvellous, rational place that eminent economists can develop mathematical models for – it starts behaving like a drunken sailor on shore leave. LTCM couldn't just dump all its contracts because they were too complex and doing so would have caused even more losses.

LTCM's problem was taken seriously enough in the USA for the Federal Reserve Bank of New York to approach some institutional creditors to suggest that they did not force the firm into bankruptcy. A group of creditors agreed to inject some $3.65 billion into LTCM to stave off the problem and give it time to unwind its positions, in return for acquiring control of the firm.

The saving of LTCM evoked a lot of criticism. While it was not technically a government bailout, the authorities had been involved. Critics argued that it set a dangerous precedent, since other, even larger, hedge funds might be tempted to take crazy risks, confident that if something went wrong in the future, they would be excused from their obligations – this is known as a 'moral hazard'. According to the free market economics that dominate US thinking, firms that make mistakes should be allowed to fail, or else the world's economy will become increasingly fragile. It is hypocrisy, they say, to save Wall Street firms while lecturing other countries on the evils of protecting their own troubled financial institutions.

Money politics in America is a very major force. Powerful financial interests are able to coax through beneficial legislation that protects them, but leaves others to suffer. Nevertheless, everyone would suffer if there was a complete breakdown in the world's financial system – the spectre of another Great Depression is always lurking. My personal opinion is that the Fed acted sensibly, given the circumstances, and has managed to keep the markets going since. It's rough justice, perhaps, but modern economies are inherently unstable, and staving off a total collapse is in everyone's best interests.

The London International Financial Futures and Options Exchange (LIFFE)

LIFFE (pronounced 'life') is a public limited company owned by its members. Set up in 1982, it provides the facilities for the financial futures and options market in London. There are about 200 members, the great majority of which are from the UK, the United States, Japan and Europe. LIFFE is regulated by the Securities and Investment Board, and almost all its members are supervised by the Securities and Futures Authority. Private investors can receive compensation for loss from the Investors' Compensation Scheme for sums up to £48,000. Like other exchanges, LIFFE runs inexpensive seminars to explain to investors how the system works.

Most of the trading used to be done using the 'open-outcry' method in 'pits' on the floor of the exchange. Today, LIFFE has been among the first to adopt electronic trading.

LIFFE ELECTRONIC TRADING

LIFFE has a website, *www.liffe.com*, where you can look up the prices of its multitude of futures contracts. You can't deal direct, though. You have to have a broker to deal for you. Because of the ease in following the market, trading has increased substantially since the introduction of electronic trading.

THE LINK TO THE CLIENT

If you want to make a deal on the LIFFE, you contact your broker, who must be a LIFFE member. You must keep a cash deposit with your broker, who deducts premiums from it, usually on the morning after the day you make a trade.

SOME LIFFE FUTURES CONTRACTS

LIFFE financial futures are usually traded in three-month cycles for delivery in March, June, September and December.

Since 2001, you have been able to buy futures contracts on individual large companies, which is interesting to the private investor who follows any of these firms closely. It is an easy way to speculate in highly liquid shares in the pharmaceutical, telecoms, technology, oil and banking sectors in the UK, Europe and the USA while avoiding stamp duty and exchange rate costs. In an announcement, Hugh Freedberg, Chief Executive of LIFFE said, 'The days of high-price, high-margin exchange trading in an environment of prohibitive taxes and regulation must surely be numbered. Free, real-time prices over the Internet will make this market even more transparent for retail brokers and smaller investors.'

At the time of writing, the following shares are available:

- France Telecom
- Deutsche
- Telecom
- Telecom Italia
- Telefonica
- AT&T
- Vodafone
- Siemens
- Alcatel
- Cisco Systems
- Nokia
- Intel

- Microsoft
- Deutsche Bank
- ING
- Banco Santander Central Hispano
- HSBC Holdings
- Citigroup
- Total Fina Elf
- Eni Spa
- Royal Dutch Petroleum Co
- BP Amoco
- Exxon Mobil
- Merck
- AstraZeneca
- GlaxoSmithKline

US futures

The world's largest and most important centre for futures is Chicago.

CHICAGO BOARD OF TRADE (CBOT)

Established in 1848, the Chicago Board of Trade developed through the latter half of the 19th century as methods of grain storage improved, allowing producers and traders to keep grain for longer periods and take advantage of price fluctuations. In this century, a wide variety of agricultural futures were introduced and, after the abolition of exchange controls in 1971, the volatility of bonds and other financial instruments gave the Chicago Board of Trade the opportunity to introduce futures trading in Ginnie Maes (mortgage securities backed by the US government) and other financial futures. The market is connected with the two other Chicago markets listed below as well as with other US exchanges.

CHICAGO MERCANTILE EXCHANGE (CME)

The CME started in 1874. Until World War 2 it traded principally in futures on onions, potatoes, cheese, eggs and butter. More foods were added in the post-war period and in 1961 the market greatly expanded with the introduction of pork belly futures (pork bellies are frozen lumps of uncured bacon). In the mid-1960s, futures contracts began to be written on live animals, such as cattle and hogs (pigs). When exchange controls came to an end in 1971, the CME began trading in foreign currencies through the International Monetary Market (IMM). The IMM has become the world's most active market in financial futures. An Index and Option Market (IOM) began in 1982.

The CME requires its members to deposit money to cover the gross margins, rather than the net as in most other markets.

CHICAGO BOARD OPTIONS EXCHANGE (CBOE)

The Chicago Board Options Exchange began in 1973, creating the world's largest options exchange. Almost all US index options are traded on the CBOE, in the Standard and Poor's 100 and in the Standard and Poor's 500. Since 1989, it has been possible to trade in options on the interest rates of US Treasury bills, notes and bonds. More recently, trading in conventional shares, warrants and bonds has been introduced.

Japanese futures

Japanese futures trading began in rice. There are now some 16 exchanges trading commodity futures and two exchanges trading financial futures. Precious metals futures account for more than 25 per cent of the total trading volume. Markets have poor liquidity and high commissions. Since 1990, foreign brokers have been allowed to become members. Although attempts are being made to streamline the multiplicity of regulations, liquidity problems are likely to continue. It is possible to trade in financial futures tied to the Nikkei Index on the Tokyo and Osaka stock exchanges.

TOKYO COMMODITY EXCHANGE FOR INDUSTRY (TOCOM)

Tocom trades futures in platinum, silver and gold using a screen system, and wool, cotton and rubber on open outcry. More futures are being introduced.

Futures in the main commodity-producing countries

New Zealand, Australia, South Africa and Canada are highly developed industrial countries which are nevertheless reliant on commodity exports. Their futures markets are dominated by mining companies and agricultural producers. The principal futures markets are:

- New Zealand Futures and Options Exchange (NZFOE)
- Sydney Futures Exchange
- South Africa Futures Exchange (Safex)
- Winnipeg Commodities Exchange.

Continental Europe

While London accounts for more than 90 per cent of the share trading in Western Europe, the next biggest markets are in Germany and France. Futures and options are traded in the following markets:

- Marché à Terme des Instruments Financiers (MATIF). With ambitions to outstrip London in futures trading, MATIF offers bond futures, futures on the Paris share index CAC-40, short-term interest rates, Eurodeutschmarks and ECU bonds, among others.
- Deutsche Terminborse (DTB), which is screen-based and is the most important options market in continental Europe, with many foreign participants, also trading German government bond futures and share futures tied to the German DAX index.
- Frankfurt Corn and Produce Exchange.
- Berne Grain and Produce Exchange.
- Vienna Commodity Exchange.
- Options Markand (OM) in Sweden, which has exchanges in London and Stockholm with links between the two for trading.
- European Options Exchange-Optiebeurs (EOE) in Amsterdam.
- Marché des Options Négotiables de Paris (Monep).

- Copenhagen Stock Exchange and Guarantee Fund for Danish Options and Futures (Futop) in Denmark.
- Irish Futures and Options Exchange (IFOX) in Eire.
- Belgian Futures and Options Exchange (Belfox) in Belgium.
- Ostereichische Termin und Optionenborse (OTOB) in Austria.
- Swiss Options and Futures Exchange (Soffex) in Switzerland.
- Mercado de Opciones Financerio Espanol in Spain.
- Mercado de Futuros Financerios (MEFF) in Spain.
- Futures markets in Padua and Bologna, Italy.

Other Far Eastern markets

These markets can be expected to become increasingly important as the Far East becomes an ever-stronger economic region:

- Singapore International Monetary Exchange (SIMEX). With a special link with the CME in Chicago, SIMEX is an important and active international market in currency futures for the yen, deutschmarks and sterling, futures in Eurodollar interest rates and some commodities.
- Hong Kong Futures Exchange Ltd. Futures traded include the Hang Seng Index, sugar, soyabeans and gold.
- The Kuala Lumpur Commodity Exchange (KLCE), which trades futures in cocoa, tin, palm oil and rubber.
- There are other small commodity exchanges in India, Thailand, the Philippines and Indonesia.

Smaller futures markets

From Turkey to the Gulf states, to Russia, China, India and Pakistan, governments are all trying to open up their economies to the delights of capitalism and financial markets. It may be fine for big Western financial institutions to be involved, but for the small investor they are hopeless.

Latin America does have some well-established futures markets, in Brazil in particular:

- Bolsa de Mercadorias de São Paulo (BMSP)
- Bolsa Mercantil e de Futuros (BM&F).

THE SMALLER FUTURES MARKETS FOR GUERRILLAS

Guerrilla investors should do their best to be well informed about what goes on in the smaller foreign markets since it will help to keep your macro-economic views up to date and may sometimes throw up clues you might otherwise have missed. Investing in these markets may be dangerous, though; not long ago, for example, the Winnipeg Commodities Exchange was the subject of a criminal investigation into alleged trading abuses. You should be aware that sharks are attracted to small markets where their nefarious activities are less likely to be stamped out. If you do decide to invest, check the charges and taxes carefully, as they vary widely. Sometimes they are lower than in the UK. In general, unless you wish to devote your life to commodities trading, there is plenty of action to be had at home and in the USA.

Guerrilla investors should do their best to be well informed about what goes on in the smaller foreign markets

Options

Share options give you the right to buy or sell a share at a certain price within a fixed time period. You pay for the option but you don't have to exercise it. You can also buy options on futures contracts, interest rates and currencies in the same way. The price you pay for the option is called the 'premium', and the price at which it is agreed that you may buy or sell the shares or futures contract is called the 'strike price' in the United States and the 'exercise price' in the UK.

The price that you pay for an option depends upon the period of time allowed until the option expires (the longer it is, the more expensive the option), and also upon the difference between the strike price and the current market price of the share or futures contract.

Options give you leverage. All you have to pay is the price of the premium to make a bet that the exercise price will be better than the market price at some point before the option runs out (in the case of traded options) or at the point that the option runs out (in the case of 'European-style' options). You don't have to come up with any more money unless you already know you have won your bet.

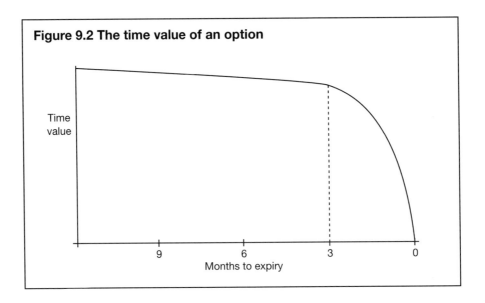

Figure 9.2 The time value of an option

There are two kinds of options, 'puts' and 'calls'. A call option gives you the right to buy, and a put option gives you the right to sell. Traded options enable you to buy or sell your option if you win the bet, instead of buying the shares or other securities themselves.

As we have seen, unlike paying the margin when you buy a futures contract, all you can lose on an option is the premium, while the possible gain can be as high as you could get in futures. Options on shares can usually be bought for between 8 and 15 per cent of the share's market price. Except for 'traded options', you cannot buy or sell an option after the initial purchase.

CALL OPTIONS

EXAMPLE

Suppose you think that shares in Company X are going to go up in the next three months. You can buy a three-month call option on 1,000 shares at, say, 184p; the premium will be 18p per share, so you will pay £180 plus dealing costs for 1,000 shares. If the share price is at 187p after three months, you could exercise the option to buy in the hope that the share price will continue to rise; you will have spent £180 + £1,840 = £2,020, so, not counting dealing costs, the shares will have to rise above 202p for you to make a profit.

PUT OPTIONS

EXAMPLE

Suppose that you think Company X's shares are going to go down in the next three months. You can buy a put option for 18p per share for 1,000 shares at 184p. If the shares go down to, say, 150p, you can exercise your option by 'putting' it on to an option dealer, forcing him to buy your shares for £1,840, which you now exercise your right to buy for £1,500, and pass them on to him. The cost to you, not including dealing charges, is £1,500 + £180 = £1,680, so your profit is £1,840 − £1,680 = £160. Since your broker can conduct both transactions quickly, you won't have to come up with all the money to buy the shares. (This applies to exercising call options as well.)

DOUBLE OPTIONS

Double options are combined put and call options, with a premium which is nearly double a normal premium. You are betting that the share price will move out of the range represented by the premium cost.

HEDGING

Suppose you own some shares which you don't want to sell, but you expect them to fall in the short term. You can buy a put option in the shares to protect them against a fall in value. In general, this kind of hedging is costly and unnecessary for the smaller investor.

WRITING OPTIONS

It is possible to 'write' options on shares that you own through your broker, who will try to find an option buyer. You get the premiums, less dealing charges, and you buy the shares when puts are exercised or sell your shares if a call is exercised. It is also possible to be a 'naked writer', which means writing options on shares you don't own – an absurdly dangerous activity if you have no money to back up the risk of loss.

TRADED OPTIONS

Traded options exist only in certain shares and their form is fixed by the options market. You can buy puts and calls at certain prices fixed around the share's market price for periods of three, six or nine months. As the share price moves, the option prices move with it. The big difference between traded options and ordinary ones is that you can buy and sell a traded option as often

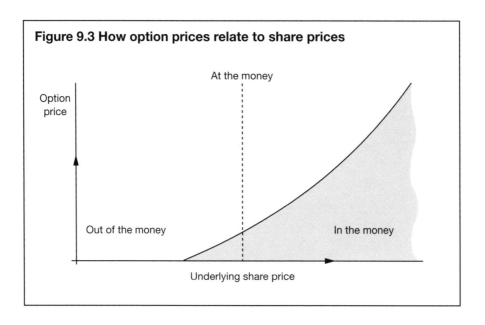

Figure 9.3 How option prices relate to share prices

as you like during its life. As well as the market in shares, you can also buy traded options based on the FTSE 100 Share Index and other indices.

EXAMPLE

Suppose you want to buy an option in Company X's shares, currently trading at 330p; put and call options may be available at 300p, 320p, 340p and 360p. The 300p and 320p prices are called 'in the money' if you are buying a call, because they are lower than the share's market price, and the 340p and 360p prices are called 'out of the money' because they are higher. Conversely, if you are buying a put, the 340p and 360p prices are 'in the money' and the 300p and 320p prices are 'out of the money'. If you bought a call at 300p, the premium might be 50p, so if you sold it immediately you would make a loss of 20p per share, even though the option is 'in the money', since you would buy the shares for 300p + 50p = 350p and only be able to sell them for 330p.

The way that the price of the option is calculated is complicated. Essentially, it is split up into two parts, the 'time value' and the 'intrinsic value'. The time value is set according to the time that an option has left to run – the longer the time left, the higher the time value – and at the moment that the option expires there will be no time value left. Time values are worked out on computer and are based on an estimate of the chances of an investor being able to exercise an option. Factors that influence time values are the time left, how near the option is to being in the money, and the volatility of the underlying share or commodity.

Intrinsic values are simply the amount by which an option is in the money, so if you had bought a call at 300p in shares selling at 330p, your option is in the money by 30p, which is its intrinsic value. The sale value of the option will vary throughout its lifetime. With a nine-month option the time value reduces fairly slowly for about six months before dropping at an increasingly rapid rate. In-the-money options tend to move in parallel with the share price, while out-of-the-money options are less responsive.

As with shares, options have a 'spread' – you pay the higher price when you buy and get the lower price when you sell – and you pay dealer's charges on top of this.

HOW TO TRADE IN OPTIONS

First, find a broker who will take you on. As with investing in shares, options brokers will offer different levels of service, such as execution only or advisory and discretionary services, which carry different levels of commission. Your broker will want you to deposit money with him, from which he will take the premiums as you deal. When you contact your broker with instructions to deal, the broker will try to get the price you ask for; if he can't, you can place a limit order for a fee. He will then do the deal for you later that day if prices make it possible to do so.

The rationale for private investors' interest in traded options is essentially the attraction of leverage combined with the limited risk of loss

The rationale for private investors' interest in traded options is essentially the attraction of leverage combined with the limited risk of loss. If you buy an out-of-the-money call and the share price rises, you make around ten times what you would have made if you had simply bought the shares, and the most you can lose is the premium, part of which you may be able to get back by re-selling the option before the expiry date. The longer the option, the more expensive it is because there is more chance of you making a profit. In-the-money options give you lower profits, but a bigger chance of making one, so they are a safer bet. Investors tend to buy puts less often than calls, perhaps because it is easier to imagine that a share is going to go up than it is to believe that it is going to go down.

FOR GUERRILLAS: WHO REALLY BENEFITS FROM OPTIONS?

The dealers certainly do. They make a profit on the transactions irrespective of whether the purchaser wins or loses. There may occasionally be moments when you are sure that a price is moving in a certain direction and can buy options at a price that will give a profit, but regularly buying traded options can be an expensive gamble, especially if you are inexperienced.

TRADED OPTIONS – A PRIVATE INVESTOR'S VIEW

A reader of the first edition of this book, Peter Hicks, has a slightly different view of the benefits of traded options; he writes that:

> 'I have found writing naked puts to be most rewarding: a way of making money without actually holding stocks and using up the annual tax-free capital gains allowance of around £12,000 for a married couple while leaving one's capital safely on deposit … In the traded options market, buyers far outweigh sellers. Many interested institutions are forbidden to be sellers by the terms of their constitutions. Loosely, there are too many 'punters' (buyers) and too few 'bookies' (sellers). Hence traded options tend to be a sellers' market, and prices favour sellers, I believe – particularly put sellers.

> 'In April [1996] I fancied Lucas. My hunch was reinforced by [an analyst's newsletter]. I toyed with the idea of buying 4,000 at about 213p – but I would much prefer to buy 4,000 at 200p! So, I 'put'myself at risk to have to buy 4,000 Lucas at 200p at any time up to November. For taking this so-called risk (I would be quite happy at 200p) I received a cheque for £420, net of all expenses – a nice tax-free bonus to add to the interest on uninvested capital. I will only have to purchase the stock if the price falls below 200p but will only lose if the price falls below 1991/2 whereas if I had bought the stock at 213p I would have lost £940 …'

Mr Hicks, an experienced private investor, keeps funds outside the market in order to back up his speculation, which, strictly speaking, does not count as 'naked writing'. He makes the following points:

- **Buyers** – no margin is required. The potential loss is restricted to the size of your initial cheque, just like placing a bet with a bookie!
- **Writers and sellers** – you are the bookie! Margin is required, but the amount depends to a large extent on the relationship between you and your broker. If you have a significant portfolio of shares lodged in a nominee account with your longstanding, friendly broker, he might not require any further margin.
- **Taxation** – option gains are subject to CGT, so you should restrict your potential gains to the annual tax-free allowance. For buyers, the tax point is the date when the gain occurs – when you sell your option for a price above that which you paid. For sellers the tax point is the expiry date of the option. This can result in a worthwhile tax holiday. In July, it is possible to sell options with an expiry date in the following April (the next tax year). The CGT 'will not have to be paid until the following year – a two-year tax holiday'.

10

the Bretton Woods system
the floating exchange rate system
the balance of payments and the black hole
the Euromarkets
the foreign exchange market
what is an exchange rate?
the forward exchange market
predicting exchange rates
the effects of exchange rates on shares
the effects of exchange rates on bonds
the effects of exchange rates on cash
the special drawing right (SDR) of the IMF
the euro – Europe's common currency
the future of the US dollar
the yen
globalization

Foreign exchange

The world has recently undergone a revolution – currencies can now be exchanged with one another more freely than ever before. This offers a great deal of scope to the guerrilla investor who wishes to take advantage of investment opportunities in currencies other than his or her own.

In this chapter we will look at the origins

and mechanisms of foreign exchange. The topics covered are:

- *The Bretton Woods system – why it was set up after World War 2, how it worked and why it has ended*
- *The floating exchange rate system – how it emerged and why it is good news for private investors*
- *The balance of payments and the black hole*
- *The Euromarkets*
- *The foreign exchange market – how currencies are traded*
- *Exchange rates – how to calculate them, and how to hedge in currencies.*
- *Arbitrage and speculation, and how to predict exchange rates*

- *The effects of exchange rates on shares, bonds and cash*
- *The special drawing right (SDR) of the IMF*
- *The Euro – Europe's common currency*
- *The future of the US dollar*
- *The yen*
- *Globalization*

The Bretton Woods system

As World War 2 drew to a close, the Allied nations and their supporters met in the United States at Bretton Woods in New Hampshire to plan an international monetary system for the post-war era. They created the International Monetary Fund (IMF) and the World Bank, and set up a system that was intended to provide stability to exchange rates. Since the United States had become by far the most powerful country in the world, the system was tied to the US dollar at $33 to an ounce of gold. All other currencies were defined in terms of dollars. If a country wanted to change its rate of exchange against the dollar, it had to make a formal announcement that it was revaluing, or devaluing, its currency. In 1949, 28 countries devalued their currencies.

Bretton Woods set the stage for the rise of socialism. Countries were able to pay for the huge cost of creating welfare states by issuing bonds, which in turn encouraged inflation. As world trade mushroomed and the economic balance between countries began to change, vast funds grew up which were highly mobile and could be switched from one country to another without the permission of governments. The demand for gold was high, and the official price of $33 to an ounce was undermined by the creation of secondary markets, where gold was traded at much higher prices. As its economic strength diminished, the United States decided unilaterally to abandon the Bretton Woods system when, in 1971, it suspended the right to convert dollars for gold at $33 to the ounce, and devalued the dollar.

The floating exchange rate system

Bretton Woods was supplanted by the floating exchange rate system, where no currency is formally linked to any other, or to gold. The rate at which you can exchange one currency for another is simply the best rate that someone will give you, so exchange rates are highly volatile (this is why they are called 'floating'). During the oil crises of 1973 and 1979, when OPEC dramatically increased the price of oil, the floating system helped to minimize the chaos, as the strain was taken by an adjustment in exchange rates (the OPEC countries' currencies suddenly became much more valuable), rather than by curtailing real economic activity, as would have happened if the Bretton Woods system had still been operating.

The floating system does have disadvantages. The principal ones are that it encourages countries to act 'selfishly' rather than cooperatively and that it greatly exaggerates the extremes in the cycle of exchange rates. Countries are tempted to manipulate their exchange rates for short-term advantage. For instance, Japan managed to keep the yen artificially low for some years in order to encourage exports, as did Britain, with less success. This kind of manipulation can only work for a few years before it becomes impossible to sustain.

The United States, too, tries to use the floating system for its own advantage. Its massive trade deficit will eventually have to be paid for with higher taxes, more unemployment and lower living standards, but the US government has staved off the evil day for some time by allowing the dollar to depreciate against other currencies. State banks throughout the world have attempted to counteract this by buying dollars to raise its rate.

The balance of payments and the black hole

Countries are like companies in that they have accounts; money flows in and out of them, and one can take a 'snapshot' of a country's accounts which purports to show its debts and assets, just as a balance sheet does for a company. Balance of payments accounts are produced each year, identifying the state's net earnings from abroad (the 'current account'), its savings or debts (the 'capital account'), and the borrowings the government may have to make to balance the books.

When a government has to borrow in order to balance its accounts, it usually goes to banks or other governments for a short-term loan. If all else fails, it must go to an international organization such as the International Monetary Fund which will insist on rigid economic controls. For this reason, governments tend to regard this last course of action as highly undesirable.

If a country's current account is negative, meaning that it has spent more than it has earned when trading abroad, it usually means that the country's currency is weakening. Conversely, if the current account is in surplus year after year, it usually means that the currency is getting stronger.

Much is made of balance of payments by politicians, economists and commentators. However, they are unreliable, just as the accounts of many companies are. If you reconcile the annual balance of payments figures for every country in the world, they should all add up. They don't – there is a 'black hole' of many tens of billions that cannot be accounted for. This black hole makes it impossible to know the true picture, and thus there can be no description of the world's economy that is entirely accurate.

The Euromarkets

The Euromarkets are a banking system that is truly international and operates beyond the control of governments. It handles huge amounts of cash belonging to companies, institutional funds, countries and wealthy individuals. The amount of money in the Euromarkets is so large that it can significantly affect exchange rates, the money supply and inflation as it moves around the world. The ease with which money can be borrowed through the system makes it attractive as a source of finance for large projects. Because of its international character, there is no central organization controlling it, and no complete figures on its size or movements. The City of London has benefited from the growth of Euromarkets because its physical location, halfway between Tokyo and New York, has enabled it to exploit its 'middle position' in the time zones.

The amount of money in the Euromarkets is so large that
it can significantly affect exchange rates, the money supply and
inflation as it moves around the world

The foreign exchange market

The important difference between doing business with a company in your own country and doing business with one abroad is that the two currencies of the respective countries will usually be involved. A German importer will usually pay a Japanese exporter in yen, an American exporter in dollars and so on. The importer will have to buy the required currency on the foreign exchange market.

The foreign exchange market is international and consists of banks, brokers and others buying and selling currencies from most of the countries in the world. Rates change very fast, so they communicate continuously. The main centres for foreign exchange trading are New York, London, Tokyo, Zurich and Frankfurt, which turn over hundreds of billions of dollars a day. The US dollar is by far the most frequently traded, and is called a 'vehicle currency'. This means that commodities such as coffee, gold and oil are normally priced in dollars. It is often cheaper for, say, a Japanese dealer who wants to buy Italian lire to buy dollars first and then use the dollars to buy lire, rather than buying them directly with yen.

The central banks in each country often try to influence the exchange rate of their currency by buying and selling in large amounts. For example, when there is an agreed target exchange rate, the central banks have to buy and sell their own currencies according to the fluctuation in supply and demand, to try to drive their currencies towards the desired rate.

The merchant banks, or commercial banks, trade in currencies for themselves, and also on the behalf of clients such as companies and large investors who want foreign currency. They trade with other banks, and also use brokers.

The brokers are used by banks because they can get the best price quicker and more cheaply than the bank itself. There are just a few authorized brokers in each financial centre.

What is an exchange rate?

An exchange rate is simply the ratio at which one currency can be exchanged for another at a given time. It can be given in two ways, either as the amount of currency A that will buy one unit of currency B, or the amount of currency B that will buy one unit of currency A. It doesn't matter which way round the ratio is expressed, as long as it is made clear which currency is being taken as one unit, though there is usually a convention for any given pair of currencies.

If the rate for marks per dollar has changed from DM2:$1 to DM2.01:$1, you will have to pay more in marks for a dollar, so the mark has 'depreciated' and the dollar has 'appreciated'. If the dollars per mark rate has changed from $0.50:DM1 to $0.51:DM1, you will have to pay more in dollars for a mark, so marks have appreciated and dollars have depreciated. This is why it can be confusing if someone says that the exchange rate has risen – which way round do they mean?

THE NOMINAL EXCHANGE RATE

The nominal exchange rate is the prevailing rate of exchange between two currencies on a given day. In other words, it is simply the price of buying one currency with another. It is sometimes given as an index relative to some base time.

EXAMPLE

If the base dollar/deutschmark rate is, say, $0.50:DM1, and some time later the rate is $0.55:DM1, the nominal index of the mark will then be 110 – the mark has appreciated against the dollar by 10 per cent.

The nominal rate doesn't tell you anything about price levels in the respective countries, however, so a formula is used to convert it into the 'real exchange rate' which does.

THE REAL EXCHANGE RATE

The real exchange rate takes the price levels of the two countries into account. The formula for calculating it is:

$$E_r = (E \times P) \div P^*$$

(where E_r is the real exchange rate, E is the nominal exchange rate given as the amount of foreign currency for one unit of domestic currency, P is the local price index and P^* is the foreign price index).

EXAMPLE

Suppose that the nominal exchange rate of dollars to marks is $0.50:DM1. If both the German and the US price indexes are 100, then the real exchange rate is

$$E_r = (0.50 \times 100) \div 100 = 0.50$$

which is the same as the nominal rate. Now suppose that at a later date the nominal exchange rate is still the same, but the US price index has risen to 110. The real exchange rate is now

$$E_r = (0.50 \times 100) \div 110 = 0.4545$$

The real exchange rate is telling you what the nominal exchange rate doesn't, in the example above that the mark will buy less goods in America than it could have previously. One problem though, is what price index is used; for instance, some indices include the prices of fast food, which are hardly a good guide to value.

THE EFFECTIVE EXCHANGE RATE

Have you ever heard a news report about your local currency going up or down against 'a basket of currencies'? What is happening is that the local, or domestic, currency is being compared with the currencies of several countries with which your country trades. The result is called the 'effective exchange rate'.

To understand the principle, let's take an example.

EXAMPLE

Suppose Japan does 60 per cent of its foreign business with the United States and 40 per cent with Germany. The exchange rate index is weighted by 0.6 times the exchange rate with the dollar and 0.4 times the exchange rate with the mark.

At the base period, the indices are all set to 100 and will look like this:

Nominal index	Nominal index	Effective index
DM:Y1	$:Y1	Y
100	100	100

If the yen subsequently appreciated against the mark by 20 per cent and depreciated against the dollar by 20 per cent the indices would look like this:

Nominal index	Nominal index	Effective index
DM:Y1	$:Y1	Y
80	120	104

The effective exchange rate index has been calculated by multiplying the nominal indices by their respective weights, thus:

$$80 \times 0.4 = 32$$
$$120 \times 0.6 = 72$$

Adding them together we get $32 + 72 = 104$, which is the effective rate index given above.

SPOT RATES

The 'spot rate' is the rate between two currencies for delivery at once. Once a deal has been done, it usually take two days before the currencies are actually exchanged because of the paperwork involved – it is a 'paper transaction' where bank notes are not physically exchanged. With electronic trading gaining ground, this process is speeding up.

The forward exchange market

If you know you want to buy yen in 90 days' time to settle a bill, but you want to be sure of exactly how much it is going to cost you, you can buy currency at the forward exchange rate, which will be different from the spot rate.

Suppose you are a German company who owes $100,000 to an American company, due on 31 June. You may decide to buy $100,000 on 1 April at the three-month forward rate, and the money will be delivered to you on the day you must pay the American company. To see why companies do this, let's look at the participants in the foreign exchange market.

HEDGING

The German company doesn't want the uncertainty of not knowing how much its American debt will cost in three months' time on 31 June. Perhaps it suspects that the dollar will cost more in deutschmarks at that time than it does now. Suppose the spot exchange rate on 1 April is $0.50:DM1 and the three-month forward exchange rate is $0.52:DM1. If it buys at the spot rate, $100,000 will cost DM200,000, and if it buys at the three-month forward rate it will cost DM192,307 now. Suppose that when three months have elapsed, the spot rate has changed to $0.53:DM1. The company could have kept its money in deutschmarks until the last moment and paid DM188,679 for its dollars instead of DM192,307, saving DM3,628. The company is more interested in being sure what its liability will be in three months' time than in speculating, so no sleep is lost over the gamble. It has protected itself against nasty surprises by making a 'forward contract'. This is known as 'hedging'.

You may wonder why companies don't simply buy the necessary currency at the spot rate far in advance of the time that they need it. This is because companies often don't want to spend the cash in advance – the money is needed for other things.

ARBITRAGE

'Arbitrage' means being able to buy something and then selling it immediately at a higher price, thus guaranteeing a profit. The communications in the foreign exchange market are so good that arbitrage opportunites only occur very briefly and require rapid trading if they are to be taken advantage of.

The communications in the foreign exchange market are so good that arbitrage opportunites only occur very briefly and require rapid trading if they are to be taken advantage of

There are two kinds of basic arbitrage:

- Financial centre arbitrage has the effect of keeping the exchange rates in different financial centres the same. If you can get $0.50 for DM1 in Tokyo, but $0.52 for DM1 in Frankfurt, you would frantically buy as many dollars as you could in Frankfurt and sell them immediately in Tokyo, making a no-risk 4 per cent profit. Every time a chance like this comes up, people take advantage of it, which brings the rates in different places back into line.

● Cross-rate arbitrage works in the same way to keep exchange rates in different currencies compatible with each other. For example, prior to the single European currency, if you were in France wanting to buy deutschmarks and you saw that the rate for yen to the mark was Y100:DM1, the rate for yen to the franc was Y40:FF1 and that the rate for francs to the mark was FF3:DM1, you could buy DM100 for FF300, or you could buy Y12,000 for FF300, and then buy DM120 with the yen for a no-risk profit. As with financial centre arbitrage, the constant exploitation of such opportunities keeps bringing the rates into line with each other.

'Arbitrageurs' are people who engage in arbitrage, the process of looking for opportunities to make profits without risk by buying and selling currencies. They are usually banks. Another kind of arbitrage opportunity they can sometimes exploit is in the difference between interest rates in different countries combined with the difference between forward and spot rates. It is also possible to find arbitrage opportunities in mispriced futures contracts.

So, why isn't everyone an arbitrageur? The reasons are that they need very sophisticated equipment, and also that the more arbitrageurs there are, the less opportunities there are for arbitrage.

FORWARD DISCOUNTS AND PREMIUMS

If the spot rate is less than the forward rate for a currency (in other words, if you get more of the foreign currency for your money by buying at the forward rate), the currency is at a 'forward premium', as it was for our German company on 1 April. If the forward rate is less than the spot rate, the currency is at a 'forward discount'.

The discount or premium of the forward rate is most often given as a percentage of the spot rate. The formula is:

Forward premium/discount = (F − S) ÷ S x 100

(where F is the forward rate and S is the spot rate). Thus, if the forward rate is $0.52:DM1 and the spot rate is $0.50:DM1, the premium is:

$$\begin{aligned}
\text{Forward premium} &= (0.52 - 0.50) \div 0.50 \times 100 \\
&= (0.02 \div 0.50) \times 100 \\
&= 4 \text{ per cent}
\end{aligned}$$

SPECULATION

Speculators are different from arbitrageurs because they are taking a risk. They try to make money on the basis of predictions about the way the markets are moving, rather than looking for momentary mismatches between exchange rates as arbitrageurs do. Speculators who think a currency is going to cost more in the future than it does now are called 'bullish' (optimistic) about the currency, and ones who think it will cost less are called 'bearish' (pessimistic).

EXAMPLE

Suppose a speculator in, say, Hong Kong (it could be anywhere) bought $100,000 in deutschmarks at the forward rate of $0.52:DM1 on 1 April, at the same time as the German company in our example, hoping to sell the dollars back into deutschmarks at the end of June for a quick profit. This is called 'going long' on the dollar. At the end of June the spot rate is $0.53:DM1. The speculator agreed to pay DM192,307 for the dollars. Changing the dollars back into marks would produce DM188,679, so the speculator has lost DM3,628 if the dollars are exchanged.

To make the principles of foreign exchange easier to understand, we haven't taken the dealing costs into account. These are small, however (fractions of 1 per cent), so they do not prevent banks and large investors from making a profit. All this is a very different business from the 'tourist rates', where paper money actually has to be moved around physically.

The frenetic activity in foreign exchange is possible due to most of the world's countries allowing free trade in currency. This has not always been the case in the past, and if free trade in currency were to be slowed by governments at some time in the future, the markets would slow down with it.

Predicting exchange rates

As we saw on page 193, it is the trading profits or losses of countries that are the main force affecting exchange rates in the long term. However, when trying to predict exchange rates, many other factors are considered:

- **Inflation**. Countries with high inflation relative to other countries find that the prices of the goods and services that they export rise also. This leads to fewer customers for their goods, a higher amount of imports, consequent trading losses and a weakening currency.

- **Monthly and quarterly trade figures**. These tend to be far less reliable than the annual balance of payment accounts, which, as we have seen, are not very reliable themselves. Nevertheless, the foreign exchange market grasps eagerly for such interim figures as they are published, in the hope of finding clues about the future.

- **Flows of capital**. If, for example, a country is trading at a loss but is enjoying a large amount of investment from abroad, its currency may not weaken as it otherwise would.

- **Interest rates**. A country which offers a higher rate of interest than others do will often attract money from abroad in the short term. However, if investors believe that the currency is likely to become worth less, they will switch their money to a safer currency.

- **Investment abroad**. Countries whose companies are purchasing or setting up businesses overseas are generally thought to have currencies that will get stronger for a decade or more, since it will take that length of time for the companies to make their profits.

- **Money flowing into a country's stock markets** is usually a sign that the currency will be strong, at least for three years or so.

- **Productivity**. A country with a high rate of productivity and economic growth is often thought to have a strengthening currency.

- **Savings**. Populations who spend everything they earn make their currencies weaker by increasing trading losses. It is notable that economically strong countries, such as Japan and Germany, have a high rate of saving per head of population.

- **Bank intervention**. A country's central bank may buy its own currency to make it stronger, or sell it to make it weaker.

- **Confidence in policies**. Investors from outside a country will look at its political situation to assess the risks of investing there. Not many people will buy bonds, for example, from a government that looks as if it is collapsing.

- **Bull and bear markets**. As with shares, if investors think that a currency is increasing or decreasing, they will invest accordingly, creating a self-fulfilling prophecy in the short term.

- **Singular events**. Wars, commodity price hikes and other one-off occurrences will have short-term effects on exchange rates.

The effects of exchange rates on shares

It doesn't occur to most people to invest outside their own countries because they have a feeling that it is risky. In fact, the reverse may be true. If you invest in the well-regulated stock markets of nations with strong currencies, you are helping to reduce the risk by spreading it across several currencies. This is of great importance to British investors, since the natural tendency to keep their money at home will almost certainly produce lower returns, as Britain lumbers towards a future of lowered international status and industrial uncertainty. Holding high-quality shares in several countries does complicate matters, certainly, but not necessarily to such a degree that it is not worth a private investor's while to do so. The main factor affecting an international portfolio is that exchange rates will affect real profits and losses.

EXAMPLE

If you are British and make, say, a 50 per cent profit investing in a Japanese company, the profits that you will actually receive if you sell and convert the money into sterling will depend on what has happened to the sterling/yen rate in the interim.

To make the sums easy, suppose that when you invested, the yen/sterling rate was 1:1, and that in the meantime the yen has depreciated by 50 per cent against the pound. If you had invested £10,000 (e.g. Y10,000), you would now have Y15,000, but since the sterling/yen rate is now 1:2, you would only get £7,500 back. However, since the future for yen is bright, it is more likely that the yen would actually appreciate against the pound. If the sterling/yen rate were now 1:0.5, you would receive £30,000 for your Y15,000. Thus, the ability to assess correctly currency trends over periods of more than five years can add value to your returns.

This kind of bet is nowhere near as risky as the short-term gambling on quarterly or annual exchange rates that the professionals go in for. If you take a global view of investment, you should be able to develop a framework for yourself by identifying the industries in different countries that are likely to prosper, the currencies that are likely to become stronger and the political outlook in those regions. Once you have done this, you can then select individual stocks in the normal way, by assessing their p/e ratios and fundamentals.

The effects of exchange rates on bonds

When the interest rates of a country falls, the value of its bonds usually goes up. As rates are currently low throughout the world, bond markets are active. When investing in bonds from other countries, care should be taken to check credit ratings and to assess the country's record on previous defaults. It is also possible to invest in foreign bonds through managed funds. Bonds in strong currencies usually offer lower interest rates than ones in weaker currencies. By convention, 2.5 per cent is the lowest acceptable 'real' rate of interest. When the average yield of interest of international bonds is higher than this figure, bonds are thought of as being good value.

When investing in bonds internationally, you must try to choose countries where the long-term exchange rates and inflation figures are improving and buy bonds there before yield rates have adjusted to the new conditions.

The effects of exchange rates on cash

When stock markets around the world are falling, many investors sell shares and increase their bond and cash holdings. Since World War 2, the value of sterling has dropped dramatically against other currencies. If you had overcome exchange controls and had invested in a spread of currencies during this period, as some have been able to do, you would have done far better than if you had stayed in sterling exclusively.

Look for a fund that is not committed to basing itself around one particular currency

There are now a number of managed currency funds which change the proportions of the various currencies they hold according to movements in exchange rates. Ideally, such a fund should produce a greater return than holding the strongest currency throughout a particular period. Look for a fund that is not committed to basing itself around one particular currency, such as that of its home country, since this may result in a poor result if the fund does not respond to a weakening trend. Usually, though, a fund will produce its final accounts in one currency, but this does not necessarily indicate a bias. Whether you are investing in a fund or on your own, you should stick to major countries or currencies that are closely tied to them.

The special drawing right (SDR) of the IMF

The International Monetary Fund's role during the Bretton Woods era was to be the lender of last resort to its member countries, which numbered about 150. Each member pays an annual subscription to the IMF which is a fixed proportion of its GDP, and this money is used to assist countries in difficulty. The amount a country pays determines the amount it can borrow, and affects its voting rights. A country can borrow foreign currency up to its subscription quota for between three and five years. Switzerland is not a member of the IMF, but does participate in the 'Paris Club' or 'Group of Ten' countries which provide further monies for countries in trouble.

The special drawing right (SDR) was invented as a way of accounting between the IMF and central state banks. It is tied to a 'basket' of several strong currencies, and the proportions of each in the basket is fixed for five years. Member countries of the IMF can pay each other in SDRs, but they are not directly convertible into any currency, and countries may only hold limited SDR reserves. It is now possible to buy bonds denominated in SDRs. As a kind of benchmark of the strong currencies, the SDR is probably the fairest of those available.

The euro – Europe's common currency

The aim of the European Union (EU) is to create a truly united federation of Europe. This is an immensely difficult task and may well not succeed, owing to the natural rivalry between its member countries.

Economic and Monetary Union (EMU) really occurred at the end of 1998, with Euroland central banks coordinating an interest rate cut. Euroland's governor of financial policy is the European Central Bank (ECB) and the European System of Central Banks (ESCB). At the time of writing, the UK has not yet joined the monetary union.

The introduction of EMU is a very important political event affecting the whole world. Although there were attempts in the 19th century to create a kind of monetary union, EMU is different because today the main way that governments try to keep the world's economy stable is through their monetary policy. We also have democracy today of a kind that did not exist in the 19th century, and EMU is intentionally part of the political process of closer union among the member states.

Much of the public debate about the rights and wrongs of the euro is fairly useless to investors.

Much of the public debate about the rights and wrongs of the euro is fairly useless to investors. Investors need to watch what is really happening, not what politicians of all hues want us to hear. George Soros, the famous billionaire trader, made much of his fortune by spotting politicians making silly mistakes by trying to impose financial policies that could not be sustained, and betting heavily against them.

As always in investment matters, be cautious and try to understand the real picture. At the time of writing, the euro has been sinking against the dollar. Now it looks as if it might start to rise substantially – if it does, it could mean that investment money pours into Europe's stock markets and drives up shares.

Whether the euro becomes the world's second most important currency, or gets into an enormous muddle and damages the EC's economy, remains to be seen. We are watching history in the making – enjoy it!

The future of the US dollar

As Japan and Germany have rebuilt their economies after World War 2, so the US dollar has weakened. After decades of being the world's 'reserve' currency, functioning as the benchmark for all others, the dollar is losing importance. One view is that consumerism, reduced exports, the costs of wars and high living standards are all playing their part in increasing the United States' debt burden and putting its economy into decline in the long term. Others believe that the USA is going to go from strength to strength as it surges ahead of others in its adoption of the 'New Economy'.

The yen

In earlier editions of this book I was incautious enough to break my own rule against trying to predict currency movements, and expressed the view that 'the yen may well become the world's premier currency within a decade'. I was utterly wrong. Japan's financial boom of the 1980s is now seen as a 'bubble economy', and Japan's industries and financial institutions are in dire need of reform, when once they were seen as setting an example to everyone else.

Globalization

With the collapse of the USSR and the immense growth in productivity of Asia, the world is plainly entering a new era. Free-market capitalism without responsible institutions has caused problems in these regions. In 1997, a currency crisis rolled across much of Asia, throwing countries into complete financial chaos. The IMF was called in, and imposed strict economic recipes in return for loans – and became demonized for its pains. In 2000, the World Trade Organization conference in Seattle and the climate control talks at The Hague failed amid wild demonstrations by anti-globalization groups.

Globalization is happening faster than people can cope with. The present system was designed to prevent another 1930s-style depression, and it has been very successful in improving living standards in many parts of the globe. Now, it seems to have allowed local economic disasters to occur, as in Russia, where people are saying that they are worse off now than they were under Communism, or in Indonesia, where a virtual civil war erupted as the Suharto regime collapsed in the wake of the currency crisis.

Whatever the merits and faults of the floating rate system for whole nations, private investors can certainly benefit from the freedom and opportunities that it offers. Take advantage of it while you can – like all previous systems, it is unlikely to last forever. No one can be sure what will replace it. There have even been proposals for a world monetary system that would allow currencies, or linked currency blocs, to move against one another within fixed ranges. Such a system might reintroduce sweeping currency controls.

11

Lloyd's of London

Until the long-running scandal that erupted in the early 1990s, Lloyd's of London had an almost legendary status as a very special investment opportunity for the very rich. It's an institution that all investors should know something about, even if you have no intention of ever becoming involved – the Lloyd's story vividly illustrates most of the fundamental issues that affect investors, especially the importance of analyzing risk. Indeed, as one of the world's great insurance underwriters, Lloyd's main business is risk, and has been for more than 300 years.

In this chapter we will look at the procedures and mechanisms of Lloyd's market and at what went wrong when thousands of investors were faced with massive losses.

The topics are:

- *The origins of Lloyd's*
- *Lloyd's structure – the agents, Names and its governing body*
- *The syndicates – how they work*
- *The underwriters and brokers – how Lloyd's chooses what to insure*

- *Becoming a Name – how private people risked their wealth*
- *The down side – open years, excess of loss and the LMX spiral*
- *The problems of asbestos, pollution and catastrophe claims*
- *The Names' rebellion*
- *Was it worth being a Name?*

Introduction

For the last decade or so, Lloyd's of London has been much in the news following a series of financial losses and the subsequent outcry from its investors, or 'Names'. It is a unique institution. Completely unrelated to its namesake, Lloyds Bank, Lloyd's of London was, until recently, entirely financed by private individuals, who gave the guarantees necessary for it to operate the world's most flexible and innovative insurance marketplace.

Until about 1950, membership of Lloyd's was virtually exclusive to the highest echelon of male society in Britain, but since then the club has expanded to include Names of both sexes, mainly from the UK, Europe, the United States, the Commonwealth and many Islamic countries. Most Names could be described as upper class, with a generous sprinkling of celebrities, politicians and aristocrats.

Origins

Lloyd's started in the 1600s in a London coffee house run by a man called Edward Lloyd. The discoveries in the New World had introduced coffee to Europe and in the 17th century coffee houses became the meeting places of the fashionable and prosperous classes. Here, political issues were discussed, news and gossip exchanged and business transacted. At Edward Lloyd's coffee house the shipping industry congregated. Gradually, a system of maritime insurance grew up whose basic principles have remained unchanged. Until the 1880s maritime insurance was virtually the only kind of insurance available, and even today it forms a major part of Lloyd's business. The idea was simple. The owner of a ship and its cargo could be wiped out if the vessel was lost through shipwreck, piracy or being seized by a foreign power, so he insured himself against total loss by paying a sum of money (a 'premium') to a large number of wealthy people who would each guarantee to pay ('underwrite') a proportion of the cost if the ship was lost. The underwriters hoped to make a profit from the premiums, the income from which would cover the occasional loss of vessels and cargoes.

The underwriters would sit in Edward Lloyd's coffee house and wait for people to come to them to ask if they would underwrite a particular risk. If they agreed to do so, they wrote their name on a 'slip' of paper, showing what percentage of the total risk they were willing to take in return for the same percentage of the total premium paid by the person seeking insurance. Thus, a 'Name' wrote a 'line' of insurance on a 'slip' of paper, terms which are still used at Lloyd's today. Naturally, the person being insured wanted to be certain that the Names would be good for the money in the event of a claim, so Names had to prove that they had enough assets to cover possible claims, and had to agree to sell all their assets if necessary in order to meet a claim. Since several Names were underwriting each risk, they realized that they were effectively in a syndicate together. After the fiasco of the South Sea Bubble in the early 1700s, laws were passed to prevent all companies except two – London Assurance and the Royal Exchange Assurance – from offering marine insurance. The laws, however, did not prevent individuals from doing the same thing, so Lloyd's grew.

As business expanded, it became impractical for Names and customers to attend the coffee house regularly, so agents were appointed to handle the business of a number of Names, while brokers sought cover from them on behalf of their clients. By 1871 there were 18,000 Names; in this year Lloyd's was incorporated as a society of private underwriters by an Act of Parliament, but continued to operate on much the same lines as it had since the 17th century. It still does so today, with a peculiar mixture of tradition, mystique and flair for inventiveness; whether you want to insure a space station or your beard, Lloyd's is the place to seek cover.

Since Lloyd's massive losses, it has set up Equitas, a 'second Lloyds', which appears to hold all the pre-1993 liabilities. Lloyd's has changed its rules to allow businesses to become Names with limited liability, and a large number of insurance companies have joined. The number of private Names has fallen substantially with corporate capital backing now a substantial part of its market capacity.

This capacity to accept insurance premiums has risen by £1 billion in 2001, reaching £11.06 billion. Most of this growth has come from corporate members trading with limited liability. Corporate members supplied £9.09 billion in 2001, while private capital with unlimited liability was £1.96 billion in 2001. About 5 per cent of world reinsurance is placed at Lloyd's

Lloyd's structure

The rules of Lloyd's are made by the Council, with an elected committee that handles details and a chairman who is elected once a year. Self-regulation by its members has always been a cardinal principle and it was with reluctance that, following a financial scandal in 1978, a 1982 Act of Parliament gave the

Council greater powers to regulate Lloyd's. The Act allowed the governor of the Bank of England to appoint four people to the Council from outside Lloyd's, as well as a chief executive. The Act also outlawed joint ownership of insurance brokers and underwriting agencies, the intention being to prevent conflicts of interest where brokers and managing agents might be tempted not to give customers – or Names – the best deal. Thus, unlike most investment services in the UK, Lloyd's is not regulated by the Financial Services Act, although this may change.

Unlike most investment services in the UK, Lloyd's is not regulated by the Financial Services Act

THE LLOYD'S COUNCIL

From 1982 until 1992, the Council consisted of 12 working practitioners at Lloyds, eight individuals nominated by other institutions (including the four appointed by the Governor of the Bank of England) and eight individuals elected by the non-working, or 'external' Names. The Council chooses a chairman and two deputies from the 12 practitioners and another member of the Council is nominated as the chief executive and third deputy.

At the time of writing, Lloyd's is considering some form of external regulation, as part of its overhaul of regulatory activities, so its structure may change.

THE COMMITTEE

The Committee consists of twelve practitioners, or working members, who manage Lloyd's on a day-to-day basis. Several sub-committees, working parties and other bodies are answerable to the main committee.

LLOYD'S SYNDICATES

Syndicates are groups of Names on whose behalf an underwriter does business. They tend to specialize in one of four areas: marine insurance, aviation, motor and non-marine. This last category is a catch-all for all kinds of risks, from fire and theft to war risks. Every syndicate keeps its yearly accounts 'open' for three years, awaiting the majority of claims, then 'closes' the year and shares out the profits on premiums to its Names. When the year is closed, the syndicate then re-insures the policies of the year into the following year's three-year accounting period, paying a premium for that year to the syndicate, which may have changed its composition of Names. This premium is based on an assessment of the future risk of claims relating to the closed year's policies. Thus, the 1990 accounts were not closed until the end of 1992.

As we will see later in this chapter, the three-year accounting system is the reason why Names do not know about losses until some time after they have occurred. The practice of re-insuring to close a year means that new Names can find themselves liable for claims against their syndicate dating back as far as the 1940s.

MEMBER'S AGENTS

Names are introduced to Lloyd's by a member's agent. After a complicated admissions procedure (see page 219), the Name must then decide which syndicates to join. The member's agent advises on this, and charges a management fee and a commission (approximately 7.5 per cent) on the Name's net profits. The idea is that the member's agent steers the Name away from trouble, spreading the risk across several syndicates and seeking out the most profitable situations. It is possible, but unusual, for a Name to have several member's agents, in which case there must be a coordinating agent who takes an extra management fee for coordinating the Name's activities. A member's agent can be linked with a managing agent or with a Lloyd's broker, or can be entirely independent.

MANAGING AGENTS

Managing agents run the syndicates, appointing the underwriters who choose which risks to insure and paying their salaries. Part of their job is to decide the proportion of 'long-tail' and 'short-tail' business. Short-tail business is insurance on which any claims will come in quickly, and long-tail business is where claims could arise many years later. Managing agents settle claims, put part of the premiums in reserve against future claims, and pay over the rest to the member's agents, who distribute it to the Names. Managing agents receive around 0.75 per cent of the premiums and approximately 15 per cent of the profits each Name on the syndicate makes, and are not allowed to own, or be owned by, a Lloyd's broker.

UNDERWRITERS

Underwriters, who can be managing agents themselves, deal with the day-to-day business of deciding whether or not to agree to insure risks brought to them by Lloyd's brokers. They are the hot-shots of Lloyd's, sitting in teams at long desks, called 'boxes', waiting for brokers to petition them for cover. Underwriters specialize in different kinds of insurance, such as shipping or aviation. A broker comes to an underwriter's box, sits on a stool at one end of it, and is pumped for information about the client, the broker's firm, and the activities of other underwriters.

A typical day at a box might consist of 20 or more brokers coming one after the other to the underwriter, seeking all kinds of insurance and re-insurance for new and old clients from all over the world. The underwriter is often highly knowledgeable about the clients and their industries and will either make a quick decision to reject or accept requests for cover, or ask for more detailed information that must be supplied later. Lines of insurance and the claims record of customers are recorded on computer as each deal is done.

Rejections are made on various grounds. For instance, US courts tend to award very high sums to claimants, so underwriters tend to be wary of insuring risks where claims may arise in the United States. This is no reflection on the client, only on the prevailing conditions in the United States. Clients who are financially weak may be rejected on the grounds that they may go into liquidation soon and fail to pay the premiums. Clients with poor claims records, or whose industries are considered too risky, are also likely to be rejected.

THE BROKERS

Brokers must be accredited by Lloyd's in order to approach the underwriters. A broker will seek cover from insurance companies as well as Lloyd's – the bigger the risk, the more it will be spread across the whole insurance market, including Lloyd's. Brokers go to the Lloyd's building and enter the 'Room' (actually several floors) where they may have regular meetings with certain underwriters, and have made specific appointments with other ones. The underwriters are at their boxes between mid-morning and mid-afternoon. Frequently, there is a queue of brokers waiting to see them. The broker explains the kind of cover he is looking for and gives information about the client. If the underwriter agrees to a line of insurance, the slip (actually a large paper sheet folded several times) is stamped and signed by the underwriter.

The slip describes the client, the cover and the premium on its left-hand side. Below it are more details of the cover and any special conditions, together with information about the client, such as its number of employees. Below this are blank folded sections where the underwriters put their stamps and signatures. Next to their stamps, underwriters write the percentage of the total risk that they are willing to cover. The first underwriter on the slip is called the 'lead underwriter'.

The broker goes from one underwriter to another until 100 per cent of the risk is covered. The slip then forms a binding agreement. When all the broking has been done, the broker returns to the office to contact clients and complete the day's business.

THE LLOYD'S BUILDING

Lloyd's is housed in an ultra-modern building on Lime Street in the heart of the City of London. The old underwriting 'Room' now takes up four huge floors. Above them are housed the offices of the administration, including the famous

Adam Room, an 18th-century wood-panelled room designed by Robert Adam. On the ground floor, the Lutine Bell, recovered in 1859 from a sunken frigate insured by Lloyd's, is traditionally rung once for good news and twice for bad. Near to it sits a man dressed in red who calls out messages for people in the underwriting Room, and close by is an open casualty book in which the day's disasters are written with a quill pen. The Room is filled with brokers and underwriters plying their trade.

Becoming a Name

In the 1980s, you had to show evidence of personal assets worth at least £100,000 to become a Name (except for 'mini-Names' and 'working Names', at whom we will look later). In 1991, this requirement was raised to £250,000. The rules about what assets are eligible vary, but essentially they are:

- At least 60 per cent of the assets must be in stocks and shares or in gold bullion and coins (but not more than 30 per cent in either of these categories), or cash at a building society or bank, or premium bonds, life assurance policies, interests in trust funds, National Savings certificates or guarantees from banks, insurance companies or building societies.
- In the case of gold, the valuation for the means test is 70 per cent of its current market value.
- Your principal residence, antiques, jewels, livestock, private company shares, cars, boats, pictures and house contents are not accepted unless supported by a letter of credit or bank guarantee.
- The remaining 40 per cent of the assets can be in the equity of freehold property, or leasehold property having more than 50 years left in the lease and where the length of the lease and the age of the Name totals more than 100 years.

You can probably see that these rules were designed for a single purpose: to ensure that Lloyd's can convert the Name's assets to cash at the accepted value as quickly as possible should it become necessary to do so.

THE APPLICATION PROCESS

Prospective Names have to apply for membership by the end of August of the year preceding the one in which they begin underwriting, and Names resigning must do so by the same date. The paperwork must be completed by the end of November in order to start underwriting by the following January.

Prospective Names must have two sponsors who are members of Lloyd's, one who vouches for the person's character and the other who is a partner or director of the member's agency that the new Name is joining. Members' agents are allowed to pay Lloyd's members to sponsor new Names.

Once you are over these hurdles, you are then summoned to a 'Rota Committee' in the Adam Room where all the risks of being a Name are explained in grave terms. No one can truthfully say later that they did not know that they had agreed to unlimited liability.

No one can truthfully say later that they did not know that they had agreed to unlimited liability

DEPOSITS AND PREMIUM LIMITS

Once new Names are accepted, they must undertake to keep the value of their assets above the level set by Lloyd's. If the value of the assets goes down, the Name must declare the fact and either produce evidence of more assets to reach the required £250,000 minimum or withdraw from Lloyd's. The Council can check on the value of a Name's assets at any time.

The Name decides how much insurance to underwrite each year – this is called the 'premium limit'. In 1992, for example, the minimum value of premiums a Name could underwrite for was £50,000 and the maximum was £2,000,000. Having agreed a premium limit, the Name must deposit 20 per cent of the value of the limit in a 'failsafe' deposit held in trust by Lloyd's. Another 10 per cent or so must be deposited either in a reserve controlled by the member's agent or in a reserve run jointly by the member's agent and Lloyd's.

The failsafe deposit can be in the form of cash, letters of credit, shares, life policies and other liquid instruments. The interest in the deposit is either paid to the Name or deposited in the Name's personal reserves. Lloyd's rules make it difficult for the Name to withdraw capital gains on such deposits.

On 31 December every year, Lloyd's makes a solvency test on every Name, consisting of a check on the true value of the Name's reserves held at Lloyd's and by the member's agents. Often changes in the value of shares and foreign currencies bring the value of a Name's reserves below the required limit. If this happens, the Name's premium limit is reduced for the following year.

When agreeing their premium limits, Names fall into several categories:

- **Category 1** members have assets of more than £250,000 and have deposited a minimum of £25,000. Their premium limits can increase by £25,000 each year to a maximum of £2,000,000, in which case they must have deposited reserves of £600,000.

- **Category 2** members have assets between £100,000 and £250,000. This can occur when a Name's assets have decreased in value due to factors such as share fluctuations. Category 2 members can also be individuals working at Lloyd's (in other words, a perk for Lloyd's workers is a reduction in the net wealth requirement). They must deposit at least £25,000 into the failsafe and reserves, and the deposits must be at least 40 per cent of their premium limit. The allowable premium limit is between £50,000 and £600,000.
- **Category 3** members are Names whose assets have fallen below £100,000 or Lloyd's workers with assets below this figure who are allowed to become Names as a perk. Failsafes and reserves must total 50 per cent of the premium limit and the premium limit cannot be more than £190,000.
- **Category 4** members are Lloyd's workers who are not required to show any wealth at all. They must deposit at least 50 per cent of their premium limit and the limit cannot be more than £100,000.

Names who are working in the market are known as 'working Names' and those who do not have to show assets of £250,000 are called 'mini-Names'. Names who are not otherwise connected with Lloyd's are called 'external Names' or 'non-working Names'. These rules may seem very wise and cautious, but two things are obvious. First, that external Names can, contrary to what is often said, use their principal home as 60 per cent of the wealth requirement by providing a bank guarantee or letter of credit, and they can use the equity in a holiday home for the remaining 40 per cent. In the UK property boom of the 1980s you didn't have to be very wealthy at all to have the value of two houses meeting the means test. Second, the perks for working Names could be said to be provided to the detriment of external Names.

Open years

As we have seen, syndicates usually 'close' their accounts for a particular year after three years inclusive (e.g. 1992 is closed at the end of 1994), the rationale being that most claims will have been made by then. The year is re-insured to close, and any other claims that subsequently arise will be met by the re-insurers, who are the syndicate members for the following year.
If, however, a large number of claims have been made and are in dispute, the year cannot be re-insured to close and must remain open indefinitely.

Names on an open year cannot resign – they remain liable for all valid claims that may arise against the year. In such cases, it is often impossible to estimate what the total liability may be, so Names must just wait and hope, while, in the meantime, they are called upon to come up with cash sums to replenish their reserves.

Excess of loss (XOL)

In the last two decades, Lloyd's has been up against increasingly strong competition from other insurance companies, and has been losing its market share. This has led a number of underwriters, particularly newer ones, to seek profit in the field of 'excess of loss insurance', or XOL. To understand XOL, think what happens when you insure a car. You will probably find that if you agree to pay an 'excess' of, say, £100 of the cost of car repairs in case of an accident, the insurer reduces your premium; you have agreed to pay the first £100 of the claim and the insurer has agreed to pay anything above that. XOL works the same way, except that it is a deal between two insurers. The first insurer agrees with the second, the 're-insurer', to pay for, say, the first £1 million of any claim and the re-insurer agrees to pay for the rest. The re-insurer may then re-insure again with a third insurer in a similar way. This process can continue with yet more insurers.

The LMX spiral

The market in London (not just at Lloyd's) for excess of loss cover is called London Market Excess, or LMX. In the 1980s, the LMX boomed as some Lloyd's underwriters dived into it, re-insuring and re-insuring again, taking a cut of the premium and earning commissions each time. This became known as the 'LMX spiral'; it seemed good business at the time, but when a number of natural catastrophes occurred (see page 223) and re-insurers became liable, the complexity of unravelling which re-insurer would be liable for what was so great that each syndicate involved had to assume the worst and call on its Names to boost their reserves with more cash. The result of this is that, overall, Names have had to deposit much more money than necessary in their reserves while they wait for the unravelling process to finish.

Lloyd's in trouble

Despite Lloyd's hitherto grand reputation and aura of effortless success, there have been many scandals and losses during its three centuries of existence – being a Name has never really been 'money for old rope'. Lloyd's present troubles, which may yet be life-threatening, have a number of causes, which we will examine here.

THE SINS OF THE FATHERS

As the world enters a new millennium, it is undergoing a 'paradigm shift', a profound change in its understanding of the effects of industrialization. Gone is the boundless faith in progress, science and the inevitability of economic growth. It is now plain that many industrial practices have caused the world enormous harm, and that they cannot be allowed to continue unchecked. The insurance business is sensitive to this change; as the claims pour in, insurance companies wake up to the trends behind them.

Asbestos

Asbestos is a general name for a number of naturally occurring mineral fibres that are highly resistant to heat. Between about 1870 and 1960 it was used in an enormous variety of products, more than 3,000 of them, such as building materials, fire-resistant fabrics, electrical equipment, motor parts and insulation materials. In World War 2 thousands of workers laboured in an atmosphere filled with asbestos dust fitting out warships.

Like many other minerals, asbestos has a nasty characteristic: quite a brief exposure to it can cause fatal lung diseases that may not manifest themselves for 50 years or more. It is often said that the dangers of asbestos were not known – not known by whom? They were certainly known, at least in part, in Britain in 1931, when the Asbestos Industry Regulations set out rules for asbestos dust extraction in the workplace. They were known by the US Navy in 1943, when it issued a pamphlet laying down minimum safety standards for working with asbestos. Nevertheless, the world went on using asbestos, and in the first half of the 20th century companies were able to obtain general liability insurance that covered possible claims against industrial disease.

Although insurance companies have long ago given up offering general liability cover, many of the old policies are still valid. By the late 1970s, a huge series of asbestosis claims had begun in the United States, and courts were making vast awards to sufferers. Lloyd's was hit badly.

Underwriters at Lloyd's had re-insured excess of loss cover against general liability policies dating back decades. As the US courts made awards against employers, they in turn sought to claim on their policies. Since so many Lloyd's underwriters had re-insured their excess of loss cover with the small number of syndicates who had been willing to take the business, the huge burden of liabilities fell mainly on them. Richard Outhwaite, an underwriter who had re-insured only 32 contracts covering asbestos risk in 1982, on behalf of a syndicate numbered 317/661, had to announce in 1985 that the 1982 year could not be closed due to the large number of asbestos claims coming in.

The syndicate's 1982 year was still open in 1992, with more claims arriving, resulting in frequent calls for more funds from its Names, each Name paying amounts proportionate to the premium limit for the 1982 year. Many of the Names were celebrities; among them were former British Prime Minister Ted Heath, golfer Tony Jacklin and tycoons John Ritblat and Robert Maxwell. Nine hundred and eighty-seven of the Names went to court, eventually receiving a settlement in 1992. Another 627 Names on the syndicate, who didn't go to court and were now time-barred from doing so, got nothing. Claims are expected to continue for some time – the average potential loss per Name has been estimated at £625,000.

Pollution

Some say that the worst is over for asbestos claims, but a new monster is on the insurance horizon. Governments want to do something about industrial pollution and most have adopted the view that the polluter should pay. Once again, the movement started in the United States, where the Carter administration introduced the Comprehensive Response Compensation and Liability Act (CERCLA), in 1980. Under CERCLA, a 'Superfund' was formed, consisting of a levy on industries, principally chemicals and oil, which is administered by the Environmental Protection Agency (EPA). The Superfund brief is to clean up polluted sites, ruthlessly pursuing any company that has been involved for the cost. Lloyd's syndicates that have re-insured old general liability policies are in the firing line, and with estimates of the cost of the clean-up running as high as $750 billion, they have become enmeshed in a web of complex litigation.

Insurers have sought to establish in the US courts that they are not liable; if they win, they can walk away from the problem, leaving the companies to slug it out with the EPA alone. The problem has become a 'lawyer's party' – the EPA has spent most of its budget so far on litigation. Every US State court can take its own view on whether insurers are liable, and what for. With up to $750 billion at stake, it is worth everybody's while to spend hugely on legal costs – the overall results will not be known for several years as the cases creep their way up towards Supreme Court appeals.

While Lloyd's insurers fight to escape liability in the United States, they have also been calling on their Names to produce cash so that reserves can be built up in case they lose. Sharpened by their experience in fighting asbestos claims, Lloyd's seems to be in with a chance of surviving the assaults of the Superfund, but in the meantime Names are forced to increase their reserves.

Where the United States leads, others follow. GATT, the World Bank and the EU are all making moves to go 'green'. The political ramifications are enormous and many governments would rather chase corporations for the clean-up costs than introduce green taxes. The insurance industry is in for a hard time and many Names may suffer.

CATASTROPHES

Since 1987 there have been a series of natural disasters and accidents that have wreaked havoc at Lloyd's. In that year the first hurricane to strike Britain in 200 years devastated the south of England, costing Lloyd's hundreds of millions of pounds. Added to this, the so-called 'Black Monday' of October 1987, when stock markets around the world crashed, greatly reduced the value of many Names' assets, compounding their difficulties.

There were 19 other serious accidents and natural disasters in 1988, costing the whole London insurance market around £1 billion. The Piper Alpha accident, where an oil rig exploded, costing 167 lives, accounted for more than half of this figure. The complexity of the LMX spiral forced Lloyd's syndicates to build reserves to £12 billion until the true liability, around £370 million, could be allocated. Piper Alpha settlements were delayed by the shock experienced by survivors of the disaster. Also in 1988, a Pan-Am jet exploded over Lockerbie in Scotland, resulting in claims totalling £100 million. In September 1989, Hurricane Hugo caused enormous damage across the Caribbean and Carolinas. The next month, there was an earthquake in San Francisco. In December there was another one in Australia. In the spring of the same year, 95 people died in the Hillsborough football stadium; in August, 51 people were killed at a party on the River Thames when the *Marchioness* was rammed by a barge; while in March an oil tanker, the *Exxon Valdez*, polluted the coast of Alaska.

It was no better in 1990. Another hurricane hit England, followed by another in Continental Europe. The total cost is estimated at £8 billion. When Iraq invaded Kuwait, Lloyd's had to pay a large part of the $300 million claim for lost Kuwaiti planes. In the wake of these losses, thousands of Names resigned from Lloyd's, while only hundreds have been signed.

THE NAMES' REBELLION

The number of Names at Lloyd's has fallen dramatically since 1988, when there were about 32,000 of them. Over 15,000 Names, a majority of the remaining members, are stuck on one or more open years. They are drawn from all walks of life, including some 50 British Members of Parliament, former prime ministers and Cabinet ministers, celebrities, foreign businesspeople, bankers, farmers, professionals and entrepreneurs. Lloyd's is a pillar of the establishment and being a Name has high social status.

As the non-working Names began to receive calls for tens, in some cases hundreds, of thousands of pounds to cover losses and build reserves, they began to ask questions. A huge proportion of the losses were centred on a few syndicates, which were made up of mainly external Names, many of whom were new. The older syndicates at Lloyd's had been harder to get on to, since they were generally already fully subscribed. In the boom of the 1980s, Names were confident of profits, but when the losses began, many of them found themselves unable to meet their cash calls from Lloyd's. Many turned to the law, issuing writs against their member's agents and managing agents, alleging negligence. Others turned to the Hardship Committee, set up by Lloyd's to help Names raise the necessary money. The Committee requires Names to agree to keep the details of their help secret, and not to sue Lloyd's. The Committee does not pay Names' debts for them, but requires that applicants fill out a highly detailed questionnaire about their, and their spouses', financial circumstances, after which it may arrange attachments to Names' salaries, charges on their houses and so on as ways of meeting cash calls. The deal is generally that the Name must pay 25 per cent of the debt up front and make an agreement to pay the rest over a long period – in some cases, a lifetime. Most of the hardship cases are older people, with low premium limits and few means. The Committee agrees not to dispossess these individuals of their only home, especially if it is modest and they have no other assets.

Despite it being 'bad form', many external Names ignored official appeals for cooperation and decided to fight it out. Committees of external Names banded together to sue the 'insiders' of Lloyd's, alleging that they had been misled and badly advised by their agents. In the United States and Canada, many Names were able to avoid their obligations on legal technicalities, and bit back – Lloyd's found itself under investigation by the FBI over alleged violations of the notorious RICO anti-racketeering laws, while Names struggled to freeze Lloyd's Names' deposits held in North America to prevent them being drawn on by Lloyd's.

External Names complained of the lack of information given them by Lloyd's, the activities of touts who earned commissions from the recruitment of new Names, and that some agents had advised Names not to resign, resulting in further losses. There is a feeling that many underwriters and agents were neither bright, efficient, nor honest, and that there was a general attitude among insiders that external Names are punters who can be taken advantage of. Following the Outhwaite settlement, Lloyd's has become a little more cooperative towards external Names and a process of reform of its systems is underway. Whether or not Lloyd's will survive in the long term remains to be seen. As government policies and the insurance markets change, conditions may well improve. For the hundreds of ruined Names, though, this is small consolation.

In 1996, Lloyd's made Names a settlement offer of £3.1 billion, called 'Reconstruction & Renewal' (R&R). Names were required to pay £1.4 billion in losses, forego £1.5 billion in litigation awards and agree to give up all present and future litigation. In September 1996, Lloyd's reported that 82 per cent of 34,000 Names had accepted unconditionally.

There is a feeling that many underwriters and agents were neither bright, efficient, nor honest

The battle rages on, however, as non-accepting Names, led by Sir William Jaffray, continue to fight Lloyd's through the courts, in the UK and elsewhere.

Was it worth being a Name?

The row at Lloyd's has been ugly, as you might expect when a large number of people have been bankrupted. But how could they have let themselves become so exposed in the first place? Being a Name is not really an investment in the normal sense of the term. Short of becoming a fugitive, a Name stands to lose everything, not just the deposit, because of the unlimited liability. In contrast, if you invested in shares, all you can lose is what you paid for the shares.

Being a Name has had quite a social cachet, which perhaps blinded some Names to the nature of the arrangement. Some Names have claimed that when they joined they were given the impression by certain individuals that the unlimited liability issue was not serious and that, in some vague way, everything would always be all right. Many Names have been interviewed in television documentaries, and some have plainly not been people with much business sense, or the capacity to really understand the nature of the risk they were taking.

Today, with much of the capital capacity supplied by limited-liability corporations that can cease trading at any time, the whole concept of unlimited liability looks deeply flawed – a relic, perhaps, of a bygone, more honourable, age.

12

Fraud, sharp practice and the regulatory bodies

In this chapter we examine:

- *The UK regulators – a new, improved system*

- *The Securities and Exchange Commission (SEC) in the United States*

- *The stopping of an unauthorized derivatives trader*

- *Two perennial scams: The hard sell and conning the law breakers*
- *A Barcelona-based investment business*
- *Pensions 'mis-selling'*
- *Insider trading in the 1980s – Milken, Boesky and Levine*

Introduction

There is a big difference between blue-collar crime and white-collar crime. White-collar criminals are far less likely to be caught and, when they are, they don't usually go to jail for very long. This is true in most countries: the more capitalist a country is, the more it seems to be true.

It is sometimes argued that financial fraudsters are an unavoidable evil in a free market, and that it is so difficult to catch them that the degree of supervision necessary would stifle business activity. While this may be true, it is also true that many professionals in the financial world spend their lives trying to work out ways of circumventing the rules, and for such people it becomes quite difficult to distinguish between theft and 'good business'.

As private investors, we must face reality: the different financial centres of the world have different methods of trying to keep the market fair, and they enforce them with varying degrees of severity. Some markets are fairer than others, but none of them offer a 100 per cent guarantee that you won't be ripped off. If you buy something in a shop and it turns out to be faulty or shoddy, it is usually possible to get redress quite quickly, but once you have handed money over for investment, it can be an expensive process trying to get it back, and you cannot often be confident of success.

Guerrilla investors have to look out for themselves. Despite the valiant efforts of the regulators (discussed below), there is always a chance that you'll come up against a crook. While anyone may be unlucky enough to be cheated, however careful he or she is, often it is the investors' own weaknesses that make them vulnerable. Here are a few of the things that seem to increase your chances of being ripped off:

Often it is the investors' own weaknesses that make them vulnerable

- Believing in a scheme because it has been discussed positively on a radio programme for small investors (as the disastrous Barlow Clowes firm was).
- Trusting people just because they are 'posh' (as some disgruntled Names claimed about Lloyd's of London).
- Trusting people just because they are not 'posh'.
- Investing in schemes you haven't thoroughly checked out.
- Doing something illegal that involves trusting someone you don't know.
- Investing for ideological reasons.
- Investing to keep up with the Joneses.
- Failing to study the deal in the context of world markets.

- Believing that the regulators will always protect you.
- Having faith in booms.
- Putting all your eggs in one basket.
- Being too eager to get rich quick.
- Being seduced by schemes that involve a lot of trading.
- Getting into schemes that you haven't first made sure you can get out of.

This may all sound rather negative but it isn't really. The point is simply that it is your money and you need to take responsibility for your actions. Self-defence is always better than running to the regulators after something goes wrong.

The regulators

THE FINANCIAL SERVICES AUTHORITY (FSA)

Since the last edition of this book, the UK's regulatory system has been overhauled and it looks as though at last we will have a regulator that is competent, fair and fully informed. What's more, we will now have unified regulation – hitherto, the bitty nature of regulation allowed all kinds of bad practices to flourish.

The new reform of financial services regulation in the UK was announced by the Chancellor of the Exchequer on 20 May 1997. Banking supervision and investment services regulation are being merged into the Securities and Investments Board (SIB) and the SIB has formally changed its name to the Financial Services Authority (FSA). The Financial Services and Markets Act transfers the responsibilities of a number of other organizations to the FSA:

- Building Societies Commission
- Friendly Societies Commission
- Investment Management Regulatory Organisation (IMRO)
- Personal Investment Authority (PIA)
- Register of Friendly Societies
- Securities and Futures Authority (SFA).

The FSA will also regulate aspects of mortgage lending.

THE SECURITIES AND EXCHANGE COMMISSION (SEC)

The Securities and Exchange Commission in the United States regulates the US stock markets and has more teeth. It may be a matter of taste, but the SEC's rigorous and determined approach to catching and disgracing the rule-breakers contrasts strongly with the less direct approach of the British. The role of the SEC in cracking high-level insider dealing in the 1980s is discussed later in this chapter.

The hard sell

The scope that commodities offered a fraudster was considerable in the past. Here's one way investors have regularly been fleeced over the years.

You are telephoned by a member of a telephone sales team working from a carefully written script. You are asked if you want to invest in the commodities market, and the benefits are explained to you. If you seem interested, you are asked how much you want to invest. The salesperson then tells you that he or she will call you back if a good investment opportunity comes up. An hour or two later you get another call – the firm's analysts have identified a 'positive buy signal' in some commodity. If you don't want to buy, the salesperson passes you over to a 'chief analyst' who explains everything to you, frequently in domineering or patronizing tones. You are pressurized to come up with a cheque. If you resist, the salesperson lets you go.

On the same day, you get another call; sadly, the opportunity has gone – you would have made a fortune already if you'd invested on margin. Fortunately, there is another 'positive buy signal' in some other commodity and you are pressurized into coming up with some money, which may be collected by a motorcycle messenger. If you part with your money, you receive an agreement form to sign, containing clauses that protect the broker against your future ire.

Your money really does go into the commodity, minus some hefty commissions; if you make a paper profit you are encouraged to let the broker keep trading for you, and if you make a loss, the broker asks you for more money to keep the contract open. The fraud is in the fact that the broker is decidedly not making every effort to find you a good deal – he couldn't care less what happens to your investment, as long as he gets some commission. Proving such a fraud in court is extremely difficult indeed.

This hoary sales technique is well known in all fields of business – it is called the 'hard sell'. It means bullying people into buying overpriced goods and it pops up anywhere that is under-regulated. The commodities market in the UK has been tightened up so the hard sell probably won't be tried again, but watch out for it in other areas. Anyone who promises miracles should be regarded with suspicion – if it sounds too good to be true, it probably is too good to be true. If someone is desperate to get you to invest in something, offer to lend them the money in return for cast-iron security of greater value to which you can get good title. Usually this is enough to make the promoter evaporate, but if it is not, you may end up with a bargain house or shareholding. This of course, is a sound method of banking!

If it sounds too good to be true, it probably is too good to be true

AN UNAUTHORIZED DERIVATIVES TRADER IS STOPPED

In mid-2000, the FSA successfully prosecuted John Dudley, who had been operating an unauthorized investment business. Dudley agreed to pay £170,500 in restitution to cover investors' losses, and £20,000 towards the FSA's costs.

From 1997, Dudley had been giving investment advice and arranging deals in futures and options contracts. The Court declared that he had recklessly made 'statements, promises or forecasts' that were misleading. Fifteen investors were named who had lost about 80 per cent of their invested money.

Conning the law breakers

Here's a fraud that has been perpetrated on investors from continental Europe:

Like many successful European businesspeople, you have a substantial sum of money that you have not declared to your tax authority. A compatriot approaches you, telling you of the wonderful investment opportunities in London-based options. If you agree to invest, your money is passed though a chain of companies and an account is opened for you in London. Every time a commodity is purchased for you, the price you pay is, say, more than double the price actually paid. After some time, the fraudsters disappear with the money. Many Europeans are unaware of the ease and cheapness with which companies can be formed in the UK, and tend to assume that limited companies are as well regulated as they are in their own countries.

This is an example of how people who try to evade tax become vulnerable to fraud. Strangely, people like this never seem to check out the schemes they invest in very carefully.

A BARCELONA-BASED INVESTMENT BUSINESS

Again in 2000, Barcelona-based Fraser Lindhardt & Webb plc, incorporated in the Seychelles and trading as Trident Market Advisers, was ordered to stop carrying on investment business in breach of the Financial Services Act 1986 and its assets were frozen. These were interim injunctions pending a trial.

Trident sold share dealing and investment advice services aimed at UK investors. It sought business by mailing shareholders in a quoted company (which is publicly available information). The mailing offered an analyst's report on the relevant quoted company, and people who replied received a call from Trident offering its services.

The FSA allege that the company did not obtain approval for its investment advertisements and was not able to rely on the 'overseas persons exemption' in the Financial Services Act. It also alleges that Trident made misleading 'statements, promises or forecasts'.

If you want to check whether a firm is authorized in the UK, you can check the FSA's website at *www.fsa.gov.uk*.

Pensions mis-selling

If you are employed (not self-employed) and your employer offers a pension scheme, it is usually a better choice than taking out a personal pension. Back in the bad old days, people who were not eligible for an employer's pension scheme had no adequate pension option, so in the 1980s the personal pension was introduced to help them. A predictable sequence of unsavoury events followed (people did predict it, and people did complain about it at the time, but nothing was done until much later). Between 29 April 1988 and 30 June 1994, a number of firms sold pensions to people who would have been better off staying in, or joining, their employer's scheme. This is now euphemistically defined as mis-selling. The firms, and their eager-beaver young salespeople, many of whom were new to financial services, made profits by doing this.

Firms that mis-sold have been ordered to contact everyone who took out personal pensions between these dates who might be affected. They have to put things right if they broke the rules then in force and the customer has suffered a loss in consequence.

The mis-selling review started at the end of 1994. A vast number of cases had to be checked and some were rightly given a higher priority because, for instance, they were people who had already retired or were about to retire.

At the time of writing, the firms are still checking younger people's cases. It has only taken over five years to get there! If you purchased a personal pension during the relevant period, you should have been contacted at least once by the relevant firm to ask if you wanted to have your case reviewed. A deadline of 31 March 2000 was given for review requests. You still may have some redress if you missed this date. The first place to check for further information is the FSA's website at *www.fsa.gov.uk*.

To prevent abuses in this kind of case, the law says that you must do all you can to reduce the size of any loss you have suffered if you want some redress. The FSA has suggested that joining or rejoining your current employer's scheme, if you can, is a way to reduce the loss.

BAD FOR THE HEALTH?

In his excellent book about genetics, *Genome* (Fourth Estate, 1999), Matt Ridley writes about heart disease as a symptom of lack of control in an individual's life and remarks that:

> *'It explains why unemployment and welfare dependency are so good at making people ill. No alpha-male monkey was ever such an intransigent and implacable controller of subordinates' lives as the social services of the state are of people dependent on welfare.'*

Anyone who has ever been on the dole knows how true this is. I would add dependency on the state and state-protected financial institutions for your pension to his list. Giving up control is bad for your health as well as for your wallet! A few years ago, when I wrote the first edition of this book, the idea that surrendering control was a bad idea was a wild heresy. In those days, 'they' knew best, and 'they' would make everything all right. Now, we know better, and the financial press is making a good living ferreting out wickedness, even where it doesn't exist. Consumer power is in fashion and everyone is posing as a defender of people's rights. The trend is welcome, but watch out – giving up control to someone who says they will protect you against the people to whom you gave up control earlier is simply changing one master for another. Guerrilla investors of the world, throw off your chains!

Insider trading in the 1980s – Michael Milken, Ivan Boesky and Dennis Levine

Boom times are good times for fraudsters as well as for the rest of us, and a series of dramatic prosecutions on Wall Street in the late 1980s brought to light well-organized wrongdoing on a massive scale. In 1986, Dennis Levine, an investment banker of limited ability who was a director of Drexel Burnham Lambert Inc., a highly successful New York stockbroking firm, was arrested on charges of insider trading.

Levine had indeed been trading on inside information, purchasing shares in companies just before a takeover bid sent their value rocketing. This was done through an account at the Swiss Bank Leu in the Bahamas, which the SEC was able to pressurize into revealing details of its client after an anonymous tip-off led them there. Levine was eventually sentenced to two years in prison, paying over nearly $12 million in illegal profits to the SEC, but not before he revealed the names of a group of individuals employed within different companies on Wall Street with whom he had swapped privileged information over several years. One of the names was startling – Ivan Boesky.

Ivan Boesky was an 'arbitrageur', a business that was originally to trade on the price differences of shares being sold on more than one stock market, but had become a high-risk, daring game of buying heavily into companies in the hope that they would be taken over. Boesky seemed to have a magic touch. He had accumulated net assets of over $130 million through the control of his arbitrage fund, through an apparently miraculous ability to anticipate takeover bids before they were announced. The truth was more prosaic: he had become deeply involved in illegal schemes with another powerful figure of the period, Michael Milken, the 'junk bond king'.

Michael Milken had become interested in 'junk bonds' while still at university. Junk bonds are corporate bonds that are considered too risky for a rating by the two main rating systems, Moody's and Standard and Poor's. When Milken started out in Wall Street in the 1970s, junk bonds were in bad odour, but through his high degree of technical ability he began to persuade investors that these bonds, which offered higher rates of interest than normal, would outperform the blue chips. By 1977 Milken was in control of nearly a quarter of the junk bond market, enabling him to improve the bonds' liquidity by acting as a market maker. He promised his clients that he would buy back bonds when they wanted to sell them; these he was able to pass on to other investors at a wide profit margin. Milken worked for Drexel, a Wall Street firm, but was able to operate semi-independently by locating his offices in his native California. Drexel had an investment banking department and Milken soon saw the opportunity to earn huge advisory fees for the firm by helping client companies raise finance through the issuing of junk bonds, a market that he increasingly controlled.

Although Dennis Levine eventually got a job at Drexel, his connection with Milken was tenuous. While still very junior, Levine had decided to develop a network of contacts throughout Wall Street with whom he could exchange inside information. A spell in Paris alerted him to European private banking methods and on his return to the United States he was able to put his plan into action. Curiously, Levine never mastered the mathematical skills necessary for the mergers and acquisitions field in which he now worked. Dominating his associates, he began to trade on his own account through his secret bank account in the Bahamas, purchasing shares in US companies that he expected to shoot up. Occasionally, he was even able to persuade his cronies to let him into their offices after hours so he could search files for confidential information. Not content with his private profits, Levine also used the information at work, telling his bosses that they should offer their investment banking services to companies that he knew were soon to be the subject of takeover bids, and claiming that he had acquired these insights through careful financial analysis. Once at Drexel, Levine desperately tried to ingratiate himself with Boesky by feeding him inside information and asking for nothing in return. In fact Boesky, by this time deeply involved in illegal activities himself, reciprocated with useful information of his own.

When Ronald Reagan became president in 1980, the financial community received clear signals that there would be little government interference during Reagan's term of office. As the markets freed up, the takeover field boomed. In 1981 Boesky was able to double his firm's capital, perfectly legally, by buying shares in Conoco, an oil company, during a bidding war. He earned some $40 million on the deal by using borrowed money, or 'leverage'. In 1982 he attempted to repeat this coup by taking a huge position in Cities Services in similar circumstances. This time the deal collapsed and Boesky narrowly escaped insolvency through conducting a complicated exchange of options with a Wall Street associate. Two weeks later, another bid for the company caused the shares to rise again, and Boesky was able to cut his losses and get out.

This painful experience appears to have prompted Boesky to take his first serious steps into illegality. Determined that he would never again take such a risk, Boesky approached an investment banker, Martin Siegel, offering cash payments in return for advance information on takeover bids. An additional benefit to Siegel was that Boesky's arbitrage activity would help to 'soften up' target companies, which would help Siegel's clients launch their bids.

Boesky wanted to become more involved in leveraged buy-outs but he needed more capital. Gaining control of Vagabond, a company partly inherited by his wife that owned the Beverly Hills Hotel, Boesky renamed it Northview Corporation and raised $100 million by issuing junk bonds through Drexel. Drexel took massive fees and a large number of warrants to buy Northview shares. Other deals with Drexel followed. In 1983 a corporate raider named Victor Posner, a client of Drexel, was in difficulties. He had signed an agreement not to increase his holding in the Fischbach Corporation, a building concern, which he had attempted to merge with one of his own companies. Milken asked Boesky to buy shares in Fischbach, guaranteeing him against any losses. When Boesky bought over 10 per cent of the company, he filed a statutory disclosure form with the SEC, the '13-D', giving false information. This action freed Posner from his obligations and allowed him to continue his attempts to take over Fischbach. The '13-D' form is meant to protect stock market investors since it involves the public revelation of the buying of large stakes in a company, and the purchaser is supposed to disclose his or her intentions and associations with regard to takeovers.

Milken continued his contact with Boesky. Soon he asked him to buy into Diamond Shamrock on the understanding that they would secretly share any profits. Boesky did so, but took large losses which Milken had guaranteed. By 1985, however, Milken had paid back Boesky for all his losses. Both men were setting their sights higher than ever before. While Boesky was able to control his own staff by a 'divide and rule' policy, Milken ensured loyalty by paying his employees huge bonuses. 'I think greed is healthy,' Boesky told an audience of students at the University of Southern California's business school, a phrase that was much used by commentators to symbolize the mood of the 1980s. He even wrote a book, *Merger Mania*, a detailed exposition of the technical aspects of arbitrage which gave no hint of his cavalier attitudes to the law.

Milken began to use his network of junk-bond-buying clients, who by now included savings and loan and insurance companies, as a pool of finance with which to exploit the craze for leveraged buy-outs and mergers. Many companies that hoped to become 'raiders' had no hope of raising the requisite capital without Milken's junk bond skills. Every year Milken presided over a conference in Beverly Hills, dubbed 'the Predator's Ball', at which he waxed lyrical on the joys of junk bond financing to an audience of institutions, clients and illustrious financiers, such as Sir James Goldsmith and Rupert Murdoch. Since Milken now dominated the junk bond market, he was able to buy back bonds from clients of Drexel, who were not in a position to assess their true value, then sell them on to Ivan Boesky; Boesky would sell the bonds back to Drexel at a large profit, and Drexel was able to sell the bonds to other customers at still higher prices.

When the founder of CNN, Ted Turner, came to Milken for help in financing a takeover bid for MGM/United Artists, the film company, also a client of Drexel, Milken asked Boesky to buy MGM shares, creating the illusion that the company was already the subject of a bid, which helped to persuade junk bond purchasers that MGM bonds were worth buying. Boesky made a profit of $3 million, sharing it with Milken, while Drexel earned some $66 million in financing fees from Turner. By this time Boesky and Milken had become dependent on one another, but Milken was gaining the upper hand, as it was he who supplied all the information. Boesky was becoming Milken's tool.

Milken helped Boesky to raise a vast amount of capital for an arbitrage fund, insisting that Boesky pay over large amounts of money now due from their illegal activities before the deal was closed. In his eagerness to get the fund off the ground, Boesky paid Milken $5.3 million that he was unable to explain to his accountants until Milken supplied an invoice after the fact. This was one of the slips that forced Boesky into a corner when he finally came under suspicion from the SEC.

When Levine was arrested in 1986, Boesky and Milken met to discuss how to avoid the attention of the SEC. Agreeing to tread carefully in the future, Boesky returned to New York to instruct his book-keeper to destroy records of illegal transactions. In August, Boesky was served with a subpoena by the SEC, demanding records and his testimony; he came clean with his own lawyers, describing the insider trading, tax frauds, manipulation of the market and false statements he had made in concert with Milken. Following negotiations, he signed a 'plea bargain' with the US Justice Department, agreeing to plead guilty on a single count of conspiracy to commit securities fraud, to pay the SEC $100 million, and to cooperate fully with the investigation. To safeguard the $100 million, and to avoid chaos in the markets, the SEC allowed Boesky to begin selling off his share portfolio. Boesky agreed to telephone other market players in an attempt to incriminate them, and had a secretly recorded meeting with Milken in which he engaged in a discussion on how to avoid detection. In November, Boesky was arrested and charged.

In 1987 Levine was sent to prison, paying $11.6 million to the SEC and a fine of $362,000. Released in 1988, he started a firm offering financial advice and still appears to be affluent. Following the 'Black Monday' October stock market crash, Milken fought tirelessly to keep the junk bond market alive, despite being under investigation, along with his employer, Drexel. Boesky was sentenced to three years in prison in December 1987, but was released after two years. He still remains wealthy. Milken mounted a costly and spirited defence, but when other associates signed plea bargains he was abandoned by Drexel. In 1990 Drexel finally collapsed and Milken was brought to trial, eventually being sentenced to ten years in prison.

Milken is now at large and is fast becoming a respected figure in some financial quarters, not entirely without reason. He did, after all, brilliantly transform the bond industry, and he is a technical master in his own field. Financial professionals often say that he was punished while many others who committed similar, or worse, deeds, went scot-free. This is no doubt true. The world of finance attracts the greedy in the same way as the entertainment world attracts the vain; it goes with the territory.

The world of finance attracts the greedy in the same way as the entertainment world attracts the vain

If there is a conclusion to draw from this tortuous story, it is surely that although the crooks may have their wings clipped eventually, it can take a very long time for regulators to catch up with them. Cheating in the markets is not a victimless crime – it is stealing from the millions of ordinary people who save through the institutions, and from the private investors struggling to understand the reasons for price movements.

13

spreading assets across countries
tax havens
offshore trusts and companies – are they worth it?
dual nationality for guerrillas
working abroad
banking offshore

Overseas investment

Active overseas and 'offshore' investment is one of the best ways both to increase your assets and to protect them. In fact, overseas investment becomes almost a necessity as an individual's wealth increases. If your net worth is less than £200,000, active overseas investment is probably not for you, yet, although working abroad for a few years can be a way of accumulating capital faster, if you are working in a low-tax jursidiction.

In this chapter we will look at the following:

- *Why people invest overseas*
- *Tax havens, what they are and how they work*
- *Offshore trusts and corporations*
- *How to avoid the sharks*
- *Working abroad*
- *Banking offshore*

Spreading assets across countries

Once you are in possession of a large amount of capital, your thoughts inevitably turn to how to keep it safe from all the unrelenting forces that are continually trying to take bites out of it. The world looks different to the wealthy; they are much more interested in international political and economic patterns than most people, since these have a bearing on the future of their money. Obviously, it is vital to be as well informed as possible, but before we look at the benefits of moving money around the world, we should consider the reservations that many people have about taking a step outside the conventions of their own country. People often think that there is something wrong with investing abroad, but there is nothing necessarily odd or improper about doing so – in fact, it is an essential part of the global economy.

Unlike continental Europe, where centuries of wars, revolutions and expropriations have made people wary of their own countries, in the UK and the United States the popular view is that one is better off keeping one's money at home. This perception is sustained by a variety of commercial and political lobbies in whose interests it is that the public continue to think this. Most countries want to keep their citizens' money where they can control it – inside their own borders. Sometimes laws are passed that prescribe dire penalties, even death, for individuals holding investments outside their own borders. When the situation is that bad, citizens are often not allowed to leave their own countries, except with the greatest difficulty; they must resort to drastic measures to remove themselves and their money to freer places, often running the risk of reprisals against their relatives and friends whom they leave behind. Many desirable countries will only let in a few people, often basing their immigration policy on the amount of money the immigrant has. Latin America, Asia and the Middle East abound in regimes that limit the amount of money their nationals can take abroad, and the wealthy rack their brains to find ways of getting money out. Even clean, civilized Sweden is the enemy of the rich, with its draconian tax laws, and many wealthy Swedes have found it necessary to leave permanently.

The reason why people take their money abroad is generally to protect it, rather than out of greed for more

Most people, perhaps, would like to keep their money at home, all things being equal. The reason why people take their money abroad is generally to protect it, rather than out of greed for more: having everything in one place makes it vulnerable, as history has proved over and over again.

Tax havens

A tax haven is simply a country or territory that has low taxes. Some countries have made being a tax haven their main business, going out of their way to attract companies and private investors from other countries by developing sophisticated financial services combined with taxes that are deliberately set at rates well below those in the investors' countries of origin. Many of the world's largest companies and banks use tax havens as a matter of course, often basing their headquarters in them. As well as saving tax, this can also give the advantage of having part, or all, of the business outside the jurisdiction of bigger, more tax-hungry governments.

The important thing to remember about tax havens is that they are vulnerable to change. Simply putting your money in a tax haven and forgetting about it is unwise; you have to keep on top of developments that may affect your investments. Each tax haven has different laws and different prospects, and all are vulnerable to pressure from foreign governments. To make a tax haven work for you, you generally have to be resident there, or to form a company based there. This doesn't mean that you have to live there all the time – you can usually qualify by simply renting a property on a long lease. Holding an investment portfolio through a bank or trustee in a tax haven, and keeping the physical securities in another country, gives you the benefits of low or no taxes and freedom from any future currency controls, and protects you from the dangers of expropriation. Thus, since your deal-making and income-earning abilities are likely to be confined to a higher tax country, the best time to make the move is when you can afford to live off your investment income indefinitely – hence the large numbers of retired people in tax havens. Tax havens offer some opportunities to people who are still trying to accumulate capital, but it is an expensive system and can be difficult legally, especially if you find that you have to return home permanently at some point.

If you are intrigued by tax havens and want to investigate them further, it is worth visiting them in person. Detailed information is easier and cheaper to get on the spot rather than going to consultants in other countries, and many schemes and wrinkles cannot be advertised in the countries where they are of most interest. Remember that many countries don't tax money held abroad unless it is 'repatriated', so if you spend income from your overseas assets abroad you may not need to move to a tax haven.

THE TAX HAVENS OF EUROPE

You may wonder why it is that the EU countries allow such a variety of tax havens, almost like pirate strongholds, to exist on their doorsteps. When I put this question to an eminent international tax lawyer, he replied that 'the politicians and big businessmen of Europe are corrupt and they have to have somewhere to put their money'. While this may be so, it would seem wiser for anyone resident in Europe to take their money further afield to the havens of the Americas, well away from any possible EU legislation in the future, and to regard the European tax havens as halfway houses for specific operations. In the same way, North American investors may be wiser to keep their money in the European tax havens rather than in the Caribbean.

The UK

Curiously, the UK is technically a tax haven – but not if you're British. Because of the arcane distinctions between 'residence' and 'domicile' (see page 281), someone who was born in another country, or whose father was domiciled in another country at the time of birth, can live in the UK for many years without having to pay tax on investments held outside the UK, as long as the income is not brought into the country. The rules allow such a person to hold property and businesses in the UK via a company incorporated abroad, so capital gains tax and inheritance tax can also be legally avoided. Why does the government allow this? Simply because it wishes to attract wealthy foreigners into Britain. The UK has an advantage over many tax havens in that it is relatively large and offers a wide range of business and professional opportunities.

Switzerland

Switzerland is a small country with good natural borders. For centuries it has survived by playing complex economic games with its more powerful neighbours and since World War 2 has acquired a worldwide reputation as a haven for capital. An ultra-conservative society with a world-class financial sector, Switzerland does not, in fact, let people settle within its borders easily. If you are a millionaire you can probably get citizenship, at a cost of £200,000 or so, as long as no objections about your morality or other civil virtues are made, although cheaper schemes appear occasionally. The main attraction is the famous 'secret' banking system which hitherto has enabled third-world dictators and other notorious types to hide their money. Since the collapse of the USSR, Switzerland is allying itself more closely with the rest of Europe. While it is true that a lot of money is hidden in Switzerland, it is by no means completely safe since Swiss banks with branches in other countries have been known to succumb to pressure from foreign governments, particularly from the United States. Taxes are relatively high, so while Switzerland may still be a haven for capital, it is not really a tax haven.

Monaco

Monaco is a tiny principality on the Côte d'Azur, surrounded by France but very close to Italy. The French do their best to tax assets in Monaco. It's relatively easy to acquire residence there, but it is probably wise to keep your assets elsewhere. Monaco is an eyesore of skyscrapers – its *fin-de-siècle* romance is long gone – and even the casinos are just for tourists.

The Channel Islands

By an accident of history, these islands are subject to the British Crown but have their own governments; in theory, the British government cannot tell them what to do. The larger islands, such as Jersey and Guernsey, are awash with millionaire lawyers and accountants. Income tax is set at 20 per cent on money brought into the country, there is no capital gains tax or VAT, and the cost of living is delightfully low. For wealthy Britons, making a permanent move to the Channel Islands gives immediate benefits, and is close enough to the UK for it to be easy to make short trips home, but it costs. You have to be a multimillionaire to settle in Jersey and on Guernsey you must buy a house for at least £200,000. The tiny island of Sark allows you to become domiciled there if you rent a property for more than a year, which is a cheaper option. Jersey and Guernsey have highly sophisticated banking and financial facilities. Running a Channel Islands-based company costs about £2,000 a year, which is on the high side.

Other Euro tax havens

Territories such as Andorra and Gibraltar offer similar advantages to the Channel Islands: cheap living, expensive property and low taxes. Gibraltar is popular as a base for offshore companies, but its close ties to the UK make it undesirable for British nationals. Luxembourg and Liechtenstein are not really tax havens, but they are excellent places to keep money and to trade from, probably better than Switzerland in most cases.

TAX HAVENS IN THE AMERICAS

These are mostly in or near the Caribbean – the Cayman Islands, the Bahamas, Bermuda, the Dutch Antilles and Panama are the best known. The big international banks all have a presence there, as do thousands of corporations. They are more vulnerable politically than European tax havens but you can often obtain residency cheaply, and Europeans are generally more welcome than Americans, owing to the pressures applied by the US bureaucracy.

FREE TRADE ZONES

These turn up from time to time and often don't last for very long. They have something of the atmosphere of the frontier bar full of piratical aliens in the movie *Star Wars* – one is never quite sure what is going to happen next. The United Arab Emirates (UAE) has set up the Jebel Ali free zone which offers a financial playground with minimal controls and very low taxes to all comers. The Gulf Arabs have been good at money for millenia – although they haven't always had much of it – so there is no reason to regard this haven as more doubtful than the others, but its advantages are really for highly sophisticated investors with plenty of wealth who can get out quickly if the balloon ever does go up.

LANGUAGES

People who don't speak another language are shooting themselves in the foot. The best opportunities are for the multilingual investor, so take the trouble to learn a language or two and don't be afraid to go to countries where they don't speak your native tongue.

The best opportunities are for the multilingual investor, so take the trouble to learn a language or two

Offshore trusts and companies – are they worth it?

I believe that the short answer to this question is generally 'No'. There are hordes of parasitical professionals who are only too keen to set you up with any number of paper entities which have a curious tendency to be expensive to run. Usually you must appoint company officials and trustees who are resident in the tax haven concerned, and while you can make every effort to ensure that such individuals are honest, they may be vulnerable to outside pressure in a crisis. If your objective is principally to protect your capital and you are prepared to live a fairly mobile life, it is generally cheaper and safer to keep control of your assets as far as possible by gaining domicile in a tax haven, understanding the tax regimes of the countries where you spend your time, and carefully diversifying your portfolio, trading through banks and brokers situated in tax havens other than your own. Trusts are examined in detail in Chapter 15; if you are committed to remaining in your own country there is a case for having a trust in a tax haven in favour of dependents in order to avoid inheritance tax.

AVOIDING THE SHARKS

People who are trying illegally to evade tax in their own countries are the prime targets of sharks. The reason is simple; if a shark steals their money, the tax evaders can do nothing about it without inviting the attentions of their tax authorities. Some people are always trying to be too clever and are 'suckers' for complicated schemes that they don't really understand. Changing your domicile is a far cheaper, safer and, above all, legal move than setting up over-complex schemes that may not be accepted by the tax collectors.

People who are trying illegally to evade tax in their own countries are the prime targets of sharks

Dual nationality for guerrillas

While governments and passport officers don't particularly like dual nationality, having two passports gives the private investor enormous scope for 'arbitrage', in the sense that it is possible to exploit differences in the regulations between different countries. The United States is one of the few countries where it is usually illegal to hold dual nationality.

There are many ways to obtain a second passport. The cheapest methods are through marriage, ancestry or religion. Specialist immigration lawyers can advise on your particular needs and opportunities. Clearly, some passports are worth more than others – try travelling around the world on an Israeli, Lebanese or Syrian passport, or on one from an African country, if you want to experience how the less advantaged half of the world lives! Many people are eager to get US nationality but, while it may be better than being, say, from Paraguay, my view is that most other First World passports are an infinitely better bet. Most countries are hypocritical enough to give passports to people who are able to pay for them, often by 'investing' in the country concerned, and this may be worthwhile as a last resort.

Working abroad

If you have the chance of working abroad in a low-tax country for a few years, don't disregard it – it might be the best chance you ever have of building savings fast. Many expatriates are paid more than they are at home, pay less tax and have lower living expenses. While you are abroad, you can avoid paying UK tax, subject to certain restrictions, by making deposits in tax haven banks or investing in offshore funds. The gains you make will accumulate tax free, which is like an ISA, but better.

EXAMPLE

Elaine works for five years in one of the Gulf states. She is paid £7,000 a month, more than double what she gets at home, and is not liable for local tax. Life is dull and expensive, but she is still able to save £3,000 a month. She puts this in respectable investments based in a tax haven.

When Elaine decides to return to the UK, her investments have grown to £200,000. Since she already has a home and assets in the UK, she decides to leave the fund where it is.

A few years later, Elaine gets married and decides to move to America permanently. Her fund has grown even more, and provides an excellent nest egg with which to start a new life. Once the money is in America, it will be subject to US tax, but until that point it has grown faster than normally because it has been tax free.

Banking offshore

Most respectable offshore jurisdictions are swarming with the branches of well-known banks. Remember, there is nothing illegal about having an offshore bank account, so long as you declare it to the Inland Revenue and pay any tax that becomes due.

The main reason for a private person to have an offshore account is so that you can transfer money between countries easily and cheaply.

HOW TO OPEN AN OFFSHORE BANK ACCOUNT

It isn't very difficult to open an offshore account, as long as you can show that you are a respectable, law-abiding person.

1.   Draw up a shortlist of banks in the tax haven of your choice. You can research these via the internet and also from bank directories available in large public libraries.
2.   Write a letter to each of the banks you have shortlisted, telling them how much money you will deposit initially and an estimate of roughly how much money will be going through the account annually. Some banks don't accept small accounts, so you need to give this information. Ask for information about the bank, such as its annual report.
3.   Look up the finance ministry, chamber of commerce and similar bodies based in the relevant tax haven on the internet. If the information is inadequate, write to them asking about guarantee schemes in case of a bank's failure, and details of the tax system.
4.   You will find that banks vary a lot. Some banks are very snooty and don't want you unless you are rich, but won't say so openly. Others leave you with the impression that they are run by cutlass-brandishing buccaneers with parrots on their shoulders. Now that globalization is becoming more respectable, you should find banks that offer you the services you want and will take your business. If you don't, look at another tax haven.

EXAMPLE

Rob works in England but has a villa in Italy, and finds it best to keep money to pay the domestic bills in another currency in an offshore account. He doesn't like keeping a lot of cash in Italy because a few years ago the Italian government, without any warning, took a large sum of money from his Italian account as part of an emergency measure during one of Italy's frequent economic crises.

   Rob has a card from his offshore bank that lets him withdraw cash from cash machines in Italy in Italian lire at a lower rate than if he changed the money at a bank, so he pays for most of his costs in Italy this way. If he has to pay an Italian bill while he is in the UK, he instructs his offshore bank to transfer the money direct to the payee.

14

property
collectables and alternative investments
your own business
the Enterprise Investment Scheme (EIS)
pensions
investments linked to insurance
other financial packages
asset allocation and retirement for guerrillas
a radical retirement solution for guerrillas

Other investments

In this chapter we will examine some of the investment opportunities outside the stock market. There are four main kinds:

1. Businesses, where you must take an active role and take risks in the hope of reaping substantial rewards.

2. Financial products, which offer a high degree of 'security' but may be expensive

and can reduce your ability to respond to changing economic conditions.

3. Collectables – objects of unclear value and with inefficient markets.

4. Property is not normally termed an 'alternative investment' since it is generally thought to be essential for most investors to own their own home. It shares some of the characteristics of 'alternative investments' but is probably less risky.

The topics covered in this chapter are:

- Property – its advantages, how to profit from its unique qualities, and the varieties of property

- Collectables – why most people fail to make money in 'things', what you must do to have a fighting chance and the dangers of the collectables markets

- *Your own business*
- *The Enterprise Investment Scheme (EIS) – the successor to BES (the Business Enterprise Scheme), this is a tax incentive programme in the UK designed to attract higher-rate taxpayers to invest in new companies*
- *Annuities – why they are bad news for retired people*
- *Pensions for guerrillas*
- *Insurance-based investments – the varieties on offer, and how to profit from the trade in second-hand policies*
- *Asset allocation and retirement for guerrillas – a radical solution*

Property

Property, or 'real estate', has to be a good investment for most people. You can see it, live in it and let it. It is part of life – even if you are not a natural handyman, there is an enormous amount you can do yourself to improve its value, simply through physical work. You'll improve your health in the process. As a property owner you are well protected in most stable countries and can participate in a market in which the powerful of the land have an important stake themselves. In addition, the property market is an inefficient market in which good deals appear all the time for those who seek them out.

The property market is an inefficient market in which good deals appear all the time for those who seek them out

As in all businesses, to succeed you must avoid the consumer mentality. Many home buyers are unsophisticated: they are willing to pay the market price for a property even when the income they could get if they let it would be far lower than the cost of the mortgage. They will tell you that gains in the equity of a property are 'cancelled out' because you must always pay an equivalent price for any house that you move to. This is plainly false. As an illustration of the consumer mentality in property, consider the UK property crash of 1989. In the preceding years, almost everyone saw huge gains in the value of their property, far outstripping inflation. Thousands of people in their twenties felt that they would never be able to buy a home if they didn't buy immediately. It seemed as if prices would continue to rise forever, and the industry professionals, including estate agents, solicitors and money lenders, did everything that they could to encourage this belief. It was easy to get a mortgage and one could borrow larger sums than normal. Controls were lax and borrowers were able to exaggerate their incomes to lenders in order to increase the amounts they could borrow.

When interest rates rose and the crash came, the effects were disastrous for home-owners at the bottom of the ladder. People had paid upwards of £60,000 for revamped slum dwellings in the grimmest parts of London in 1988; in 1994, these properties were going for around £25,000 at auction. Lenders repossessed thousands of homes and sold them for prices lower than the outstanding mortgage; many of the people who had lost their homes found that they still owed the balance of what they had borrowed. Some were prosecuted for fraud for exaggerating their incomes on the mortgage applications.

Predictably, the government and institutions worked to mitigate these effects and the UK market improved. The sufferings of the worst hit could have been avoided if they had been more cautious about their borrowing levels and more sceptical about the trend in prices and interest rates. First-time buyers who bought after the crash have benefited from low interest rates and low prices.

Property prices move in cycles. During a slump, or stagnation, owners must simply sit it out until things improve. There are other disadvantages to owning property; the principal ones are poor liquidity, high trading costs, the dangers of legislation and the possibility of expropriation. Before looking at the different types of property, we should examine these characteristics in more detail.

THE RISK OF EXPROPRIATION

It may sound a bit far-fetched in the UK, but there is always at least a slight risk of expropriation anywhere. Property owners are most vulnerable to it during wars and revolutions. Property is conspicuous and immovable; it is very easy for a government to take it away, either directly or through taxation. Unless you see this coming early, there is little you can do. Sometimes there is a 'window of opportunity' when you can borrow money against the property and move it abroad. The good news, though, is that you can probably see such disasters coming in good time if you are alert and objective. If the worst comes to the worst, cut your losses and leave before you lose your liberty and your life as well as your assets.

LEGISLATION AGAINST PROPERTY OWNERS

Many societies seem to be in two minds about property. On the one hand, they want everyone to benefit from ownership and on the other they want to limit profits, particularly those of landlords and developers. Most Western countries have some kind of 'rent control' legislation, ostensibly to protect tenants from their landlords. These laws produce all kinds of absurdities. In the UK, as in many other countries, some tenants are able to rent properties permanently for tiny sums, while others must pay well over the odds with virtually no security of tenure. If rent controls become too draconian, invest in a country with better laws. Despite the difficulties, a working knowledge of the law and the careful selection of rental property still enable landlords to profit from their investments in many places.

As we will see below, renting out commercial property, such as shops and offices, is generally regarded as a better investment than renting out residential property, on the grounds that it is easier to evict a business than a private person. My own view is that the degree to which you specialize is more important than the category of property in which you invest.

The tax rules are always changing. In the UK at present, you pay no capital gains tax (CGT) on your own home. This means that you can accumulate a large amount of tax-free capital by moving up through a series of increasingly more valuable houses (not necessarily increasingly larger houses) by means of leverage (see page 9). It is not impossible to accumulate £1 million in this manner over a period of years, provided that you are always able to service your debt and are not sentimental about moving. There are various quirks to this CGT relief that can benefit owners of more than one property. Anyone who intends to make money in property must read widely on how it is taxed and use a good accountant.

If you invest in a foreign country, you should study the rules, and their history, carefully. It is not unknown for a government to offer attractive concessions to foreign property investors, only to impose swingeing taxes once enough people have been beguiled into purchasing. This happened a few years ago in Spain when property-related taxes in Marbella and elsewhere rose by 2,000 per cent in one year.

HIGH COSTS OF BUYING AND SELLING

These vary enormously from country to country, but are considerably larger than the cost of trading in shares or bonds. In the UK, industry professionals do not give value for money, but put up a barrage of propaganda about how necessary their services are. A little research and the willingness to do it yourself can reduce costs significantly. For example, it is not obligatory to use an estate agent or a solicitor when conveying a property in England and Wales, and there are many instances where their services can be dispensed with altogether. For more information about this, read *The Conveyancing Fraud* by Michael Joseph (see Bibliography for details). Similarly, it pays to shop around when getting a mortgage since some lenders have cunning ways of increasing the costs.

LOCATION, LOCATION, LOCATION

By far the most important factor affecting property is where it is situated. A beautiful detached house in wonderful countryside miles from anywhere may well be worth considerably less than a dreary, badly built flat within commuting distance of London.

People need good jobs to pay high mortgages; the places where there are good jobs tend to have higher house prices accordingly. Once you get an eye for this, you see that this is the same in most of the world. We may bemoan the fact that some regions of the UK are economically disadvantaged, but we have to face the facts as investors: a palace in the middle of a decaying area that is getting worse is going to be worth less than a tiny studio flat in the centre of a booming metropolis.

Within a locality, location can be important too. Identical houses quite near each other may have different values because of all kinds of factors, such as noise, traffic, the proximity of public transport and so on. Do all the normal checks that people recommend and use your eyes and ears to verify any information you see in writing.

ILLIQUIDITY

Property cannot be sold as quickly or as easily as high-quality financial securities. Owners can get squeezed when taxes and interest rates increase. For this reason, it is important to make sure you always have some cash or near-cash deposits.

HIGH MAINTENANCE

It doesn't cost much, if anything, to hang on to valuable shares or bonds for many years. In contrast, it costs a substantial amount to maintain a house.

POOR INFORMATION

Everyone thinks they know all about property, but few people really do. Nobody would invest in the stock market if it had as many secrets, questionable practices and just plain lack of good market information as the property world has. *The Estates Gazette* is the property person's main trade magazine, and is worth reading.

TYPES OF PROPERTY

Legislation and the degree of commitment necessary vary according to the kind of property you invest in. Here are the main categories.

Undeveloped land

Undeveloped land is simply land that has not been built on or developed in any way. Several studies suggest that it generally keeps its value in real terms. It is a passive investment; you buy a field, walk about on it all your life, and can be confident of reselling it without loss – it effortlessly keeps pace with inflation. Raw land is illiquid and produces little or no income, but it cannot burn down or be burgled so you can sleep easily at night. You can improve its value by getting permission to develop it. With such a long-term investment, the occasional opportunity to do this can arise as local planning policies change. People have made their fortunes by simply waiting for a town to grow out as far as their property.

Most of the increase in the value of a piece of land occurs before any construction begins: the big money is in getting permission for change of use. If you buy in your own area, you will be at an advantage because you will be well informed about local affairs. Buying in decaying areas is dangerous, and you should always buy at a low or moderate price. Make sure you have the soil properly surveyed, checking drainage and stability.

Residential property

We all need to live somewhere; owning your own home will save you rent and usually give you a capital gain into the bargain. Borrowing money to buy a house is about the cheapest way to borrow there is. Improve your house and insulate it, but don't spend a lot on trendy alterations that will be out of fashion in ten years' time. In old countries like Britain there are many houses whose foundations are hundreds of years old – they've been altered again and again over the generations and always require careful maintenance, but most of them will still be standing long after you're dead.

Buying a house or flat to rent out takes more knowledge, but a home-owner has, perforce, acquired many of the requisite skills. When buying, one rough rule of thumb is not to pay more than 80 times the monthly rent you can get. This may seem impossible until you become aware of the bargains available through repossessions, deaths, divorces, and so on. Seek out a bargain in a good area that you know well, maintain it yourself and you should be able to cover the mortgage, tax and maintenance costs with the rental income. Wait for a capital gain if inflation pushes up prices and reduces your debt.

Being a landlord is a business, requiring effort on your part

Being a landlord is a business, requiring effort on your part. However, it will not take up all your time unless you own a large number of properties. Your main headache will be the management of tenants. In the UK at present one can offer tenants an Assured Shorthold Tenancy for a minimum of six months; the rules allow for relatively easy eviction in case of rent default or, in any case, at the end of the lease, but the rules are strict and you must make sure that you follow them to the letter. Failing to serve notices at the proper time, for example, can result in tenants acquiring the right to stay indefinitely, which will greatly reduce the value of the property. There are unscrupulous local authorities and charitable agencies that encourage tenants to exercise their rights in this regard, so get it right. Choose your tenants carefully. Specializing in a certain kind of tenant, such as Japanese business families, military personnel or some other group who are motivated to behave well, can be mutually rewarding. As a landlord you will be faced with the reality of society's inequities, not with its myths.

There are other types of residential tenancy. Letting to limited companies was popular before the introduction of Assured Shorthold Tenancies because you could get the tenant out, but be careful to check that the company is genuine, or the tenant may be able to get security of tenure. Licences are appropriate for flat sharers, but you should get expert advice. Fully protected tenancies should be avoided at all costs, except where you are acquiring an occupied property and are certain that you can buy the tenant out.

Commercial property

As mentioned earlier, the law regarding the letting of business premises is less weighted against the landlord. However, if you are considering shops and offices, you should be aware that it is extremely hard for a small business to stay solvent in the current regulatory environment: the vast majority of new businesses fail within two years. This means that you are likely to have problems with tenants defaulting, and you must factor in the costs of dealing with this when budgeting. The treatment of bankrupts has become so mild in the UK that you cannot count on personal guarantees, although you should always attempt to get them. These problems will be exacerbated if you lock tenants into long leases at high rents at the peak of a boom, or persuade a tenant to rent a shop in a poor position. Give them a chance to make a living and they will be far more reliable. As always in property, the location is of prime importance, so take great care when purchasing.

Time sharing and property bonds

Purchasing a time share gives you the right to a fixed period of time in a property in perpetuity. They may sometimes result in a profit, but they are essentially a scheme for consumers, not investors. Property bonds are insurance-based schemes offering holiday accommodation on a points system. Again, they are for the unsophisticated investor and would appear to be of doubtful value.

INVESTING THROUGH THE STOCK MARKET

You can buy shares in publicly quoted property companies, subject to the same risks as any kind of equity investment.

DEVELOPING PROPERTY

The tycoon Jacob Astor used to say 'neffer develop'. It's a rough and risky business even for the professionals, but some people find they have a talent for it. Very small developments, such as converting a house into flats, are realistic projects for the amateur, but it is hard to control costs and stay on the right side of all the red tape.

GROUND RENTS AND FREEHOLDS

In England and Wales there is an interesting trade in the freeholds of buildings that have been sold off, usually as flats, on leases of 99 years or so. The leaseholders pay you an annual 'ground rent', which can be raised every few years, and when the lease expires your building becomes yours again, so you can resell the lease. It is possible to buy parcels of such freeholds at auction at prices that may allow a profit on the ground rent income. The value of any improvements carried out by the tenants become yours at the end of the lease, and can be taken into account when selling a new lease. If the building has become dilapidated, most leases require tenants to restore the building to its original condition, which can be a substantial benefit to the freeholder. A leaseholder may generally renew the lease by agreement before the term is up, and will usually pay a large premium for doing so. The Leasehold Reform, Housing and Urban Development Act 1993 has introduced new rights enabling many long leaseholders to compel landlords to sell them the freehold. Contact the Leasehold Enfranchisement Advisory Service (1st Floor, 6–8 Maddox Street, London W1; tel. 020 7493 3116) for more information.

PROPERTY FOR GUERRILLAS

'Property is the best way, the safest way, and indeed, the only way to get rich', wrote an American president nearly a century ago. This has a nice ring to it, and quite a lot of truth. As a business, property is relatively much less demanding than most others because of two unusual characteristics – the ability to borrow large sums as gearing, and the time factor. In a long deflationary period, when prices are on their way down, this can work against you; despite dire warnings of the doomsayers, there is no sign of this happening at present in the UK. Conceivably, though, there might come a time when there were fewer young people getting on to the bottom rung of the property ladder, and property prices then might start to sink. When there is even slight inflation, however, the borrowed money on your property helps you to increase your returns as long as property prices keep pace with inflation.

When property people come a cropper, it is usually because they have borrowed too much and cannot make the repayments on their loans. Opinion is divided over how much is too much borrowing, but you should definitely always keep back some cash to deal with maintenance crises and times when there are no tenants. Don't be in a rush to make money – overextending yourself is dangerous.

Suppose you have several properties in the UK and a huge CGT liability if you sell. One way around this is to borrow against the properties – this way, you have a large chunk of cash you can move into other investments, perhaps overseas. Making sure that the rents you receive cover the mortgage repayments is the formula most dealers use to stay solvent until the day comes when they can sell their property for a profit.

Collectables and alternative investments

PROBLEMS

'Alternative investments' are things like diamonds, sapphires, Scotch whisky, wine, stamps or precious metals. These are often sold by aggressive telephone salesmen operating from abroad. If it's a con, it is usually that the price you pay is too high and that it is difficult to resell the item. Don't rely on the salesman to tell you what a fair price is, or how to resell – find out for yourself, and make very, very sure of the market before you get involved.

Collectables are works of arts, antiques, memorabilia and similar objects. Unless you are highly knowledgeable they are not a good investment. Here are the principal reasons why.

Illiquidity, no income and doubtful increase in value

Being objects, they do not produce a cash income. You hope to make money on resale alone. Changes in fashion make speculation, even in the highest quality art, very uncertain. For example, the works of many of the most fêted Victorian artists sell for less now, in real terms, than they did in their own lifetimes. You may find that you cannot sell an object at any price if it is not in vogue.

High maintenance costs

Valuable objects must be maintained, stored and insured at high cost. They are easily stolen or damaged. There is nothing more burdensome than having to be suspicious of tradespeople and strangers who are in your home. Their admiring glances at your beautiful possessions can become a real strain.

Careful selection doesn't work

Only professionals and experts can really succeed consistently in spotting winners.

It is hard to find bargains

We have all heard the stories of the person who recognized a hugely valuable antique at a low price in a provincial shop, or the discovery of a famous signature on an apparently worthless painting. It does happen, but you must invest a lot of effort and time in the search, so it's more like prospecting for gold than investing. If you really enjoy this kind of thing, consider it as a hobby or as a full-time business.

The traders are against you

The collectables world makes the stock market look like a convent. There is very little regulation and a lot of dishonesty. Unless you are knowledgeable, you are a punter who, in the eyes of many professionals, deserves to be fleeced.

Unless you are knowledgeable, you are a punter who, in the eyes of many professionals, deserves to be fleeced

Forgery

Forgery is a very real problem, especially with high-value objects. Many forgers are brilliant artists in their own right who cannot get the recognition they deserve. Anything can be forged – the museums and galleries of the world are full of forgeries.

SUCCESSFUL STRATEGIES

If you still want to dabble in collectables, here are some strategies that are said to work.

Fashions can be cyclical

If you really do have good taste, and are fascinated by, say, mediaeval Indian miniatures, you can buy when they are completely out of fashion, wait 50 years or so and make a killing. Of course, it may be your children who make the killing – but they'll have had to avoid inheritance taxes on your collection to do so.

Things can 'become' art

American folk art, Buddhist temple paintings and African sculptures were all considered curios rather than art at one time. Now they have great value. If there is a category of attractive objects that you really like, and can buy for less than it would cost to have made at the present time, then they may increase in value dramatically one day.

Wine

Suppose you spend £10,000 on fine wine in a vintage year and store it. A few years later, it is ready to drink, and you can sell part of your purchase to recover your £10,000, and drink the rest for free. That's the theory, and in recent years it has worked for buyers of fine French clarets and vintage ports. No other wines are thought to be safe bets – even champagne, which the uninitiated might think of as an investment, isn't really safe, because it is past its best after about 20 years. The investment market in wine is basically limited to the products of about 30 chateaus in Bordeaux

Joining in with the hype

The great game of the professionals is to collude in the collection of objects when they are cheap and then to hype them in as rigorous and expensive a manner as it takes to launch a consumer product on to a mass market. This is the world of glamour, publicity, high-profile exhibitions and auctions. It's not for the amateur, but a full-time career in collectables may be very rewarding.

Your own business

Some people seem to be born knowing how to run businesses, but most people who succeed have to learn it the hard way. Business is almost always difficult, and many people find it boring. Be very careful of the sharks who prey on naive beginners – 'business opportunities' that are advertised to you as a neat little package are generally mediocre at best. Franchising, for instance, although a proven route to business success, is little regulated and full of people who want to take an up-front fee from you for a business that may not work.

Pyramid Schemes, where you pay a large fee to join a selling scheme and are asked to recruit new members, don't often work, because most of the money comes from new members, not real customers. Recently in the Far East, I was approached by two respectable Chinese ladies, whom I'd known slightly for years. They wanted me to sign up for a 'multi-level marketing scheme' where the products were gold coins. They gave a very slick presentation and were probably sincere in their belief in their wares. The trouble was that they couldn't really answer the question of how to sell the gold coins, or what their market value really was. The flip chart they showed me was full of slogans like 'guaranteed profits' and 'no risk, high rewards'. In reality the reverse was probably true – 'high risk, low rewards'. They had both had to shell out a fairly large sum to purchase 'sample' coins – and that was the clue to how the promoters make their money. How do you sell an expensive item that doesn't move easily, like specially minted gold coins? To people who think they can sell it to someone else, of course!

Back in 1940, a Wall Street broker wrote:

> '*Most businessmen imagine that they are in business to make money, and that this is their chief reason for being in business, but more often than not they are gently kidding themselves. There are so many other things that are actually more attractive. Some of them are: to make a fine product or to render a remarkable service, to give employment, to revolutionize an industry, to make oneself famous or, at least to supply oneself with material for a conversation in the evening.*'

Fred Schwed, *Where are the Customers' Yachts?*
Simon and Schuster, 1940

This is still true today. Remember, businesses aren't just there to give you a wage – you could do that if you had a job. Businesses are supposed to make profits over and above a fair wage for all your blood, sweat and tears.

The Enterprise Investment Scheme (EIS)

The EIS was introduced in 1994 as the successor to the Business Enterprise Scheme (BES). Both schemes are supposed to give investors a chance to 'get in at the ground floor' on new and expanding businesses – you get a tax break, the new company gets its capital cheaply, and, hopefully, everyone profits hugely after the five-year lock-in period. It's a mug's game. Britain is a country that is so inimical to business start-ups that it is a surprise that any succeed; the extreme over-regulation, the absurd employment laws, the ubiquitous monopolies, the high costs of professional advice, the lack of fast, inexpensive legal remedies for businesses kill most new businesses. Little wonder, therefore, that BES promoters looked for ways to offer greater security.

They found them in a variety of property schemes where the profit came from sales after the five-year lock-in period and offered a reasonably secure investment. This provoked howls of public protest – the BES was supposed to help businesses that would create employment and bring about other social benefits, not to provide an opportunity to make money on one-off deals.

Hence the EIS was introduced, with rules that are supposed to limit investment under the scheme to 'genuine' trading companies.

Few companies have tried to raise capital in this way. Why? Because it is very, very risky to start up a 'genuine' trading business in the UK.

Some time ago the managing director of one EIS company told me, 'One in ten EIS companies will do well, so you should put £1,000 into 20 different EIS companies. If the share prices in the two good companies go from 50p to £2 in five years, you have more than covered any losses that you might have made in the other companies.' Frankly, I can think of better investment propositions than this blarney. If the £2,000 that you have invested in the two best-performing companies quadruple their value, you have made £6,000 with which to cover any other losses, which, presumably, could be as high as £18,000. 'It's high risk,' he enthused, as if that justified the mediocrity of his business and its management. Knowing his particular company and its background well, and being determined not to invest in such a poor prospect, I was surprised to see hundreds of small investors, many of them lower-rate taxpayers, buy shares in the company. Apparently it was the triumph of the gambling instinct over the evidence.

Pensions

ANNUITIES

This is where you pay an insurance company a lump sum in return for a regular income for either a fixed number of years or for the rest of your life. The fixed-term variety can be useful if you are planning to pay for school fees or to fund some other savings plan. The payments are partly from the capital, which is tax free, and partly as interest, which is taxed as income. Most annuities give no protection against inflation, so the real value of the payments reduce over the years, and you are locked in forever – there is no way to change your mind and get your money back. Having watched an elderly relative being slowly reduced to penury by buying an annuity because she 'didn't want the bother' of looking after her investments actively, I have a horror of them as a retirement plan.

PENSIONS FOR GUERRILLAS

The developed countries of the world have ageing populations; there may be fewer people of working age to support a much larger population of pensioners in the future, and it seems likely that scandals, rule changes and collapses will occur. National Insurance, for instance, is not really insurance at all. It is simply a tax – there is no solid guarantee that a state pension will be paid to you when you are old.

Pensions are intended to provide money for you after you have retired; they are very tax-effective but are not necessarily the best way to provide for your old age. If, for instance, you build up a large fund through ISAs, you might find yourself in possession of a capital sum that would provide you with a much higher retirement income than a pension could. With a pension, you get tax relief on the money you put in, but you get taxed fully on your eventual income when you retire, and you have to buy an annuity. With an ISA, you don't get any tax relief on your contributions, but the pension income is tax-free and you can use the fund as you wish.

Private pensions tend to lock your money in until you retire and most of the capital is turned into an annuity on your retirement, depriving you of control. Most personal pension plans and AVCs are expensive and overrated.

One possible route is to take out a stakeholder pension, without going through an intermediary, that uses an index tracking fund. This reduces charges and you'll probably outperform the majority of pension investments, while enjoying tax relief on contributions.

If you work for the government or a large, benevolent company that offers you an ultra-generous pension, then it is probably worthwhile to have a pension, since the employer's contributions will make a huge difference to the growth of the fund. Most people, however, are not in this position – and pension schemes tend to hurt people who change jobs several times. Today, the rapidly changing economy means that many of us may change careers more than once, let alone our jobs, so the post-war system based on a job for life and a pension to go with it is a thing of the past.

Investments linked to insurance

There are a number of investment products that are dressed up in insurance policy clothing; generally they are unitized, in the same way as unit trusts are, but they receive different tax treatment. You can contribute to these schemes either by paying regular premiums or by investing a lump sum. They can be unit-linked, where the money goes into an investment fund and the policy will vary in value according to the value of the units, or they can be 'with profits', which means that they are guaranteed not to reduce in value and you may also get annual and terminal bonuses.

SINGLE-PREMIUM BONDS

These are where you invest a lump sum. Usually, you receive life cover, guaranteeing the return of the capital, or a larger amount, if you die. The initial charges can be as much as 6 per cent, with a 1 per cent annual management fee, which are higher than the charges for unit and investment trusts. Unlike unit and investment trusts, the insurance company's fund is subject to capital gains tax and they are all subject to income tax. In addition, investors who make withdrawals from a single-premium bond of over 5 per cent may be subject to income tax on these. They can be attractive to higher-rate taxpayers, who can 'roll up' the gains until they retire when they may be taxed at a lower rate. A variation of this kind of bond is the 'broker bond', where the fund is managed by a professional in return for additional fees; the advantage of these is doubtful, to say the least.

QUALIFYING LIFE POLICIES

Most policies where you pay regular premiums are qualifying life policies, which means that they are tax-free when they mature or when you surrender or assign them. The premiums must be payable for at least ten years and the policy gives a degree of death cover. Not many people realize that it takes more than five years for a life policy investment to beat saving in a building society and that more than a third of the people who buy life policies end them within three years, and lose money in doing so.

It takes more than five years for a life policy investment to beat saving in a building society

One variety, the endowment policy, is frequently used to repay a mortgage, but it is often not the best way to do this. More than 70 per cent of endowment policies are surrendered early and the insurance companies offer low surrender values.

SECOND-HAND LIFE INSURANCE POLICIES (TEPS)

An interesting, and relatively unknown, investment is to buy someone else's life assurance policy. These are known as traded endowment policies (TEPs). The system works because the surrender values offered by the insurance companies are low to discourage early encashment. It is worth buying them at a higher price than the surrender value and taking over the annual payments since you will receive the full maturity value and all the bonuses due. It is also possible to re-sell the policy before maturity. The capital growth is subject to capital gains tax but you can use your annual CGT allowance and organize losses to offset the rest of the gain. Essentially, you are profiting from someone else's inability to keep up the payments. Specialist companies dealing in these policies – sometimes they are auctioned – advertise in magazines such as the *Investor's Chronicle*.

The market for traded endowment policies is worth around £200 million and there is a row about whether TEP prices are too high. The Association of Policy Market Makers (APMM) gives you quotations from three of its members. Some firms belong to the APMM and others to the Association of Policy Traders (APT).

When dealing with a trader, remember to check that the firm is:

- regulated by the FSA
- has a compensation scheme
- has indemnity insurance.

Other financial packages

Schemes combining several financial products, such as back-to-back policies, capital conversion plans and school fees plans are usually heavily sold and rotten value. You should usually be able to achieve better results by arranging the underlying deals yourself.

Asset allocation and retirement for guerrillas

Asset allocation is a fancy way of saying dividing your wealth across different asset types. We all do this anyway, because the system forces us to. A youngish professional might have:

- a flat
- a car
- an ISA
- a cash deposit
- a pension scheme.

That's asset allocation. The concept becomes more important if you become richer, which tends to happen in middle age – say between 45 and retirement. At this age, most people start thinking about their future and how they want to spend the rest of their lives. They are probably at the peak of their careers and income-earning power, and they want to make their wealth grow as fast as possible, so they have more when they retire. This is the time of life when people are most able to take a bit more risk, with the chance of improved returns. Ironically, people who get rich during this period are often able to go on getting richer and richer long after retiring, because they have the 'risk capital' available to take advantage of investment opportunities across the world as and when they appear.

A RADICAL RETIREMENT SOLUTION FOR GUERRILLAS

In Western countries, the outlook for retired people is not altogether promising. In the UK, if elderly people can no longer look after themselves, they go into nursing homes and are gradually stripped of their assets to pay for the high cost of care. When everything has been sold and there is no money left, the state grudgingly foots the continuing bills.

Marc Faber, a colourful Swiss fund manager in Hong Kong, has this to say about the problem:

> *'If I can give one piece of investment advice, I would say ... as an alternative to ending your days in cold New York, London or Munich, deprived of any help, you could retire in a community in Thailand, North Africa, the Caribbean or in Latin America with, say, three servants ... Some people might say that in northern Thailand, for instance, you don't have the medical attention you have in New York, but I don't care ... maybe you have better attention in the sense that you have a doctor who is nice to you and some nurses who are nice to you, whereas if you go into a hospital in the West, nobody cares.'*

> *quoted in Trading the World's Markets,*
> *Wiley, 2000)*

Personally, I think this is the best investment advice I have ever heard!

15

income tax
tax avoidance and tax evasion
capital gains tax (CGT)
inheritance tax (IHT)
trusts
hidden taxes
starting a company

Tax

Tax is a burden on everyone in society, from the richest to the poorest, and the rules are Byzantine in their twisted incomprehensibility, although it has to be said that they have been simplified somewhat in recent years.

Use an accountant, even if you don't have much money: a good one – often these are provincial and charge very reasonable fees –

will stop you getting into a mess and should be able to save you substantial amounts of money. Some people think that you can 'monkey' with the Inland Revenue in the way that you can with some other government organizations. Don't – you won't have a prayer. When it comes to collecting its revenue, the state apparatus loses its kindly face and gets very tough indeed. Nevertheless, there is scope for considerable tax saving if you are prepared to study the rules. This chapter can only scratch the surface of the subject, but it should give you some food for thought. Remember, though, that the rules are always changing, so always check for latest figures and take professional advice.

In this chapter we will look at:

- *Income tax – the current allowances and reliefs in the UK*
- *Tax avoidance and tax evasion – why avoidance is legal and desirable*
- *Residence, ordinary residence and domicile – how these different categories affect your tax status*
- *Capital gains tax (CGT) – how to reduce your liability*
- *Inheritance tax – why it is never too early to make a will, and some ideas on how to plan for passing on your estate*
- *Trusts – the varieties of trust and their uses*
- *Tax avoidance through starting a limited company*

Income tax

The income tax rates often change, so always check for the latest figures. The main allowance for 2000/01 is:

	Personal allowance
Up to age 65	£4,385
Aged 65–74	£5,790
Aged 75+	£6,050

This personal allowance is free of income tax. The income limit for age-related allowances is £17,000.

TAXABLE BANDS

Money that you earn over and above your personal allowance is taxed in 'bands' at different rates:

Taxable income (after deduction of allowances)	2000/01
£0–1,520	10% (the 'starting rate')
£1,521–28,400	22% (the 'basic rate')
Over £28,400	40% (the 'higher rate')

EXAMPLE

Fiona is a 30-year-old self-employed software developer and earns £32,785 in the 2000/01 tax year. How much income tax does she have to pay and will she have to pay the dreaded 'higher rate'?

Income	£32,785
Less personal allowance	£4,385
Taxable income	£28,400
Tax on the next £1,520	10% of £1,520
	= £152
Tax between £1,521 and £28,400	22% of remainder
	= £5,914

Fiona's total tax payable is £6,066. If she earned any extra money in that year over and above £32,785, she would have to pay 40 per cent of it in tax – but note that the higher rate is only on the extra money. If she earned an extra pound, she would have to pay 40p extra in tax.

INCOME TAX ON INVESTMENT INCOME

Investment income is principally the money you receive as interest and dividends.

Interest is usually taxed at source, which means that whoever is holding your money, such as a bank or a building society, deducts 20 per cent of your interest and pays it to the Inland Revenue (the extra 2 per cent of the 22 per cent basic rate is ignored). If your total income, including investment income, puts you in the 40 per cent tax band, you'll have to pay the extra yourself. Only higher-rate tax-payers have additional tax to pay on taxed interest.

Non-tax-payers, who earn less than the personal allowance, can either reclaim the 20 per cent deducted tax that the building society has deducted or use a special form to arrange to receive interest gross.

Dividends are not taxed at source. No income tax is payable on dividends if your total income (including the dividends) is below the higher rate of tax because of a tax credit system too complex to explain here.

If you are a higher-rate tax-payer, you must pay 25 per cent of the amount of dividends received (32.5 per cent of the grossed-up value including the tax credits).

This means that if you have investments that generate net dividends to you of up to £29,507 in the 2000/01 tax year and you had no other income, you would not be liable for income tax. Note, however, that most large quoted companies presently do not pay high dividends, so to achieve this level of dividend income you might have to have some pretty unusual and risky investments.

Tax avoidance and tax evasion

Tax avoidance is when you make efforts to reduce or avoid paying tax legally by exploiting the complexity of the rules. Tax evasion is the same thing, except that you break the law. The right to avoid tax is well established and, to paraphrase Lord Clyde's comments in a famous tax case of 1929, a person does nothing wrong by arranging his or her affairs to take advantage of the rules, so long as they are not broken. The extraordinary complexity and unfairness of tax legislation mean that, in practice, there are many circumstances in which a layperson could not possibly tell the difference between avoidance and evasion. Nevertheless you should make sure you use the very best adviser you can find and do all that you can to stay within the law.

The right to avoid tax is well established and a person does nothing wrong by arranging his or her affairs to take advantage of the rules, so long as they are not broken

Expatriates probably have the greatest scope for mitigating tax. In certain circumstances, you may be able avoid a large CGT liability by becoming non-resident, but the rules are getting tougher. Tax planning is essential so that you can make full use of all the tax avoidance opportunities – and you'll need professional help to do this.

RESIDENCE OUTSIDE THE UK

If you are not 'resident' or 'ordinarily resident' in the UK, you are not subject to UK income tax but for a few minor exceptions (there always seem to be exceptions!). Low tax jurisdictions and tax havens charge their residents little or no tax, and wealthy people have often found it necessary to move to a tax haven for this reason. Residence has nothing to do with nationality or passports.

There is definitely scope for tax reduction if you are enterprising enough to work abroad for a few years, or if you have a foreign spouse. You should always seek the advice of a good accountant, if not an expensive specialist tax lawyer, before making any decisions that could affect your tax situation. Mitigating tax in this way is *not* a DIY matter, and the topic can only be covered in outline here, so do get professional advice.

You are treated as resident in the UK if you are 'physically present with the intention of being resident'. At present, the tests are as follows, but do check for the latest tests because they do change:

- If you are physically present for 183 days in any one tax year (6 April to 5 April), you are resident in that year.
- If you are physically present for an average of more than 90 days in any year over a four-year period, you are resident from the fifth year; unless you are shown 'to have formed the intention to continue coming to the UK for that period' in which case you are treated as resident from the tax year in which the intention arose.

Ordinary residence

'Ordinary residence' is a strange notion, quite distinct from residence. As it is the main criterion for capital gains tax (CGT), it is important to get the Inland Revenue to agree that you are 'not ordinarily resident' before you make a capital gain, if you want to avoid the tax. You can be resident in more than one country at the same time but 'ordinarily resident' in only one country at a time. It's relatively easy to work through this nonsense if you are leaving for ever, but it can cause serious problems if you return to the UK within a few years, since the Inland Revenue may decide that you were ordinarily resident in the UK for the whole time you were away and ask for the CGT on any capital gains you made during that time.

Ordinary residence is usually defined as 'habitual residence', so, for instance, you can be ordinarily resident in the UK but non-resident in a particular tax year by being absent for the whole of that particular tax year.

Domicile

Domicile is another strange notion, quite distinct from 'residence' or 'ordinary residence'. You can have only one domicile at a time.

There are two kinds of domicile: domicile of origin and domicile of choice. Your domicile of origin is usually the country where your father was domiciled when you were born. If you have a domicile of origin outside the UK, you may be able to live in the UK for a long time without ever having to pay UK tax.

Domicile of choice is more tricky: you have to be resident in a country and have 'the intention of permanent or indefinite residence' there. If you want to change from a UK domicile, you must intend never to return for anything more than brief, infrequent visits, or the Inland Revenue will say that you haven't changed your domicile. Domicile does not have to be the same thing as residence or nationality – for instance, you may have lived in the UK for decades and still be domiciled elsewhere.

Unlike many other people, the British seem to have a curious fear of working abroad or emigrating. It really is not as bad as it sounds – life in many other countries can be better than in the UK, especially if you are able, affluent and capable of adapting. Nor will you lose out on culture or modern conveniences; in fact, you may find more of them in other countries than there are in Britain.

Capital gains tax (CGT)

Capital gains tax is tax on the profits you make on an asset. Almost all assets will be chargeable to either income tax or to CGT. However, it is possible through tax planning to influence how money is treated, to take advantage of the different reliefs that apply to the two taxes. Gambling winnings and damages awarded for defamation are tax free. Cars are also exempt from CGT, since most cars are sold at a loss. If you invest in classic cars, and can convince the Inland Revenue that you are not trading in them, you can keep your profits from their sale tax-free.

For 2000/01, you have an annual exemption of £7,200 which is free of CGT. Any net taxable gain in the year, after deducting all reliefs and the exemption is added to total income from other sources in the year to determine the tax band applicable. The tax bands are the same as the ones for income tax and the rates are 10, 20 and 40 per cent.

The CGT rates for 2000/01 on taxable gains (after deducting the exemption) are:

Size of taxable gain	CGT rate
£1–1,520	10%
£1,521–£28,400	20%
£28,401 and over	40%

THE MAIN RELIEFS ON CGT

From March 1982 until 6 April 1998, an indexation allowance was given on CGT which allowed, for instance, the cost of shares to be adjusted by the change in the retail price index, thus reducing the gain. It could not be used to create a loss.

Shares were 'pooled' so that if you made several purchases and sales of shares in the same company, the cost per share was calculated as the average purchase price of all of them, plus indexation. If you bought shares during that period, you can still apply indexation for purchases up to 6 April 1998.

For purchases after 6 April 1998, both pooling and indexation are abolished. Taper relief now applies, which makes a deduction from the gain based on the number of years you held the shares.

Taper relief applies differently to business assets and non-business assets. Business assets are treated more generously – you get a reduction in the gain of from 12.5 per cent after one year building up to 75 per cent for business assets held for over four years. Non-business asset taper relief gives you a a reduction of from 5 per cent after three years up to a maximum of 40 per cent of the gain after ten years.

The maximum CGT on a business asset share for a higher rate tax-payer is 10 per cent, and 24 per cent on a non-business asset share.

AIM-listed companies and shares in companies not listed on the stock market are treated as business assets, as are most employee share schemes. If you buy shares in listed companies in the normal way, they count as non-business assets.

EXEMPT ASSETS

The main assets not subject to CGT are:

- government securities (such as gilts)
- qualifying corporate bonds – mainly interest-based corporate loan stocks
- venture capital trusts – but with special rules
- enterprise investment schemes – but with special rules
- ISAs
- transfers between spouses.

DISPOSALS

You aren't liable to CGT on an asset unless you 'dispose' of it, but that doesn't only mean selling it. If you give an asset to someone, it is often judged to be a disposal at market value and potentially liable to CGT.

SALE AND REPURCHASE OF SHARES

Once known as 'bed and breakfasting', this is done to realize a gain or loss in order to raise the base cost of the shares by using your annual CGT exemption or to create a loss to set off against other capital gains you have made during the same year.

Currently, the rule is that you have to wait more than 30 days between selling the shares and buying them back. The share price may, of course, have changed in the meantime. If you are married, however, you can sell your shares and have your spouse buy them simultaneously and then have your spouse transfer them back to you, free of CGT because transfers between spouses are exempt. You will have incurred dealing costs, though.

Index funds are pretty much the same, so you could sell one index fund and buy another to use up your annual CGT exemption and raise your base cost

Here's a new wrinkle based on the increasing popularity of index funds (see page 46). Index funds are pretty much the same, so you could sell one index fund and buy another to use up your annual CGT exemption and raise your base cost.

USE YOUR ANNUAL EXEMPTION!

Everyone, including children, gets the annual CGT exemption (£7,200 for 2000/01) on your net capital gains. Net gains are your gains minus your losses after deducting all the reliefs, including losses brought forward from previous years. If you make net losses in a year you can carry them forward indefinitely to set against any future gains.

What you can't do is carry forward your annual exemption – you must use it up each year or lose the benefit of it.

For example, if you make no profits for four years and make a profit of £30,000 in the fifth year, you will have to pay CGT. If you made capital gains of £6,000 every year for five years, you would use up most of your annual exemption and not be liable for tax. A good accountant may be able to help you plan your sales of assets to take advantage of this.

Inheritance tax (IHT)

If you have any money and you care at all about the people you will leave behind when you die, it is extremely selfish not make a will. Intestacy, or dying without a will, causes a great deal of expenditure and unnecessary suffering for your heirs – the state and the professionals will profit at their expense. Despite this, a very large number of people with assets die intestate, often, it seems, because of a superstitious feeling that making a will may somehow hasten death. Making a will is inexpensive and there are even standard forms you can buy to do the job, so it is really inexcusable not to make provision for how your possessions will be divided up after your death.

It is better not to use a standard form, though – use a solicitor when drawing up a will, because it is easy to make a mistake that renders it technically invalid. The fee should not usually be more than £100 (they get you at the other end if you are unwise enough to appoint them as an executor).

Intestacy causes a great deal of expenditure and unnecessary suffering for your heirs

The key points to remember when drawing up a will are:

- **Choose executors whom you trust**. An executor is a person who agrees to take the responsibility for seeing that the legal formalities of dividing an inheritance are done properly. I believe that you should never appoint a solicitor, bank or other professional as an executor. Their fees are likely to be out of all proportion to the value of the work they do, and in the despair of bereavement no one will want to fight them over their fees. It is extraordinary how often estates are shamelessly ransacked in this way. Any reasonably responsible person can do the executor's job, and a solicitor can always be engaged (at a much lower rate) to advise on technical matters. Have at least two executors, to avoid problems if one dies at the same time as you, or is too busy to do the work.
- **Think long and hard about who you want to leave your money to**. Don't try to play God, punishing the 'bad' ones of your family and rewarding the good – this may result in disputes after your death. If possible, leave everything to one person, such as your spouse, on whom you can rely to care for the others whom you want to help.
- **Plan carefully to avoid legally as much inheritance tax as possible**. This is discussed in more detail below. The main point to remember is that proper planning can massively reduce the bite the state will take out of your money. Regularly review your will with an accountant and a solicitor, and adjust it to take any new legislation into account.
- **Have a substitute beneficiary in your will** in case the first ones die at the same time as you do – in a car crash, for example.

A dead person's assets (the 'estate') are taxed in three ways: through inheritance tax, income tax and capital gains tax. Inheritance tax must be planned for; it is a tax not only on the 'final disposal', which is the amount you leave when you die, but also on some gifts made during your lifetime. It's no good handing over all your money to your heirs on your death bed to avoid IHT – it won't work.

HOW IHT IS CALCULATED

For 2000/01, the threshold for inheritance tax is £234,000. If your estate is worth less than this, no IHT is payable. Anything above the threshold is taxed at 40 per cent. Your 'estate' is the total value of all your assets when you die, including any chargeable transfers you made within seven years prior to death.

Shares and bonds are easy to value, but property sometimes isn't, since the Inland Revenue may disagree with the valuation the executors obtain. If, incidentally, a solicitor or other professional is an executor, an argument over a valuation will cost you money in fees, even if your valuation is finally accepted. Arguments can be lengthy.

IHT EXEMPTIONS

These include:

- **Transfers between spouses**. You can leave your estate to your spouse entirely free of IHT.
- **Gifts to other people**, up to a limit of £3,000 per tax year.
- **Small gifts** of up to £250 per tax year to any one individual.
- **Marriage gifts**. A parent of the bride or groom can give up to £5,000 to the couple free of IHT, while a grandparent or 'remoter ancestor' can give up to £2,500. Anyone else can give up to £1,000.
- **Gifts to charities**.
- **Gifts that you make earlier than seven years before your death**.

Gifts above the annual limits are called potentially exempt transfers (PETs). There is a sliding scale of tax rate depending on the length of time between the gift and your death if you die within seven years.

PET sliding scale

Time between gift and death	Percentage taxable (above the annual exemption limits)
0–3 years	100%
3–4 years	80%
4–5 years	60%
5–6 years	40%
6–7 years	20%

PETs are valued at the date you made the gift, not the date of death.

IHT RELIEFS

Estates that have business or agricultural property enjoy reliefs of 100 per cent on those parts of the estate. As you can imagine, the rules defining business and agricultural property are complicated.

If someone dies and leaves the money to someone else who dies shortly after (within five years), you don't have to pay IHT twice because of Quick Succession Relief, which reduces the tax payable on the second death according to a tapering scale.

PLANNING THE ESTATE

A married couple can make wills so that when the first spouse dies, a sum equal to the exemption goes to children or other beneficiaries and the rest goes to the surviving spouse. No IHT to pay. When the surviving spouse dies, the estate also has the exemption, so the couple have saved some £93,600 (40 per cent of the 2000/01 threshold).

For people with assets far above the threshold for IHT, estate planning can be extraordinarily complex. It is therefore worth paying for the best advice you can get. Trusts may play an important part in the plan. Becoming resident in a tax haven with no death duties is a serious option.

Most people are reluctant to give away large sums long before they die: inflation, the increased health expenses and lack of earning power in old age can easily get you into trouble when you are at your most helpless. One doesn't know when one is going to die, so it is foolhardy to budget at retirement age for one's own death at, say, 85, when one might hang on until the age of 93. In addition, you may well feel reluctant to give control of large sums to family members who are not mature enough to handle them. Human development being what it is, many people don't really 'grow up' until their parents die.

Trusts

Trusts separate the control over assets, the entitlement to capital and the entitlement to income. You must appoint trustees of complete integrity as they will be responsible for the administration of the trust's assets, and you can instruct them on who will get the income and who will get the capital.

Trusts were invented centuries ago to protect assets from the depredations of the Inland Revenue and other undesirables such as irresponsible or immature beneficiaries. The Victorian man of property would go to great lengths to make sure that his assets would be managed by responsible businesspeople after his death, while the proceeds could be enjoyed by his unworldly descendants. Today, the main advantage of UK trusts is their use in reducing the amount of inheritance tax.

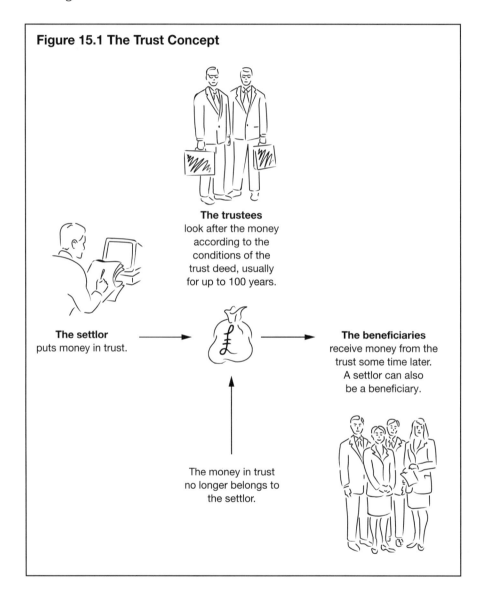

Figure 15.1 The Trust Concept

The trustees
look after the money according to the conditions of the trust deed, usually for up to 100 years.

The settlor
puts money in trust.

The beneficiaries
receive money from the trust some time later. A settlor can also be a beneficiary.

The money in trust no longer belongs to the settlor.

The players in a trust are the settlor, who is the person transferring the assets, the trustees, who administer the trust, and the beneficiaries, who receive the benefits of the assets. Trusts are normally set up to run for about 80 years.

The settlor can retain some control over a trust by retaining the right to appoint new trustees, or by making the trustees get consent before taking certain actions. The trustees have a legal duty to act in the best interests of the beneficiaries and have many other heavy legal obligations. A settlor can be a trustee, but this can give rise to tax liabilities. A settlor can also be a beneficiary.

BARE TRUSTS

With bare trusts, the trustees act as nominees who hold assets for someone else, who still legally possesses them. They can be useful to higher-rate tax-payers who want to accumulate money for their children; a child can possess the assets, held by the trustee who re-invests the income. Because this income belongs to the child but is not paid to the child, it is tax free up to a certain limit.

FIXED-INTEREST TRUSTS

In this kind of trust, the beneficiaries receive income from the trust that is liable for income tax. If the trust deed allows it, the settlor or trustees can cancel this if the beneficiaries behave in a way that they don't like.

DISCRETIONARY TRUSTS

This is where the trustee has the power to decide the amount of money a beneficiary can receive. The trust's income is taxed, but a beneficiary who is a lower-rate tax-payer can get part of this back from the Inland Revenue.

ACCUMULATION AND MAINTENANCE TRUSTS

These are for beneficiaries up to the age of 25 and have special advantages for inheritance tax.

CAPITAL GAINS TAX ON TRUSTS

Trusts pay CGT at a lower rate and have a lower annual exemption than people do, unless the settlor or the settlor's spouse has an interest, in which case their own exemptions come into play.

Trusts pay CGT at a lower rate and have a lower annual exemption than people do

'Hidden' taxes

As well as income tax, capital gains tax and inheritance tax, there are also all kinds of taxes on things that you buy, such as VAT. They don't seem to be taxes because they are included in the price, but they are taxes nevertheless. Another 'hidden' tax is National Insurance, which is definitely a tax and most definitely not insurance in any sense. Spend your money in lower tax countries if you can!

Starting a company

If you are not business-minded, it may never have occurred to you that forming a limited company to hold some or all of your assets, including shares, can be a useful way of reducing taxes. Company law is complicated and cannot be dealt with in full in this book, but here are some of the advantages.

CHANGING FROM BEING SELF-EMPLOYED TO HAVING A COMPANY

If you are self-employed and your earnings are increasing, there may come a point when it becomes worthwhile to transfer the business into a limited company to keep profits taxed at 20 per cent, which is the 'small companies' rate of corporation tax on profits up to £300,000, rather than having to pay income tax at higher rates. Another advantage is that because self-employed people are taxed on a preceding year basis, it is possible, with careful planning, to choose to cease trading as a self-employed person at a time when you are making large profits and avoid paying tax on a large proportion of them due to the 'drop out' effect. Get your accountant to explain how this works. You can then transfer your business to your new company.

TAX RELIEF ON BORROWING

If you withdraw a large sum of money from your company and it then borrows the same amount from a bank, the company's borrowing attracts tax relief on the total interest paid, which makes it cheaper than if you borrowed it personally. You have to do this in the order described; it's no use having your company borrow the money first and then withdrawing it for your own use as the Inland Revenue may deny you the relief.

Bibliography

Jules Abel, **The Rockefeller Millions: The Story of the World's Most Stupendous Fortune**, 1967

Consensus Research & Ernst and Whinney, **Attitudes of Companies in Britain to Fraud**, 1987

Peter Bernstein, **Against the Gods**, Wiley, 1996

Rowan Bosworth-Davis, **Too Good To Be True**, Bodley Head, 1987

J. Carswell, **The South Sea Bubble**, Cresset Press, 1960

Simon Cawkwell, **The Profit of the Plunge**, Rushmere Wynne, 1995

Richard Eels and Peter Nehemkis, **Corporate Cultures**, Macmillan, 1984

Kenneth Fisher, **100 Minds that Made the Market**, Business Classics, 1995

Philip Fisher, **Common Stocks and Uncommon Profits**, John Wiley, 1996

J.K. Galbraith, **The Great Crash**, Penguin, 1975

Leo Gough, **The Financial Times Guide to Business Numeracy**, Financial Times Management, 1994

Leo Gough, **Going Offshore**, Financial Times Management, 1995

Leo Gough, **25 Investment Classics**, Financial Times Management, 1998

Leo Gough, **Investing in Internet Stocks**, Wiley, 2000

Leo Gough, **Trading the World's Markets**, Wiley, 2000

Benjamin Graham, **The Intelligent Investor**, HarperPerennial, 1973

John Guiseppi, **The Bank of England: A History from its Foundation to 1964**, 1966

S.L. Hays, A.M. Spence and D.V.P. Marks, **Competition in the Investment Banking Industry**, Harvard University Press, 1983

Michael Joseph, **The Conveyancing Fraud**, Michael Joseph 1989

J.M. Keynes, **The General Theory of Employment Interest and Money**, Harcourt, 1936

Richard Koch, **Selecting Shares that Perform**, Financial Times Management, 1995

V.P. Lane, **Security of Computer Based Information Systems**, Macmillan, 1985

Edwin le Fevre, **Reminiscences of a Stock Operator**, John Wiley, 1994

L.H. Leigh, **The Control of Commercial Fraud**, Heinemann Educational Books, 1982

Michael Lewis, **Liar's Poker**, Penguin 1990

Ferdinand Lundberg, **The Rich and the Super Rich**, Thomas Nelson & Sons, 1969

Peter Lynch, **One Up on Wall Street**, Penguin, 1989

Burton G. Malkiel, **A Random Walk down Wall Street**, W.W. Norton & Co., 1991

Mark Mobius, **Mobius on Emerging Markets**, Financial Times Management, 1995

James Morton, **Investing with the Grand Masters**, Financial Times Management 1997

C. Northcote Parkinson, **Parkinson's Law**, John Murray, 1958

Patrick Philips, **Inside the Gilt-Edged Market**, Woodhead-Faulkner

Robert Prechter, **At the Crest of the Tidal Wave**, New Classics Library, 1995

W. Proctor, **The Templeton Touch**, Doubleday, 1983

Jim Rogers, **Investment Biker**, Random House, 1994

Anthony Sampson, **The Money Lenders**, Random House, 1968

Jack Schwager, **Market Wizards**, HarperCollins, 1993

Fred Schwed, Jr, **Where Are the Customers' Yachts?**, Simon and Schuster, 1940

Adam Smith, **The Money Game**, Vintage, 1976

Ralph Lee Smith, **The Grim Truth About Mutual Funds**, Putnam, 1963
George Soros, **Soros on Soros**, Wiley, 1995
Kathryn F. Staley, **The Art of Short Selling**, Wiley, 1997
Michael Stolper, **Wealth, an Owner's Manual**, HarperBusiness, 1992
Tolley Publishing Company, **Tolley's Tax Guide**, annual
John Train, **Preserving Capital and Making It Grow**, Penguin, 1983
John Train, **The New Money Masters**, Harper & Row, 1989
Charles Vintcent, **Be Your Own Stockbroker**, Financial Times Management, 1995

Useful addresses and websites

USEFUL FINANCIAL WEBSITES

www.moneycentral.msn.com *Microsoft's financial pages*
www.cbs.marketwatch.com *CBS, American TV financial* news
www.bridge.com *Bridge delivers financial news*
www.fool.co.uk *The Motley Fool*
www.yahoo.com *Yahoo has a good financial section*
www.news.ft.com *Financial Times*
www.investorguide.com *Investor Guide*
www.fisher.osu.edu/fin/ *Ohio State University's Virtual Finance Library*
www.bloomberg.com *Useful market information from Bloomberg*
www.marketxs.com *Good for US and European company data*
www.comdirect.com *Market focus section is good for international research*
www.offshore.net *Information for offshore investors*
www.ftmarketwatch.com *A Financial Times site*
www.magicnumbers.com *Promotes financial calculations for research and has a useful list of US and European company websites*

SELECTED INTERNATIONAL STOCK, COMMODITY AND FUTURES MARKETS

Australia

Australian Stock Exchange Centre
20 Bond Street
Sydney, NSW 2000
Tel: 29 227 0000. Fax: 29 235 0056.
www.asx.com.au

Sydney Futures Exchange (SFE)
30–32 Grosvenor Street
Sydney, NSW 2000
Tel: 29 256 0555. Fax: 29 256 0666.
www.sfe.com.au

Belgium

Belgian Futures & Options Exchange
(BELFOX)
Palais de la Bourse
Rue Henri Mausstraat 2
Brussels 1000
Tel: 2 512 80 40. Fax: 2 513 83 42.
www.belfox.be

Brussels Stock Exchange (Société de la
Bourse de Valuieres Mobilieres de Bruxelles)
Palais de la Bourse
Rue Henri Mausstraat 2
Brussels 1000
Tel: 2 509 12 11. Fax: 2 509 12 12.
www.stockexchange.be

EASDAQ (European Association of
Securities Dealers Automated Quotation)
Rue des Colonies 56, Box 15
Brussels 1000
Tel: 2 227 6520. Fax: 2 227 6567.
www.easdaq.com

Brazil

Brazilian Futures Exchange (Bolsa
Brasileira de Futuros)
Praca XV de Novembro 20, 5th Floor
Rio de Janeiro RJ 20010–010
Tel: 21 271 1086. Fax: 21 224 5718

The Commodities & Futures Exchange
(Bolsa de Mercadoris & Futuros)
BM&F Praca Antonio Prado 48
São Paulo SP 01010–901
Tel: 11 232 5454. Fax: 11 239 3531.
www.bmf.com.br

Rio de Janeiro Stock Exchange (Bolsa de
Valores de Rio de Janeiro)
Praca XV de Novembro 20
Rio de Janeiro RJ 20010–010
Tel: 21 271 1001. Fax: 21 221 2151.
www.bvrj.com.br

São Paolo Stock Exchange (Bolsa de
Valores de São Paolo)
Rua XV de Novembro 275
São Paolo SP 01013–001
Tel: 11 233 2000. Fax: 11 233 2099.
www.bovespa.com.br

Canada

Montreal Exchange (ME) (Bourse de
Montréal)
The Stock Exchange Tower
800 Square Victoria, CP 61
Montreal H4Z 1A9
Tel: 514 871 2424. Fax: 514 871 3531.
www.me.org

Toronto Futures Exchange (TFE)
The Exchange Tower
2 First Canadian Place
Toronto M5X 1J2
Tel: 416 947 4487. Fax: 416 947 4272.
Toronto Stock Exchange (TSE)
The Exchange Tower
2 First Canadian Place
Toronto M5X 1J2
Tel: 416 947 4700. Fax: 416 947 4662.
www.tse.com

Vancouver Stock Exchange (VSE)
Stock Exchange Tower
609 Granville Street
Vancouver V7Y IHI
Tel: 604 689 3334. Fax: 604 688 6051.
www.vse.ca

Winnipeg Stock Exchange
620 – One Lombard Place
Winnipeg R3B 0X3
Tel: 204 987 7070. Fax: 204 987 7079

China

Shanghai Stock Exchange
15 Huang Pu Road
Shanghai
Tel: 216 306 8888. Fax: 216 306 3076

France

MATIF (Marché a Terme International de
France)
176 rue Montmartre
Paris 75002
Tel: 33 1 40 28 82 82. Fax: 33 1 40 28 80
01. **www.matif.fr**

MONEP (Marché des Options
Negociables de Paris)
39 rue Cambon
Paris 75001
Tel: 1 49 27 18 00. Fax: 1 9 27 18 23.
www.monep.fr

Paris Stock Exchange (Bourse de Paris)
39 rue Cambon
Paris 75001
Tel: 1 49 27 10 00. Fax: 1 49 27 13 71

Germany

Bavarian Stock Exchange (Bayerische
Boerse)
Lenbachplatz 2(A)
Munich 80333
Tel: 89 54 90 45 0. Fax: 89 54 90 45 32.
www.bayerischeboerse.de
Berlin Stock Exchange (Berliner
Wertpapierboerse)
Fasanenstrasse 85
Berlin 10623
Tel: 30 31 10 91 0. Fax: 30 31 10 91 79

Deutsche Terminborse (DTB)
Boersenplatz 4
Frankfurt-am-Main 60313
Tel: 69 21 01 0. Fax: 69 21 01 2005.
www.exchange.de

German Stock Exchange (Deutsche
Boerse AG)
Bersenplatz 4
Frankfurt-am-Main 60313
Tel: 69 21 01 0. Fax: 69 21 01 2005.
www.exchange.de

Hamburg Stock Exchange (Hanseatische
Wertpapierboerse Hamburg)
Schauenburgerstrasse 49
Hamburg 20095
Tel: 40 36 13 02 0. Fax: 40 36 13 02 23

Stuttgart Stock Exchange (Baden-
Wurttembergische Wertpapierboerse zu
Stuttgart)
Konigstrasse 28
Stuttgart 70173
Tel: 7 11 29 01 83. Fax: 7 11 22 68 11 9

Hong Kong

Hong Kong Futures Exchange Ltd (HKFE)
5/F, Asia Pacific Finance Tower
Citibank Plaza
3 Garden Road
Tel: 2842 9333. Fax: 2810 5089.
www.hkfe.com

Hong Kong Stock Exchange (SEHK)
1st Floor
One and Two Exchange Square Central
Tel: 2522 1122. Fax: 2810 4475.
www.sehk.com.hk

India

The Stock Exchange, Mumbai
Phiroze Jeejeebhoy Towers
Dalal Street
Bombay 400 001
Tel: 22 265 5860. Fax: 22 265 8121.
www.bseindia.com

Japan

Tokyo Commodity Exchange (Tocom)
(Tokyo Kogyoin Torihikijo)
10–8 Nihonbashi
Horidome-cho
Chuo-ku 1-chome
Tokyo 103
Tel: 3 3661 919l. Fax: 3 3661 7568

Tokyo International Financial Futures
Exchange (TIFFE)
1–3–1 Marunouchi
Chiyoda-ku
Tokyo 100
Tel: 3 5223 2400. Fax: 3 5223 2450.
www.tiffe.or.jp

Tokyo Stock Exchange (TSE) (Tokyo
Shoken Torihikijo)
2–1 Nihombashi-Kabuto-Cho
Chuo-ku
Tokyo 103
Tel: 3 3666 0141. Fax: 3 3663 0625.
www.tse.or.jp

Korea (South)

Korea Stock Exchange (KSE)
33 Yoido-dong
Youngdeungpo-gu
Seoul 150–010
Tel: 2 3774 9000. Fax: 2 786 0263.
www.kse.or.kr

Luxembourg

Luxembourg Stock Exchange (Société
Anonyme de la Bourse de Luxembourg)
11 Avenue de la Porte-Neuve
L-2227
Tel: 47 79 36–1. Fax: 47 32 98.
www.bourse.lu

Malaysia

Kuala Lumpur Options & Financial
Futures Exchange (KLOFFE)
10th Floor, Wisma Chase Perdana
Damansara Heights
Jalan Semantan
Kuala Lumpur 50490
Tel: 3 253 8199. Fax: 3 255 3207.
www.kloffe.com.my

Kuala Lumpur Stock Exchange (KLSE)
Exchange Square
Bukit Kewangan
Kuala Lumpur 50200
Tel: 3 206 7099. Fax: 3 206 3684.
www.klse.com.my

Mexico

Mexican Stock Exchange (Bolsa Mexicana
de Valores, SA de CV)
Paseo de la Reforma 255
Colonia Cuauhtemoc
Mexico DF CP 06500
Tel: 5 726 66 00. Fax: 5 705 47 98.
www.bmv.com.mx

Netherlands

AEX-Stock Exchange
Beursplein 5, PO Box 19163
Amsterdam 1000 GD
Tel: 20 550 4444. Fax: 20 550 4950.
www.aex.nl

Singapore

Stock Exchange of Singapore (SES)
No. 26–01/08, 20 Cecil Street
The Exchange 49705
Tel: 535 3788. Fax: 535 6994.
www.ses.com.sg

Spain

Bilbao Stock Exchange (Sociedad Rectora
de la Bolsa de Valores de Bilbao)
Jose Maria Olabarri 1
Bilbao 48001
Tel: 4 423 74 00. Fax: 4 424 46 20.
www.bolsabilbao.es

Madrid Stock Exchange (Bolsa de Madrid)
Plaza de la Lealtad 1
Madrid 28014
Tel: 1 589 26 00. Fax: 1 531 22 90.
www.bolsamadrid.es

Spanish Financial Futures Market (MEFF
Renta Fija)
Via Laietana 58
Barcelona 8003
Tel: 3 412 1128. Fax: 3 268 4769.
www.meff.es

Sweden

Stockholm Stock Exchange Ltd
(Stockholm Fondbors AB)
Kallargrand 2
Stockholm SE-105 78
Tel: 8 613 88 00. Fax: 8 10 81 10.
www.xsse.se

Swedish Futures and Options Market
(OM Stockholm AB)
Box 16305, Brunkebergstorg 2
Stockholm S-103 26
Tel: 8 700 0600. Fax: 8 723 1092.
www.omgroup.com

Switzerland

Swiss Exchange (SWX)
Selnaustrasse 32
Zurich CH-8021
Tel: 1 229 21 11. Fax: 1 229 22 33.
www.bourse.ch

Swiss Options & Financial Futures
Exchange AG (SOFFEX)
Selnaustrasse 32
Zurich CH-8021
Tel: 1 229 2111. Fax: 1 229 2233.
www.bourse.ch

Taiwan

Taiwan Stock Exchange
Floors 2–10, City Building
85 Yen Ping Road South
Taipei
Tel: 2 311 4020. Fax: 2 375 3669.
www.tse.com.tw

Thailand

Stock Exchange of Thailand (SET)
2nd Floor, Tower 1
132 Sindhorn Building
Wireless Road
Bangkok 10500
Tel: 2 254 0960. Fax: 2 263 2746.
www.set.or.th

Turkey

Istanbul Stock Exchange (ISE) (Istanbul
Menkul Kiymetler Borasi)
Istinye
Istanbul 80860
Tel: 212 298 21 00. Fax: 212 298 25 00.
www.ise.org

United Kingdom

International Petroleum Exchange of
London Ltd (IPE)
International House
1 St Katharine's Way
London El 9UN
Tel: 0207 481 0643. Fax: 0207 481 8485.
www.ipe.uk.com

London International Futures & Options
Exchange (LIFFE)
Cannon Bridge
London EC4R 3XX
Tel: 0207 623 0444. Fax: 0207 588 3624.
www.liffe.com

London Metal Exchange (LME)
56 Leadenhall Street
London EC3A 2BJ
Tel: 0207 264 5555. Fax: 0207 680 0505.
www.lme.co.uk

London Securities and Derivatives
Exchange (OMLX)
107 Cannon Street
London EC4N 5AD
Tel: 0207 283 0678. Fax: 0207 815 8508.
www.omgroup.com

London Stock Exchange (LSE)
Old Broad Street
London EC2N 1HP
Tel: 0207 797 1000. Fax: 0207 374 0504.
www.lse.com

United States

American Stock Exchange (AMEX)
86 Trinity Place
New York NY 10006–188
Tel: 212 306 1000. Fax: 212 306 1802.
www.amex.com

Chicago Board of Trade (CBOT)
141 West Jackson Boulevard
Chicago IL 60604–299
Tel: 312 435 3500. Fax: 312 341 3306.
www.cbt.com

Nasdaq Stock Market
1735 K Street NW
Washington DC 20006–150
Tel: 202 728 8000. Fax: 202 293 6260.
www.nasdaq.com

New York Stock Exchange (NYSE)
11 Wall Street
New York NY 10005
Tel: 212 656 3000. Fax: 212 656 5557.
www.nyse.com

REGULATORS

Association of Chartered Certified
Accountants
29 Lincoln's Inn Fields
London WC2A 3EE
Tel: 0207 242 6855

Building Societies Commission
25 The North Colonnade
Canary Wharf
London E14 5HS
Tel: 0207 676 1000

Financial Services Authority
25 The North Colonnade
Canary Wharf
London E14 5HS
Tel: 020 7676 1000. **www.fsa.gov.uk**

Friendly Societies Commission
25 The North Colonnade
Canary Wharf
London E14 5HS
Tel: 0207 676 1000

Institute of Actuaries
Staple Inn Hall
High Holborn
London WC1V 7QJ
Tel: 0207 632 2100

Institute of Chartered Accountants in
England & Wales
Silbury Court
412–416 Silbury Boulevard
Milton Keynes MK9 2AF
Tel: 01908 546335

Institute of Chartered Accountants in
Ireland
Chartered Accountants House
87–89 Pembroke Road
Dublin 4
Tel: 00 353 1 668 0400

Institute of Chartered Accountants of
Scotland
27 Queen Street
Edinburgh EH2 1LA
Tel: 0131 225 5673

Law Society
113 Chancery Lane
London WC2A 1PL
Tel: 0207 242 1222

Law Society of Northern Ireland
Law Society House
98 Victoria Street
Belfast BT1 3JZ
Tel: 01232 231614

Law Society of Scotland
The Law Society's Hall
26 Drumsheugh Gardens
Edinburgh EH3 7YR
Tel: 0131 226 7411

Registry of Friendly Societies
Victory House
30–34 Kingsway
London WC2B 6ES
Tel: 0207 663 5244

Securities and Exchange Commission
(SEC)
450 Fifth Street, NW
Washington, DC 20549
(telephone Office of Investor Education
and Assistance:
(202) 942–7040. **www.sec.gov**

Glossary

Account
Fortnightly, or sometimes three-weekly, trading period on a stock exchange.

Actuary
A statistician, usually employed by an insurance company, who calculates risk.

Advisory broker
A stockbroker who advises clients on their investments as well as buying and selling on their behalf.

Agency brokers
In the UK, broker/dealers who act as agents between market makers and investors.

Allotment price
In a tender for gilts, the price allotted to successful tenders. In a gilts auction, non-competitive bids are allotted a price that is the weighted average of successful competitive bids.

Annual charge
Management fees levied on investments, often as a percentage of their value.

Annual Percentage Rate (APR)
A standardized way of expressing interest rates which make them comparable with one another, and include hidden charges and other extras.

Anti-trust
Anti-monopoly legislation, originally aimed at US trusts used to create monopolies.

Arbitrage
Taking advantage of the difference in price of the same product or rate in different places.

Arbitrageurs ('ARBS')
Generally, but incorrectly, used to mean speculators who buy shares in a company in the hope that it will be taken over. This is not strictly arbitrage, since some time elapses between purchase and sale, and in theory one should not know the future price. If you do, it's cheating!

Asset
Anything that has a monetary value.

Auction
For gilts, an auction is where new issues are bid for in one of two forms competitive or non-competitive.

Audit
The process of inspection of a company's books by independent accountants.

Averaging
'Averaging' a particular share holding is achieved by buying more on a fall or selling some on a rise in value.

Back-to-back loan
Hedging against interest rate changes by borrowing in one currency against the security of a deposit in another currency.

Backwardation
This is when the spot or near-term price of a commodity is higher than its forward price, sometimes caused by shipment delays.

Balance of payments
The difference between the total value of money entering a country and the total leaving it in a year.

Balance of trade
The difference in total value between a country's annual imports and exports.

Balance sheet
A statement of a company's financial

situation at the end of the last financial year.

Bargain

A transaction on a stock exchange.

Basket currency

An invented currency based on several national currencies, such as the ECU and Special Drawing Rights.

Bear

Someone who thinks the share market will go down.

Bearer bonds

Bond certificates that can be held anonymously and used almost as freely as cash.

Bed and breakfast operation

Selling shares and then buying them back to mitigate capital gains tax. Now no longer possible because of a rule change (see p 283).

Bell-wether share

A share in a company that is regarded as likely to move in line with market trends.

Beneficial owner

The true owner of a security who may not be named in the register of ownership.

Bid price

The price at which a unit trust manager or market maker is willing to buy shares.

Blue chip

The top 100 or so companies on the stock market, reputedly stable investments.

Boilerhouse operations

Firms who use high-pressure tactics to obtain investments of doubtful value.

Bonds

Securities, usually paying a fixed rate of interest, which are sold by companies and governments.

Bonus issue

The issue of additional shares by a company to its shareholders at no cost; also called a 'scrip issue' or a 'capitalization issue'.

Bretton Woods

The place in New Hampshire, USA, where the post-war system of foreign exchange was agreed in 1944.

Bull

Someone who thinks the share market will go up.

Bulldog bonds

Bonds issued by governments in sterling, other than British government gilts.

Call option

The right to buy shares at an agreed price within a certain time.

Capital gains tax (CGT)

A tax on the increase of value of assets realized in a particular year.

Capitalization

The total value at the market price of securities issued by a company, industry or market sector.

Capitalization issue

See 'bonus issue'.

Cash and carry

When a dealer buys a commodity for cash and sells the futures contract at a profit, possibly when the spot price is more than the forward price, interest, storage and insurance costs.

Central Gilts Office (CGO)

The Central Gilts Office in the UK is where trade in gilts is processed on computer.

Central Moneymarkets Office (CMO)

The Central Moneymarkets Office in the UK is where trade in money market instruments is settled on computer.

Chartist

Someone who studies charts in the hope of predicting changes in stock market prices.

Chinese Walls

The attempt to keep confidential information from passing from one branch of a securities house to another.

Churning

Trading with a client's portfolio in order to generate extra commissions dishonestly.

Clean price

The price of a gilt, not including rebate interest or accrued interest.

Clearning house

A system for making sure that buyers and sellers meet their obligations.

Closed-end fund

A fund where the size of the total investment is fixed. All investment trusts are closed end.

Commercial bank

A 'high street' bank which deals mainly with the public.

Commodity

Any raw material.

Common stocks

The US name for ordinary shares.

Concert party

An informal group of investors who try to obtain control.

Consideration

The value of a share transaction before the costs of dealing are paid.

Contango

The normal situation in the futures market where the spot price is less than the forward price.

Contract note

Written details of an agreement to buy or sell securities.

Contrarians

Investors who act against consensus views.

Conventional option

Options that are not traded.

Conventional stocks/bonds

Bonds with fixed interest rates and repayment dates.

Convertible loan stock

A security paying a fixed rate of interest which may be changed in the future for ordinary shares.

Corporate governance

A jargon term for the fashionable issue of how companies should be run, in the context of society as well as the law and best practice.

Corporate issue

A bond issued by a company.

Coupon

The nominal interest rate on a fixed-interest security (bond), or a warrant which is detached from a bearer bond or bearer share certificate to be used to claim interest.

Cum

The Latin word for 'with'. For instance, 'cum dividend' means 'with dividend'.

Currency hedging

Trying to reduce or eliminate exchange rate risks by buying forward, using financial futures or borrowing in the exposed currency.

Dealing costs

The cost of buying and selling shares, including the broker's commission, stamp duty and VAT.

Debenture

A bond issued by a company, paying a fixed rate of interest and usually secured on an asset.

Deep discount

Bonds that have been issued in the UK after 14 March 1989 at a discount of more than 0.5 per cent per annum or 15 per cent in total are said to have a 'deep discount', and the discount is to be taxed as income. No such bonds have yet been issued.

Derivative

These include options, forward contracts and the like. They are often said not to be 'real' assets, because they may expire and become worthless.

Designated territory

The UK's Department of Trade and Industry (DTI) terms certain tax havens 'designated territories', meaning that they operate proper controls over their financial industries. They include the Isle of Man, Luxembourg, Jersey and Guernsey.

Devaluation

The formal reduction in the value of a currency against other currencies.

Dirty floating

The practice of a state intervening to influence or manipulate exchange rate movements.

Discount broker

A stockbroker who deals for clients but gives little or no advice and charges low commission rates.

Discounted cash flow

A way of estimating the value of an investment in today's money by adjusting future returns to get their present value.

Diversification

The act of spreading capital across different investments in order to reduce risk.

Dividend

A regular payment out of profits by companies to their shareholders.

Domicile

The country where you are resident for tax purposes; it is difficult, but not impossible, to change your domicile.

Double dated stock

UK gilts that can be redeemed by the government between two specified dates.

Double taxation treaty

Treaties between countries to offset a person's tax liabilities in one country against those in another.

Dragons

The economies of Thailand, the Philippines, Malaysia and Indonesia.

Earnings

The net profit of a company that is distributed to its shareholders.

Earnings per share (EPS)

The profits of a company, after tax, divided by the number of shares.

Enfacement

The process by which a UK bond passes from a CGO member to a non-member. *See also* 'Central Gilts Office'.

Equities

Another name for shares.

Eurobond

A stock that is issued by a syndicate of banks and is usually bought and sold outside the country in whose currency it is denominated.

Eurocurrency

Deposits of a currency that are held outside the country in which the money is denominated.

Eurodollar

US dollars held outside the United States.

Euromarket

The market in currencies and securities outside the countries in which they are denominated.

Eurowarrant

A certificate linked to a Eurobond which entitles the holder to buy a given number of shares at an agreed price and time.

Ex dividend date

The date when a holder of a UK bond receives the next interest payment.

Ex dividend stock

UK bonds that are sold to a buyer who does not receive the next due interest payment because the deadline for registration of the transfer has passed.

External bonds

Bonds issued in the market of one country that are denominated in the currency of another.

External Names

Names at Lloyd's who do not work there.

Federal Reserve

The central banks of the United States.

Fixed assets

A company's assets that are not being processed or bought and sold, such as buildings and machinery.

Flat yield

Also called 'running yield' or 'interest yield', it is the income you earn in a year if you bought £100's market value of a bond. The figure is calculated by dividing the coupon by the market price and multiplying by 100.

Flotation

When a company first issues its shares on a stock exchange.

Floating charge

A right to priority payment from the assets of a person or company.

Floating exchange rates

Currency exchange rates that change their rate according to the activity in the market.

Floating rate note

Bonds and other debt instruments that carry a variable rate of interest, usually linked to a reference rate such as the London Inter-Bank Offered Rate (LIBOR).

Force majeure

A supplier usually has a clause in delivery contracts allowing him to break the contract when there is force majeure which is a major external event such as a strike or major catastrophe.

Forward exchange contract

An agreement to buy an amount of a currency at an agreed exchange rate on a fixed date.

FT Actuaries All-Share Index

A stock market index, divided into 40 sections, covering all shares quoted in the UK.

FT Industrial Ordinary Share Index

An index of the ordinary shares of 30 top companies.

FTSE 100 Index

The 'Footsie', the principal index for the price of shares quoted on the London stock market.

FTSE stocks

The 100 companies whose shares are represented in the FTSE 100 Index. Generally regarded as 'blue chip'.

Fundamental analysis

The assessment of the value of a share on a company's actual earnings, assets and dividends.

Fungible stocks

UK bonds that are issued after an identical issue and merged with it.

Futures

The right to buy or sell a financial instrument at an agreed price at some future time.

Gearing

The ratio between a company's share capital and its borrowings. High gearing means a proportionately large amount of debt and low gearing means a small amount of debt.

GEMM

A Gilt-Edged Market Maker.

General Agreement on Tariffs and Trade (GATT)

A group representing most nations which supervises international trade.

Gilt-edged

Securities issued by the British government, usually at a fixed interest rate. US gilts are called Treasury bonds.

Holding company

A company that controls one or more other companies.

In play

When a company is thought to be the target of a bid, it is said to be 'in play'.

Index fund

An investment fund that invests in all the shares used in a given market index, mimicking the performance of the index.

Inflation

A general increase in prices.

Insider dealing

Trading in shares when in possession of price-sensitive information that is not known to the market. Insider dealing is illegal to some degree in most markets.

Institutions

The large, managed investment funds, including pension funds, insurance funds, unit and investment trusts are known as institutional funds and are the major players in the stock market.

International Monetary Fund (IMF)

The international lender of last resort, set up by the Allies in 1944.

Investment bank

Called a 'merchant bank' in the UK, a bank that works as a financial intermediary, offering such services as takeover and merger assistance, and the placing of new share and bond issues.

Investment trust

A company that manages share portfolios and whose own shares are quoted on the Stock Exchange.

ISAs

Individual Savings Accounts. These provide a tax-free shelter for UK tax-payers.

Junk bonds

Company bonds that are not rated by credit-rating agencies. They are 'low quality' and offer a higher rate of interest than other bonds.

Kerb trading

Trading that occurs after a stock market has officially closed for the day.

Kondratiev Wave

A theoretical economic cycle lasting approximately 60 years.

Less developed country (LDC)

A polite way of saying a poor country.

Liquidity

The degree of ease with which an asset can be turned into cash.

Lloyd's of London

An insurance market.

London Inter-Bank Offered Rate (LIBOR)

The rate of interest offered by commercial banks to other banks on the London Inter-Bank Market.

Longs
British government securities that are to be redeemed in 15 or more years' time.

Management charges
Fees taken by fund managers to cover their overheads. These can be too high.

Margin
In the market, a cash deposit against a sum invested on credit.

Market maker
Formerly 'jobbers', these are dealers in securities in their own names on a stock exchange.

Marketability
The degree of ease and speed with which a security can be sold.

Mediums
British government securities that are to be redeemed in between five and 15 years' time.

Merchant bank (See 'investment bank')

Money supply
The available money in a system and the rate at which it circulates.

Mutual funds
The US name for unit trusts.

Name
An investor at Lloyd's of London.

National Savings Stock Register (NSSR)
The cheapest way to buy gilts.

Net asset value (NAV)
The net assets of a company divided by the number of shares it has issued gives the net asset value per share.

Net margining system
Used by some stock exchanges in the United States, this system reconciles the total margins due to each broker so that the difference, rather than the total, is passed to the clearing house.

Net present value (NPV)
A figure that represents the total of future cash inflows from a project, less cash outflows, inflation, and/or a required rate of return.

Net worth
The value of an individual's assets after all debts have been subtracted.

NIC
A newly industrialized country, for example South Korea.

Nominal value
The value of a security printed on its certificate. Also called 'par' or 'face value'.

Nominee
A person or company that is registered as the owner of a security in order that the true owner's identity is kept secret, or to make dealing easier.

Non-competitive bid
In a gilts auction, a bid for between £1,000 and £500,000's worth of stock which will receive an allotment at a price that is the weighted average of the successful competitive bids.

Offer price
The price at which a unit trust manager or market maker will sell a stock or share.

Open-ended
A fund that has a variable amount of capital and doesn't have to match its buyers with sellers. *See also* 'unit trusts'.

Open outcry
A system of face-to-face trading where brokers shout their bids and offers out loud; now only used in some commodity and derivatives markets.

Option
The right to buy or sell a security at an agreed price within an agreed timespan.

Ordinary share

The most usual type of share, called 'ordinary' to distinguish it from other kinds, such as 'preference' shares which pay a fixed dividend.

Organization of Petroleum Exporting Countries (OPEC)

An association of some of the major oil-producing countries that tries to regulate oil production and prices, thus affecting the world oil market.

Over the counter (OTC)

Any market that does not work through an exchange-based system.

Par value

The nominal value of a share or bond, as stated on its certificate. This is not its market value.

Pari passu

Latin for 'at the same rate', 'equal ranking'.

Pit trader

A dealer who works on the floor of an exchange, usually a futures exchange, that uses the 'open outcry' system.

Portfolio

A collection of securities held by one investor or fund.

Preference shares

Fixed dividend shares giving preference, as a creditor, over ordinary shareholders but behind bond holders.

Price/earnings (P/E) ratio

The market price of a share divided by its earnings (e.g. profits) gives the p/e ratio, which is the most commonly used measure of the 'value' of a share.

Prior charges

Interest paid on loan stock and debentures that is settled before the distribution of dividends to shareholders.

Private placing

An issue of new shares to institutions and large private clients rather than to the general public.

Programmed trading

Investors who give standing instructions to their brokers to buy and sell at pre-ordained price or growth levels.

Proxy

A person who votes, with permission, in the place of a shareholder at company meetings.

Put option

The right to sell a security at an agreed price within an agreed time limit.

Quotation

The price of a security currently fixed by a stock exchange market maker.

Rating of bonds

This is done according to risk: the least risky bonds are rated AAA and the highest risk bonds are rated D. Junk bonds are too risky to be rated.

Redemption yield

Any one of several methods of calculating what interest rate is necessary for the market price of a bond to equal the net present value of the remaining interest payments and redemption value.

Reserve currency

The currency that is most used by governments and institutions for holding cash reserves. Currently, it is the US dollar.

Reverse auction

When a bond issuer invites bond holders to sell their bonds back to the issuer.

Rights issue

When a company offers new shares pro rata to its own shareholders, usually at a discount.

Saitori

Members of the Tokyo Stock Exchange

who work as intermediaries between brokers. They are not allowed to deal on their own accounts or for non-members of the Exchange.

Savings and loan (S&L)

The US equivalent of British building societies.

Scrip issue

See 'bonus issue'.

Seat

Having a seat on an exchange means being a member of the exchange.

Securities

These are any financial instrument traded on a stock exchange, such as shares and bonds.

Self-regulating organizations (SROs)

These are financial organizations that regulate, with varying degrees of effectiveness, the activities of their members.

Shell company

A quoted company that has few or no trading activities.

Shorts

Short-term bonds.

Special drawing right (SDR)

A basket currency used by the International Monetary Fund (IMF) which consists of weighted amounts of sterling, French francs, deutschmarks, yen and US dollars.

Speculation

Gambling on the change in the price of a security.

Spread

The difference between the prices of a share at which a market maker will buy (bid) and sell (offer).

Straddle

Making contracts to buy and sell an option or future at the same time in order to protect against big price changes.

Swap

An agreement to exchange a stream of future payments.

Tap issues

In the UK, the name for an issue of government bonds that is not fully subscribed. In such cases, the broker keeps the remainder and 'dribbles' them into the market slowly.

Technical analysis

The attempt to predict share price movements on the basis of past patterns of movement.

Tigers

The economies of Hong Kong, Taiwan, Singapore and South Korea.

Tombstone

A newspaper advertisement that sets out the details of a bond issue or major loan, and the banks that have underwritten it.

Underwriter

One who provides insurance cover or guarantees a financial transaction.

Unit trusts

UK savings schemes run by specialists for small investors; funds are invested in securities. In the United States they are called mutual funds.

Warrants

A certificate, usually attached to a bond, that gives the holder the right to buy shares at a given price and date.

Widows and orphans

Mythical creatures, a metaphor for clients who are very risk averse and financially unsophisticated.

Working Name

An investor at Lloyd's who also works as an agent or underwriter there.

Yearlings

These are short-term bonds, usually with a one-year life.

Yields

The annual return on an investment, excluding capital growth.

Zaibatsu

The Japanese word for 'financial clique'; the original *zaibatsu* was a group of powerful families who industrialized Japan in the 19th century.

Index